Springer Series on ADULTHOOD and AGING

Series Editor: Bernard D. Starr, Ph.D.
Advisory Board: Paul D. Baltes, Ph.D., Jack Botwinick, Ph.D.,
Carl Eisdorfer, Ph.D., M.D., Donald E. Gelfand, Ph.D., Lissy Jarvik, M.D.,
Ph.D., Robert Kastenbaum, Ph.D., Neil G. McCluskey, Ph.D., K. Warner
Schaie, Ph.D., Nathan W. Shock, Ph.D., Asher Woldow, M.D.

Donald E. Gelfand, Ph.D., is a professor at the School of Social Work and Community Planning of the University of Maryland at Baltimore. His interests span both basic and applied areas of aging. He is the author or editor of a number of books on ethnicity and aging, including *The Aging Network* (Springer Publishing Co., 1984), a text on programs and services in aging. He has conducted research on aging among a number of ethnic groups including Italians, Poles, Russian Jews, Salvadoreans, and Vietnamese. His recent research efforts have focused on the effects of immigration on older individuals. In 1983 he served as a Senior Fulbright Fellow in Darmstadt, West Germany. He has also served as associate director of the National Policy Center on Older Women, as a senior research associate at the National Council on the Aging and as secretary of the Social Research, Planning and Practice Section of the Gerontological Society of America.

Charles M. Barresi, Ph.D., is professor of sociology and Fellow of the Institute for Life-Span Development and Gerontology, The University of Akron. He received his Ph.D. degree from The State University of New York at Buffalo and completed postdoctoral work at the Scripps Foundation Gerontological Center, Miami University in Oxford, Ohio. His published work has appeared in numerous books and journals and has covered a number of major topics in aging. These include widowhood and its impact on the older individual, environmental factors and life satisfaction, and service providers' perceptions of the elderly. His recent research interests are in ethnicity, cross-cultural aging, and patterns of family caregiving. He was a consultant on the PISCES Project, a Robert Wood Johnson Foundation–funded study of health-impaired elderly, and he is a member of the Research Committee of the Association for Gerontology in Higher Education and a Fellow in the Gerontological Society of America.

ETHNIC DIMENSIONS OF AGING

Donald E. Gelfand
Charles M. Barresi
Editors

SPRINGER PUBLISHING COMPANY
New York

Springer Publishing Company, Inc.
536 Broadway
New York, NY 10012

89 90 91 / 5 4 3 2

Library of Congress Cataloging-in-Publication Data

Ethnic dimensions of aging.

  (Springer series on adulthood and aging; v. 18)
  Bibliography: p.
  Includes index.
  1. Minority aged—United States.   2. Old age.
3. Ethnicity—United States.   I. Gelfand, Donald E.
II. Barresi, Charles M.   III. Series.
HQ1064.U5E78   1987   305.2'6'0973   87-28611
ISBN 0-8261-5610-X

Printed in the United States of America

Contents

Part III Practice, Policy, and the Ethnic
Dimensions of Aging

Contributors

Dorothy M. Barresi, M.F.A., is lecturer in English at the University of North Carolina at Charlotte. She received her M.F.A. in creative writing from the University of Massachusetts. Winner of several national awards, she is the author of *The Judas Clock,* a collection of her poetry, and her work has appeared in numerous literary journals.

Elena Bastida, Ph.D., is an associate professor in the Department of Sociology and Social Work at Wichita State University, Kansas. She has been awarded postdoctoral fellowships from both the National Institute on Aging and the National Institute of Mental Health. Her research has concentrated on the impact of structural characteristics on individual dimensions of aging, with a particular emphasis on health and housing.

Rosina M. Becerra, Ph.D., is associate dean and professor in the School of Social Welfare at the University of California, Los Angeles. Her publications include articles on political participation of the Hispanic elderly and the cultural context of Hispanic aging and a reference handbook on how to conduct research among the Hispanic elderly.

Rita Bonar, M.S.W., is director of social services at the Montreal Extended Care Centre, Ville Marie Social Services in Montreal, Canada. Her main work consists of individual intervention with elderly ethnic individuals in a long-term-care facility. Her research focuses on sociopsychological aspects of aging in chronic care hospitals and nursing homes.

Timothy H. Brubaker, Ph.D., is professor in the Department of Home Economics and Consumer Sciences and is affiliated with the

Family and Child Studies Center at Miami University, Oxford, Ohio. Author of a number of books and articles on aging, he has also served as editor of the journal *Family Relations*. His interests are centered around the later life family.

Carole Cox, D.S.W., is presently a research associate at the Brookdale Institute on Aging and Human Development of Columbia University, New York. Formerly director of the Gerontology Program at San Jose State University, California, her research in the field of aging has concentrated on issues of ethnicity, nursing homes, and long-term care.

Milada Disman, Ph.D., is a research fellow of the Gerontology Research Council of Ontario and assistant professor in the Department of Behavioural Science at the University of Toronto, Canada. A sociologist, her recent research and writing focuses on ethnicity, aging, and mental health.

Rose C. Gibson, Ph.D., is a faculty associate at the Institute for Social Research and an associate professor at the School of Social Work, University of Michigan. She is the author of numerous articles and monographs on the Black elderly and the Black family. She has also served on the advisory board of the Carnegie Corporations' Aging Society Project.

Zev Harel, Ph.D., is professor of Social Services and director of the Center on Applied Gerontological Research at Cleveland State University, Ohio. He completed his M.S.W. at the University of Michigan and his doctorate at Washington University, St. Louis. He serves as a consultant to planning and service organizations in the field of aging and is active in a number of professional organizations in the field of gerontology.

Christopher L. Hayes, Ph.D., is assistant professor of psychology at Long Island University, Southampton, New York. He was formerly director of the Center for the Study of Preretirement and Aging at The Catholic University of America. His major areas of interest include ethnic minority aging and clinical/practice issues in working with the elderly.

Cary Kart, Ph.D., is professor of sociology at the University of Toledo, Ohio. He has published widely in sociology gerontology, including a leading text, *The Realities of Aging* (Allyn and Bacon,

1985). His main areas of research interest are aging and health, institutionalization, and the social psychology of aging.

Kathryn Kozaitis is a Ph.D. candidate in social work and anthropology at the University of Michigan. Her theoretical and research interests include ethnicity, gerontology, cultural change, urbanization, applied anthropology, and contemporary culture. She previously earned masters' degrees in social welfare administration and anthropology.

James E. Lubben, D.S.W., M.P.H., is assistant professor in the School of Social Welfare at the University of California, Los Angeles. Presently chairperson of the School's Health and Aging Concentration, his research has focused on assessing the health and psychosocial needs of elderly persons. He also serves on major committees of the Gerontological Society of America.

Mark Luborsky, Ph.D., is project manager in the Behavioral Research Department at the Philadelphia Geriatric Center in Philadelphia, Pennsylvania. He earned a Ph.D. in anthropology from the University of Rochester, New York, and has been involved in studies of ethnicity and elderly widowers and the effectiveness of interdisciplinary health care teams.

Michael J. MacLean, Ph.D., is associate professor, School of Social Work, McGill University in Montreal, Canada. His main research interests are related to ethnicity and aging, the quality of life for institutionalized elderly people, and the influence of the urban environment on aspects of aging.

Edward A. McKinney, Ph.D., M.P.H., is professor and chairperson of the Department of Social Service, Cleveland State University, Ohio. He received his Ph.D. and M.P.H. from the University of Pittsburgh and an M.S.W. from Atlanta University.

Carol M. Michael, Ph.D., is assistant professor in the Department of Home Economics and Consumer Sciences at Miami University, Oxford, Ohio. She received her Ph.D. from The Ohio State University. Her professional interests include the professional development of women and food patterns of various ethnic groups.

Robert Rubinstein, Ph.D., is senior research anthropologist in the Behavioral Research Department at the Philadelphia Geriatric

Center. He received his Ph.D. from Bryn Mawr College. His recent research has focused on the role of ethnicity in the life of elderly widowers and the meaning of home for the elderly.

Eleanor Rado Stoller, Ph.D., is professor of sociology, State University of New York, Plattsburgh, New York. A graduate of Washington University in St. Louis, her research has focused on the informal support networks of community-based elderly. Her longitudinal study of social support networks and family caregivers of community-based elderly has been funded by the National Institute on Aging.

Fernando Torres-Gil, Ph.D., is the staff director of the U.S. House Select Committee on Aging. He is on leave from the University of Southern California, where he is an associate professor of gerontology and public administration. He has written extensively on minority and Hispanic aging issues, including a recent report published by the Carnegie Corporation, "Hispanics in an Aging Society" (1986).

K. Victor Ujimoto, Ph.D., is professor of sociology and research associate at the Gerontology Research Center of the University of Guelph, Ontario, Canada. He has written extensively on Japanese Canadians, multiculturalism, and aging ethnic minorities. His most recent effort is the national research project "Comparative Aspects of Aging Asian Canadians: Social Networks and Time Budgets."

Michael Williams, Ph.D., M.P.H., is assistant professor of social work at Cleveland State University, Ohio. He also serves as the field education coordinator. He received his Ph.D. and M.P.H. from the University of Pittsburgh. His primary interest is in studying the effects of social policy decisions on minority groups, particularly on the Black elderly.

Introduction

It is always intriguing to examine current scholarly thinking from a historical perspective. This is certainly true in the case of ethnicity and race. In the 1960s the topics of ethnicity and race were on everyone's lips as the civil rights movement began to gain in importance. The civil rights acts of the period and the leadership of individuals such as Martin Luther King, Jr., helped to produce major changes in the lives of many American Blacks. In the 1970s interest in ethnicity and race peaked, except for a new resurgence of interest in the topic among White ethnics. The new assertiveness by White ethnic groups that began to appear in the 1970s has continued into the 1980s with consolidation of organizational efforts.

The discussion of the importance of race and ethnicity in American life has taken a new turn in the 1980s. Some writers have argued that with the implementation of civil rights legislation race is no longer an important variable in determining "life chances" of individuals, including the education and jobs available to them or where they are able to live (Wilson, 1980). Instead, they contend that class is now a more vital determinant of social mobility than race and that minority-group individuals who are able to attain adequate education will have access to high-level jobs and housing. If we can generalize this argument to White as well as non-White groups, ethnicity should become less important as all ethnic groups attain better education and greater social mobility. Opponents of this argument contend that discrimination still faces minorities in many fields. Downplaying the importance of race overlooks this continued discrimination.

In aging, the issue is not just mobility within one generational cohort but also mobility between cohorts. The problem of studying cohorts of the elderly is complicated. The life experiences of a particular cohort of elderly will no doubt be very different from those of the cohort of older individuals that precede them. For example, the various cohorts of older Poles now living in the United States may differ in their life experiences despite commonalities in date of birth. Some current Polish elderly may have grown up in the United States. Others may have matured in Poland, left after World War II, and come to the United States or Canada as "displaced persons."

Intercultural comparisons thus become difficult because of the varied experiences that may have shaped the older person's life. Intergenerational social mobility also requires analysis of the effects of socioeconomic changes among successive cohorts of older ethnic group members. The socioeconomic status of each of these cohorts may also be disparate. One would hope that socioeconomic status has improved with each successive generation of elderly. Unfortunately, in the area of ethnicity and aging this assumption cannot be made, particularly in relation to minority elderly.

No one effort will be able to unravel definitively all of the complex issues in the field of ethnicity and aging. The purpose of this volume is to examine critically many of the interrelationships between ethnicity and aging based on the critical thinking of researchers and practitioners. Indeed, a number of the authors in this book clearly demonstrate the complexity of ethnicity in their discussions. This complexity can be evidenced in a number of ways. First, the forms of ethnicity may change. Thus, what are regarded as indicators of ethnic identity may change over time, with the major change occurring intergenerationally. Some social indicators of ethnicity, including traditional forms of dress, may disappear entirely, and new indicators of ethnic background may be developed. Only a strong historical review of a particular ethnic group can clearly detail these changes.

On a personal level, individuals may move in and out of ethnic identity, utilizing their ethnic identity more overtly when it fulfills a need. As the authors in this volume indicate, individuals may move in and out of activities that relate to their ethnic background depending on their life situations. Drastic life changes—for example, the death of a spouse or retirement—may encourage individuals to rethink some basic issues such as their ethnic identity. It is also possible that at crucial moments individuals may assert their ethnic identity through a process of behavior that may relate to their early socialization. At these times individuals may not actually be aware of how the attitudes they are expressing or the behavior they are exhibiting is related to ethnicity. Zbrowski's (1952) famous studies of the manner in which different ethnic groups reacted to postoperative pain is an example of this relatively unconscious tendency to exhibit ethnically related behavior.

All of these issues need careful research as we attempt to hone in on the importance of ethnicity in the field of aging. We see these issues, however, as not just an exercise in interesting social or sociopsychological theory. Our belief is that understanding the relevance of ethnicity to aging is crucial for effective program planning at local levels in settings such as senior centers and nursing homes.

The issue of ethnicity and aging is also constantly being confronted at the social-policy level of state and federal government as various groups advocate for specific policies oriented to their needs. At the practice level an understanding of the importance of ethnicity and aging is vital in effectively working with older people, whether this work is in a specific training program or a clinical setting related to health and mental health.

In the late 1970s the National Conference on Ethnicity and Aging held at the University of Maryland was a first effort to focus attention on all of these issues. Neither the conference nor the publication of *Ethnicity and Aging* (Gelfand & Kutzik) in 1979 succeeded in resolving all of the issues related to ethnicity and aging. This book will also not resolve all of the difficult issues inherent in this topic, but we hope it will further illuminate many of them.

In preparing this volume we have attempted to cast our net as widely as possible. The goal was to bring together the conceptual and empirical efforts needed to provide a clear understanding of similarities and differences among individuals in specific ethnic groups as they grow older. Intensive discussions were held with researchers and practitioners around the country. They indicated that interest in ethnicity and aging has become quite strong in the 1980s despite limited funding for research on this topic. There is also important data about ethnicity and aging contained in research undertaken for a variety of purposes. Often, however, there is a need to encourage researchers or program developers to focus directly on ethnicity rather than merely viewing ethnic background as a variable that must be controlled for statistically or through sampling procedures. When ethnicity per se is focused on, the important issues related to ethnic affiliation and aging become evident.

In assembling the chapters we have worked from a number of basic principles. First, we have taken our definition of ethnicity from Gordon (1964), whose focus is on groups that are set off from society by race, religion, or national origin. The book is thus not restricted to "minority groups" and includes chapters on ethnic groups from European backgrounds. We believe this approach allows for comparisons of similarities and differences among groups that would be impossible with a more restrictive definition. It also emphasizes the possible influence of culture on the individual and the diverse cultural backgrounds found in North American society. Second, we have tried to focus on conceptual issues as well as data related to specific ethnic groups. Third, we have encouraged the authors to think through the meaning of their findings and analyses for groups other than the ones on which they have focused.

In Part I theoretical issues related to ethnicity and aging are examined, with a variety of ethnic groups providing the basis for the discussions. Although research results underlie many of the theoretical discussions in Part I, Part II is explicitly directed toward important and conceptually grounded research on ethnicity and aging. These chapters were also selected because they range over a diverse sample of ethnic groups including Jews, Finns, Blacks, Mexicans, Chinese, and Japanese. This diversity is also evident in Part III, where the difficult areas of practice and policy related to ethnicity and aging are examined. We believe that the reader will find much of the discussion relevant to many ethnic groups even if the chapter discussion is specific to one particular ethnic group.

Because of our interest in the conceptual issues of ethnicity and aging we have not attempted to provide coverage of every ethnic group in North America. No effort has been made to provide the type of data often found in needs assessments of particular groups. The gaps in coverage are readily apparent, particularly in the case of Native Americans, for whom conceptually based research in aging is still lacking. We have also made no effort to engage in cross-national comparisons. Although such an effort is very valuable, a comprehensive cross-national comparison is beyond the scope of one volume. There are, however, a number of chapters from Canadian sources. These chapters are indicative of the strong interest in ethnicity and aging among Canadian researchers, practitioners, and policymakers. This interest reflects in part the continuing immigration into Canada from a variety of sources, including European countries. We also do not view the chapters in Part III as complete in their coverage of all of the practice and policy issues inherent in ethnicity and aging.

Our hope is that this volume will assist individuals already interested in the meaning and importance of ethnicity for themselves and for the elderly. We also hope that it will awaken new interest in ethnicity and aging among those individuals who have not previously paid much attention to the topic. Only with a continued expansion of attention to ethnicity will we be able to ascertain what its role is, and will be, for the older persons of this and the next century.

DONALD E. GELFAND

CHARLES M. BARRESI

Acknowledgments

No volume of this nature could be successfully completed without the full cooperation of the individual authors. We are grateful to each one of them for the tolerance of our editorial suggestions and their efforts to comply with the deadlines imposed. We are very indebted to Kim Hunt for undertaking the arduous task of compiling the common reference list. We are also grateful to Irene Fort, Pat Conley, and Bev Riggin for their secretarial assistance and to the staff at Springer Publishing Company for their help in seeing this project through to fruition. Finally, the most indispensable support came from our respective spouses, Katharine and Lenore, who endured the many solitary hours while we were occupied with the mountains of manuscripts, and the frequent phone calls and visits required throughout the planning and execution of this book.

D.E.G.
C.M.B.

Their First America

after a photo by Jacob Riis, circa 1895

We believe in a camera giving back
what it takes, though this time
the boy in the alley is not enough
under his peanut straw cap, rat-cheeked and wary,
protecting the moon his grandmother makes
peeking over his shoulder.
She squints to pull this new danger
into her eyelashes.
Her skirt looks at least as heavy
and beaten as the wings of downed crows, but even
this detail is partly true, part lacking,
like the wooden fire escape
suspended over their heads.

Because one flight up
past the clarity of bricks and white edges,
greenhorn women take work in, blurring.
Where *mortadella* and flypaper hang
beside pictures of the saints—
each window we cannot see
offers dim faces in a kitchen,
everything close as blood.
Can't you just hear the women and children
pull basting thread from knee pants
and the insect whine of their workday
lengthening at both ends, 35¢ a pair.

It is a long way from home by steerage.
It is longer still to Queens, Long Island, the suburbs,
the next new world.
The boy shields his grandmother
and it is not enough. Already
she is untranslatable, antique, a life
lumbering eyes half-open
into a milky block of ice
we cannot chip her from.
But the boy's gaze burns! He is a small animal
transfixed by a car's high beam.
Any minute he'll summon the will or anger
to outrun what caught him
on the lower east side of his first America
in middle ground, in stubborn light.

DOROTHY BARRESI

Part I
Theory and the Ethnic Dimensions of Aging

The process of social aging is rooted in the most basic components of social structure. Age, like gender and race, is a correlate of social behavior and must be taken into account when analyzing specific social situations or relationships. Research activities cannot proceed, however, without a firm theoretical foundation. In order to understand the complexity of social aging it is necessary to examine existing theory and to develop and test new theoretical formulations that are capable of providing explanation and understanding. Matilda White Riley (1987) provides an example of the growing awareness of the centrality of aging theory to the social sciences in her presidential address to the American Sociological Association. She urges fellow sociologists to become more aware of the importance of aging as a foundation to the understanding of social relationships and social structure and calls for the continued examination and development of aging theory.

In keeping with this emphasis, the first section focuses on the uses of theory in ethnicity and aging. The integration of these two major social correlates, ethnicity and aging, provides insights into a host of social phenomena including family, work, politics, religion, and intergenerational relations, to name but a few. Although the chapters for the most part center on theory as a main concern, connections with both research and practice are clearly identified. Several of the authors illustrate their theoretical formulations with original data, whereas others rely on previous work. All, however, are solidly grounded in empirical reality.

The first chapter, by Gelfand and Barresi, details the current state of theory, research methods, and policy and practice in ethnicity and aging. In an overview of the field they point out the present problems and future challenges facing gerontologists, legislators, and service providers with regard to both old and new ethnic groups. A number of basic issues are brought to the reader's attention, including the emergent nature of ethnicity and the manner in which the "age as leveler" assumption tends to mask important ethnic differences among the aged. Of particular interest is their focus on the status of the new immigrants of Southeast Asia and the differences displayed between their experiences and those of earlier immigrant groups. Especially relevant is the discussion of two important issues: the relationship between ethnicity and social change, and the positive and negative aspects of ethnicity as it affects the aging process.

The second chapter provides an extensive examination of the life-course perspective as applied to the process of social aging in ethnic groups. Barresi notes that although ethnicity is often mentioned as a salient variable affecting the development of the individual's life course, no one to date has elaborated on its structural and procedural aspects. Whereas Luborsky and Rubinstein, in the following chapter, examine ethnicity as a life-course phenomenon, Barresi looks at the broader picture of the contribution of ethnicity as a central variable that defines and structures the many components of the life course. The model he introduces examines the relationships among individual, group, and cultural factors and the life-course process in ethnic aging. His discussions on the effect of language and meaning on ethnic life-course dynamics, and the salience of family and work activities as they impact on the life-change events, are of particular interest. Accompanied by numerous examples, these explanations provide insight into the foundations underlying the individual's dominant personal and social characteristics and the contribution that ethnicity makes in the development of his or her life course.

In the third chapter Luborsky and Rubinstein examine ethnicity as a life-course phenomenon. Data gathered from a sample of older Jewish, Irish, and Italian widowers provide the basic information for demonstrating how ethnicity acts as a variable in the life-reorganization process. Like Disman, in the concluding chapter in Part I, they also draw attention to the concept of ethnic identity, suggesting that ethnic identity in late life is based on past ethnic experiences and is organized thematically around them. Reflecting on ethnicity as a result of lifetime experiences, they suggest that the meaning of ethnicity is related to four intertwined life-course events: life-span development and family history, historical settings of key life events, the situational nature of current ethnic identity, and the continual reworking of past ethnic experiences. They conclude with the generalization that ethnicity and ethnic identity are dynamic entities that serve as vehicles by which individuals creatively transform and revitalize their social identities and selves.

The relationship between cultural systems of meaning and aging provides the setting for the fourth chapter, by Bastida. Using empirical data on the concepts of fatalism and realism in a Hispanic sample, she demonstrates how conceptual meaning is dependent on the culture and must be understood by researchers within that context. Building on this strong sociology-of-knowledge approach, she proposes the use of an interpretive model of the systems of meaning and discourse utilized by an ethnic group; this will lead to a better understanding of the dynamics of ethnic aging. This interpretive model includes both the lay interpretations and perceptions of aging as well as the more rigorous social science definitions and concepts. In closing, Bastida presents a convincing argument that this approach will provide a conceptual foundation for further research and encourage continual reformulation of the paradigms and methods used in the scientific study of culture and aging.

Part I ends with a discussion of the implications of ethnic identity as a coping mechanism in social aging. Disman utilizes the technique of life history to reveal the elderly's ethnic identity as they experience and manifest it in everyday life. Citing illustrations from personal interviews with Canadian elderly of various ethnic backgrounds, she emphasizes the importance of meanings assigned to ethnicity as one aspect of a person's identity. She discusses the concept of continuity of self in the aging process and suggests that it works to provide acceptance of the aging process and modifies one's definition of self as "old." When one's identity is secure because of continuity, then being old can be accepted. Disman contends that continuity of self is not threatened by aging as long as the person is able to maintain a dominant self, whether in work, family, or other roles. This dominant self provides the central theme around which the person's life becomes organized. The chapter concludes with a discussion of the hierarchy of selves and the effects of ethnic identity on persons for whom it is more or less important.

A number of similar themes run through the chapters in this section. Ethnic identity and its dynamics are presented by Disman and by Luborsky and Rubinstein as adaptive techniques used by ethnic elderly during the aging process. Barresi and Bastida each deal with the manner in which language and meaning become important mechanisms for ethnic elderly in coping with the aging process within their distinct cultural groups. The interplay between the individual, the ethnic group, and the host culture is thus brought into focus. Gelfand and Barresi touch on a number of these themes, including the language issue, and focus particular attention on intergenerational relations and their effect on aging for members of various ethnic groups.

These chapters clearly demonstrate the need for more concentrated attention on the problematic aspects of explanation regarding the dynamics of ethnic aging. At the same time they illustrate the valuable insights that can be gained when such endeavors are undertaken. We can only hope that the material in this section will provide the necessary stimulation and impetus to further efforts in the evaluation and development of theory in the ethnic dimensions of aging.

1

Current Perspectives in Ethnicity and Aging

Donald E. Gelfand and Charles M. Barresi

As the field of aging has grown, the complexity of the aging process and society's reaction to older persons has become more evident. To some degree this complexity results from the changing racial and ethnic composition of the American population. The numbers of native-born White, Black, Asian, Hispanic, and Native American elderly will increase dramatically over the next 50 years. The effects of these demographic changes will be compounded by the effects of current immigration patterns.

The inception of the quota system in 1924 to determine the number of new immigrants symbolized an effort to maintain domination by Northern European groups. Until 1965 immigration was limited. Quotas from southern and eastern Europe were oversubscribed, accompanied by a corresponding paucity of immigrants from northern and western Europe. As this system became riddled with exceptions (such as the acts that allowed American soldiers to bring their Japanese or Korean brides into the United States), calls for immigration reform began to be more commonly heard.

The repeal of the quota system in 1965 opened American borders to large numbers of individuals who entered the country with visas, others who entered the United States as refugees, and the large, basically uncounted numbers of individuals who continue to enter illegally. What is important is not only the numbers of immigrants but the fact that this current immigration represents an influx of Hispanics and Asians whose cultural backgrounds bring a new dimension into the society. This new immigration since 1965 has had a decided impact on the field of aging. There are now not only

older Americans with varied ethnic backgrounds but also substantial numbers of older Americans who are first-generation immigrants. This creates a mix of generations within these ethnic
groups, whose needs for services and support are varied.

Gaps in knowledge about ethnicity and aging and the questions
that need to be answered have been pointed out by Gelfand (1981) in
a general review of the literature and by Jackson (1985) in an
examination of minority aged. The questions raised in 1981 still
remain for the most part unanswered. The agenda for research and
knowledge in the area of ethnicity and aging is extensive. The lack
of information cannot be totally explained by the size of the task. In
this chapter our attention is focused on the problems that inhibit
researchers in ethnicity and aging from providing a more satis-
factory knowledge base for planning and implementing programs
and services for older individuals.

Methodological Issues in Ethnicity and Aging

The first hurdles to be overcome in probing the relationships of
ethnicity to aging are methodological. In the 1970s it was necessary
to convince investigators of the value of including ethnicity as a
variable. This problem has now largely been overcome. The majority of investigators are now careful to include Black, Hispanic, and
perhaps Asian elderly in their sampling design when possible.
When unable to accomplish this type of sampling, we at least can
expect to find disclaimers about the generalizability of the findings
beyond White elderly.

Among minority elderly the most notable gap is the sparseness
of research about older Native Americans. This situation can be
accounted for by general lack of interest in Native Americans
among the public and by the difficulties of gaining access to Native
American communities, which are generally suspicious of outsiders.
Based on the tragic history of these groups, their suspicions extend
not only to White investigators but also to cooperative Native Americans, who are viewed pejoratively as "apples" (red on the outside,
white on the inside). As infant mortality decreases and the percentage of elderly among Native Americans increases, this lack
of basic and programatically relevant knowledge will be especially
harmful.

Even with attention being paid to minority elderly, it has been
difficult to persuade researchers to focus on the differences among

White or "Euro-American" groups. This has been especially problematic with research based in the American West and Southwest where groups have often been classified by researchers as Anglos, Blacks, and Hispanics. Even in the more ethnically diverse areas of the East and Midwest, the variety of backgrounds among Whites has often been ignored, with a consequent loss of critical information about the differences in attitudes and behaviors among aging cohorts from such diverse ethnic groups as Jews, Italians, Poles, and Greeks (Barresi, 1986).

Although some of this missing information may be traced to a lack of interest in ethnic diversity, sampling problems also account for a large portion of these gaps. Unless a research project is stratified along the variable of ethnicity, it is likely that a community-based design will be applied. In such community designs the probability of finding significant numbers of White ethnic elderly from diverse backgrounds is limited. Researchers often have adequate numbers of Whites and minority elderly in a sample. What is unfortunate, however, is that among the Whites in the sample there may be only ten or so each of Polish, Greek, Portuguese, and German elderly. Reliable and valid statistical comparisons among these groups thus become difficult if not impossible. Therefore, attention to sampling of specific White ethnic groups becomes necessary if we are to obtain the type of data required to expand our knowledge of the influence of ethnicity on the lives of older Whites.

Undertaking this type of investigation is, of course, expensive because of the geographic spread of White ethnic groups. Even though Native Americans, Vietnamese, Hmong, and Korean elderly are more concentrated in ethnic communities, gaining access to their homes is also difficult. Consequently, researchers must often resort to obtaining samples from group sites where there are concentrations of older ethnic groups. Although this strategy solves the problem of obtaining a sample, it has obvious drawbacks in generalizability to older individuals who do not come to these group sites or who do not live in the area being served.

Specific attention to ethnicity as a variable and increased funding to enable better sampling procedures would help to alleviate the problems mentioned. It would be a mistake, however, to infer that the problems of ethnicity and aging are primarily related to methodological issues. Rather than being merely a reflection of methodological problems, the lack of a firm knowledge base in ethnicity and aging must be attributed to the general core of thinking within the field of aging.

Ethnicity, Aging, and Change

Social scientists have always expressed interest in the process of social change, but their work has generally failed to illuminate this process. It is not unfair to say that social scientists display the general human tendency to feel more comfortable with the world as it is rather than the world that will exist in the future. Planners and practitioners also find it difficult to consider programs for future cohorts of the elderly while struggling to develop programs that meet the needs of the present cohort of older people.

It is only recently that we have seen any clear ability to focus on change in the field of aging. Theories that have been popular in gerontology have tended to stress the years that we define as "late life" as discrete and unrelated to events from earlier times. Whether utilizing "disengagement" or "activity" approaches, gerontologists have viewed the older person as an individual entering a new status where previous attitudes and desires do not have to be taken into account. For the most part, attempts to develop theoretical approaches in gerontology have moved away from this bias toward approaches that either stress continuity between the current status of the older person with his or her past or focus on social structural factors that impinge on the older person (Hagestad & Neugarten, 1985).

Because of the tendency to view the world through unchanging lenses, variables such as ethnicity have proved problematic. These problems stem from the basic fact that ethnicity is not a static variable. When simply defined as a sense of peoplehood based on race, religion, and nationality (Gordon, 1964), it is clear that each of these three underpinnings of ethnicity can be affected by changing social, economic, and political conditions. The perceptions of persons in racial groups are altered as these groups experience changing conditions in the society. The same is true of religion. The proliferation of religious groups produces an endless round of severed and retied connections, leading to mixed loyalties and identifications. Nationality becomes even more confused among ethnic groups. For example, the links of older Italian-Americans to Italy become less clear as their connections with the "old country" recede into the distance. Not to expect change among ethnic groups would be unrealistic because ethnic groups are groups that have generally depended upon their ability to adapt in order to survive.

Ethnicity must thus be viewed as a variable that changes in response to changes in the individual's or group's life. The actual changes reflect the conditions confronted by ethnic individuals living outside their own environment, whether they are Turks living in Germany or Italians in the United States. In this sense, the "emergent" nature of ethnicity cannot be stressed too strongly (Yancey, Ericksen, & Juliani, 1976).

The focus on ethnicity as emergent calls into question the saliency of some characteristics of ethnicity that are often regarded as traditional to a specific culture. A specific example is provided by Cohler and Grunebaum (1981), who state that the notion of the extended Italian family is one that emerged after migration to the United States. In Italy the nuclear family was very protective, with few relationships to extended kin networks. The model of the traditional Italian-American family stemmed from the "chain" migration of Italians to the United States. In this migration pattern Italian men first came to establish themselves and then sent for their wives and children. At a later time sisters, brothers, and extended family members were also brought to the New World. Close familial relationships were thus established because of the need for continued support in a new and strange society and culture. This chain immigration resulted in stronger attachments among extended families in the United States than had existed previously in Italy.

If we view ethnicity as an emergent phenomenon, we then call into question the whole idea of "traditional" ethnic culture. As Rosenthal (1986) and Gelfand and Fandetti (1986) have argued, the notion of traditional ethnic culture that is used as a baseline in current research efforts may represent only an "immigrant model," with less and less relevance to our need to define clearly the contours of ethnic culture.

A recent volume by McGoldrick, Pearce, and Giordano (1982) attempts the complex task of describing a large number of ethnic group cultures and then utilizing the characteristics of each group for family therapy. Although the attention to ethnicity as a variable in family dynamics is laudable, this approach again tends to place emphasis on ethnicity as an unchanging variable. An alternative approach has been suggested by Gelfand and Fandetti (1986), in which ethnicity is viewed as a variable whose importance needs to be assessed not only for an understanding of the aging process but for the provision of services as well. In this approach a two-stage process is developed in which initially specific questions are asked about the individual regarding the following:

1. Generation of immigration.
2. Socioeconomic background.
3. Residence (i.e., do they live in an ethnic neighborhood?).

4. Language(s) (i.e., do they speak English or the so-called mother tongue or both?).
5. Involvement in traditional ethnic organizations and the ethnic church.

Answers to these questions and references to current knowledge can assist us in understanding the importance of ethnicity for the individual.

The Impact of Ethnicity

Age as a Leveler

Bringing ethnicity into the models used in studying aging has been difficult not only because of our difficulty dealing with ethnicity as a changing phenomenon but also because of the continuing strong, and often unspoken, tendency to view age as a leveler. Current analyses of drinking behavior among older persons provides an example of this tendency. When drinking behavior is discussed, the common approach is to assert that the consumption of alcohol is usually reduced among older people because of lower tolerance for alcohol and the reduction in social situations encountered in which alcohol is being served. Almost no discussion can be found in the literature about differential alcohol consumption among older ethnic group members, with perhaps the exception of alcohol problems among Native Americans. The unspoken assumption is that the reductions in alcohol usage are equivalent among all ethnic groups. This assumption has yet to be proved.

Life expectancy is one major area related to basic physical characteristics of aging where ethnic differences have been acknowledged. Statistics continue to show decreasing differences in life expectancies among White and minority elderly. Complicating the picture, however, is the so-called crossover effect in which Blacks who live into their seventies have longer life expectancies than their White peers. This difference in life expectancy is now also shown to exist among Native Americans and perhaps Asians as well (Manson & Callaway, 1985). Whether related to selective survival among these groups or to susceptibility to specific diseases, these differentials continue to be a topic of discussion among researchers (Manton & Stallard, 1984)

The lack of similar attention to social and behavioral differences among ethnic and minority aged is related to the tendency to regard age as a leveler that counteracts differences existing among the elderly. Clearly, the current tendency in ethnic research is to simplify the world in order to make it more orderly and easier to comprehend. Using the age-as-leveler bias, however, neglects important elements that shape an older person's existence. Ethnicity is for many older individuals one of the more important of these elements.

Positive and Negative Ethnicity

At times it would appear that investigators assume that the existence of an ethnic identity among their subjects is ipso facto a positive factor in their aging process. According to this view, ethnicity serves as an important link to a cultural heritage that specifies how things should be done, including thinking and behaving in old age, relationships with family, and involvement in the larger community. In a supposedly rootless world, ethnic identity provides the individual with roots not easily destroyed by the decrements associated with the aging process in industrial society.

Less attention is paid to the negative impact of ethnicity on the older person. For the older Pole, adherence to traditional ethnic culture may include an expectation of living with children. This expectation may not be met because of the distance the children live from the parent's neighborhood or the negative attitudes of adult children about having parents living in their household. For the older Vietnamese, adherence to traditional culture may include an expectation that children will provide the respect and deference they believe should be afforded elders. Faced with the demands of survival in American society, adult Vietnamese children may not have either the inclination nor the ability to afford the expenditure of time and energy necessary to fulfill these expectations (Cox & Gelfand, in press). In these two illustrations problems arise from the differences in allegiance to the traditional ethnic culture by older parents and their children. Unburdened by the demands of surviving in a foreign and strange culture, the Vietnamese family in Vietnam may not face these problems.

The traditional immigrant culture may also pose problems for the older person. Traditional values may stress disengagement, whereas the individual still desires to remain engaged in a variety of activities and organizations. In the traditional culture hostility between adult children and older parents may exist when the parent persists in maintaining control of property and decision making at a time when children would like to assume more authority.

The traditional culture thus may not create the unalloyed positive experience that many authors assume. Indeed, some recent writers have argued that the importance attached to ethnic culture as a means of identity or as a base for social mobility is a myth (Steinberg, 1981). This debate is beyond the scope of this chapter, but it is important to note that membership in an ethnic culture may be the reason for some problems experienced by older persons as well as providing a foundation for their successful aging. Understanding an ethnic culture and its effect on aging requires knowledge not only of the manner in which an ethnic culture can assist elderly in coping with the demands of late life but also of the problems that might be created by adherence to this culture.

Ethnicity as a Political Agenda

All of the aforementioned factors make the assessment of the impact of ethnicity on the aging process a difficult task. Complicating the situation even further is the fact that ethnicity is not a topic that is viewed by many with objectivity. Advocates argue for its importance in any assessment and planning activity; others argue that it has ceased to be relevant in American life except among the most recent immigrants. The rhetoric that pours forth from both camps is not merely the result of differing positions on the issue but also because of the real benefits or losses stemming from the ultimate outcome. The potential benefits include funds for programs oriented to specific ethnic groups. The Ethnic Heritage Studies Act of the 1970s has been cited as an example of the increased political clout of White ethnic groups (Mann, 1979).

Advocates for minority elderly have argued that programming must be developed to meet their specific needs (Jackson, 1980). Some of these needs stem from the greater extent of poverty, malnutrition, and poor health that minority elderly experience. Lower life expectancy among minority groups in general, when compared with the dominant majority, is a direct result of neglect in meeting these vital needs. Among the elderly, the lowest life expectancy recorded is among Native Americans. Given that life expectancy among minority groups is less than among Whites, then perhaps the definition of eligibility for programs under the Older Americans Act should be reduced from one standardized at age 60 to one more relevant to the life expectancy of each respective minority group. This would follow a suggestion by a recent census report (U.S. Bureau of the Census, 1984, p. 14) that eligibility for social service programs should take into account the number of years remaining and that "old age" moves upward as life expectancy increases.

Efforts to have services targeted for minority elderly through Area Agencies on Aging across the United States do not appear to be particularly effective. A recent report (Wiggins, 1986) notes that most Area Agencies do not evidence any particular desire to target their services to the minority elderly. Instead, these agencies assume that using the criteria of over age 75, poor, frail, and rural will include the greatest number of minority elderly in a particular area. Among White elderly, there are few indications that targeting is taking place. The reluctance to target programs specifically for White ethnic elderly upsets many advocates of ethnicity. Those who espouse the importance of ethnicity among Euro-Americans argue that differences between ethnic groups remain strong among older individuals born outside the United States as well as among older persons who are descendants of these immigrants. Acceptance of such a policy could mean an allocation of funds specifically for Euro-Americans. However, at a time when financial resources appear to be shrinking rather than growing, a division of limited resources among more recipients is not a particularly appealing prospect for many agencies.

Future Issues in Ethnicity and Aging

Despite the complex relationships between ethnicity and aging there are some important implications that can be drawn from current data on ethnic groups. These implications are not necessarily positive for all groups of ethnic aged. A survey of older individuals in New York City who arrived in the United States before 1950 indicates a strong reliance on a foreign tongue (Lee, 1985). It is reasonable to expect that these individuals have some rather specific service needs. The most recent census figures indicate that "among those persons 65 years and over speaking a language other than English at home, 1 in 5 did not speak English well and 1 in 10 did not speak English at all" (U.S. Bureau of the Census, 1984, p. 24.). This limited ability in communication makes it difficult for these elderly to avail themselves of services and also creates problems for service providers. The problem extends beyond elderly persons who speak a foreign tongue, however, to include also those who are illiterate. The rate of illiteracy varies widely among elderly ethnic groups, with the native-born of foreign or mixed parentage reporting 0.6%; foreign-born, 4.1%; and Blacks, 6.8% (Bureau of the Census, 1984, p. 92). Providing services to these elders in the near future, and for some time to come, will continue to pose special difficulties.

There are also individuals who arrived in the United States either after World War II as refugees or more recently as a result of immigration reform. These older persons may also have strong allegiance to ethnic cultures. As Gelfand (1986) notes, it is a mistake to assume that the ethnic culture that these older persons bring to the United States is the same as that of their forebears. Recent older Russian-Jewish immigrants have exhibited distinctly different attitudes toward services than commonly assumed to be present among their peers who emigrated from Russia at an earlier time.

Although the social service needs of foreign-born Euro-American older persons are extensive, their representation in the American population is declining. The majority of Euro-Americans in the United States now represents second- and even third-generation individuals whose involvement with ethnic culture may be more a question for researchers than an assumable fact. Among the elderly of these American-born ethnics, however, service needs remain high.

Among minority elderly the situation is different. Because of the effects of earlier patterns of discrimination older minority group members may suffer from both poorer health and lower income. This is reflected in the higher illness and poverty rates among minority elderly. Moreover, among groups such as Native Americans the specific living situation on the reservation may also produce conditions that are less than favorable for healthy longevity (Manson & Callaway, 1985). It is important to note that both of these groups, despite their American nativity and long family history in the United States, still display rather glaring unmet service needs.

Among Native American groups, it is possible that tribal memberships also reflect distinct attitudes toward the aging process. However, even these attitudes may be undergoing change among more recent generations of Native Americans. This assertion raises perhaps the most crucial and certainly most difficult issue for research in ethnicity; the relationship between social class and ethnicity. If upward social mobility reduces the influence of ethnicity, then it may be possible to argue that ethnicity will become less and less relevant as upward social mobility of the majority of these groups in the United States increases.

The relationship between ethnicity and aging is even more complex among Hispanics and Asians. Hispanics represent a variety of cultures and nationalities. Aggregating these groups under the term *Hispanics* also neglects the distinctions between those families who have been settled on American soil for five or six generations and recent immigrants. Even among Chicanos there are distinct differences in attitudes and cultures in various southwestern states, depending on the history of the state. As Lukas (1985) correctly notes in his analysis of the effects of school busing on three Boston families, this is not to imply that there are no differences among Blacks.

The situation among Asians is even more problematic because of both the diversity and the rapid growth of the Asian population in the United States. During the 1970s the Asian-American population increased by more than 141%, in comparison to an increase of 17% among Blacks and 39% among Hispanics. The Asian-American population is also estimated to have increased by 50% since 1980 and may be 4% of the U.S. population by the year 2000. Between 1980 and 1984 the number of legal immigrants from Asia exceeded the number of legal immigrants from Latin America (Gardner, Robey, & Smith, 1985).

Although this growth pattern is very clear, the situation becomes less distinct when we move beyond the basic figures. The first complexity is the number of ethnic groups represented under the term *Asian*. At present there are at least eight large groups and three "others" that are classified as Asian. These groups are diverse in cultural attitudes. Because of their recent immigration, the tendency is to think of Asians as primarily a young population. Even this assumption is an oversimplification. For example, the median age of Whites in 1980 was 31.3 years. The median age of Chinese Americans was 29.6 years and of Japanese Americans 33.5 years. The Chinese-American figure reflects recent immigration of Chinese into the United States, but the median age of Japanese Americans reflects the long tenure of this group in the United States. The relative needs of Chinese, Vietnamese, Filipino, or Japanese elderly will thus be different because of their differential tenure in American society and the proportion of elderly in their respective groups.

The status of the elderly may also vary according to the numbers of children available to assist the older person. On this parameter, Asian-American populations, except for Vietnamese, rank lower than Whites (1,358 children per 1,000 individuals), Blacks (1,806 children per 1,000), or Hispanics (1,817 children per 1,000 individuals). There are also differences among groups in the average size of the household. In 1980 these ranged from 2.7 persons among White families to 4.4 individuals among Vietnamese. As a recent study comparing Hispanic, Vietnamese, and Portuguese elderly indicates, however, it cannot be assumed that a larger number of individuals in the household automatically means more assistance to the elderly (Cox & Gelfand, in press).

There are some indications in these data about the future status and problems among minority elderly. The proportion of high school graduates among Asian-Americans is currently above that of Whites, Blacks, and Hispanics. A recent study notes that Asian-Americans are already well represented among managerial and professional ranks. "Among Japanese, Filipino and Asian-Indian immigrants the proportion in the highest occupational category in 1980 not only exceeded the White figure but also the proportions for the U.S. born workers in these groups" (Gardner et al., 1985, p. 32). On the basis of this information it can be expected that Asian-Americans who reach old age will have economic and social resources comparable to those of White elderly and far superior to their Black and Hispanic age peers. This is already evident from the fact that a smaller number of Asian-American families (except for Vietnamese) are below the poverty level than either Black or Hispanic families (Gardner et al., 1985).

An often disregarded but potentially important statistic regarding minority elderly is that, in 1980, 82.9% of White children under the age of 18 were living with two parents, compared with only 45% of Black children (Gardner et al., 1985). This portends a future where there may be many older Blacks who will have had little ongoing contact with their children and thus be unable to call on them for assistance in their later years. Even this brief examination of some specific indices relating to minority elderly emphasizes the fact that the impact of ethnicity on aging will not diminish as the United States moves into a society with increasingly larger numbers of older persons.

The meaning of ethnicity for the older person in American society is undergoing change. The meaning of these changes must form the basis for our research agenda over the next 50 years. Along with an aging society, the complex ethnic composition of the United States is being altered by the major numbers of immigrants from areas formerly underrepresented in the population. As the number of older Hispanics and Asians increases, the need to understand the role of ethnicity in aging will also increase.

An enhanced understanding of the importance of ethnicity for older minority group members and Euro-Americans will provide a possibility of generalizing to other groups, or at least will provide a means of extrapolating important differences that may positively or negatively affect older individuals. Ignoring the importance of ethnicity may harm the lives of many older individuals. Overstating the importance of ethnicity may also be damaging.

It is unlikely that the political issues involved in ethnicity and aging will disappear. The configuration of ethnic groups, relationships among family members, and values and attitudes may be altered among successive cohorts of older ethnic group members. The theoretical and methodological problems cited in this chapter inhibit us from coming to grips with the probability and extent of these changes. Dealing with these problems will provide vital information necessary for a full-fledged and, one hopes, rational debate on these issues.

2

Ethnic Aging and the Life Course

Charles M. Barresi

The life course perspective has long been utilized to explain differences in role adjustment during the aging process. Its major applications have been used to understand individual differences, but it can also be useful for explaining group behavior when an entire group is similarly affected in their adjustment to life events.

Social science literature contains many illustrations of the life-stage concept used to explain the development process in children (Freud, 1963; Erickson, 1950). Typically the stages identified in these theories describe the aging process in terms of a sequence of accomplishments, each dependent on the attainment of psychosocial competencies necessary to perform at that level. When the life course perspective is applied to aged persons, however, the emphasis is more likely placed on losses in the ability to satisfactorily carry out social and behavioral activities, rather than gains.

The purpose of this chapter is to explore the implications of the life-course perspective as applied to the process of social aging in ethnic groups. After a brief review and description of the life-course approach, the remainder of the chapter will examine the specific applications and effects that stem from the progressive movement through successive roles and statuses accompanying ethnicity and aging.

The Life-Course Perspective

As individuals progress in chronological age they move through a series of age-related statuses that require certain role behaviors. Over the years a number of different authors have described this process. In premodern societies, the changing nature of social roles as the person ages requires continual adaptation and the ability to carry out expected functions within the social setting (Simmons, 1945). This progression has been characterized as a "flow" of cohorts from one age stratum to another (Riley, Johnson & Foner, 1972). Each new stratum occupied by the cohort places a new set of age-related expectations as well as new rights and duties on the occupants. A more contemporary statement (Atchley, 1983) sees aging in modern society as the result of an accumulation of knowledge and skills that are used to adapt to the changing role demands with which the individual is faced.

The preceding authors have utilized the life-course perspective in a general sense; others such as Buhler and Massarik (1968) have made a more specific application of the concept. Using a time grid, they represent the actual amount of time respondents spend in various role activities. Review of the graph for any given individual's life course identifies the major role changes experienced in terms of the respective time commitments observed. Other researchers (Back & Bourque, 1970) have used the life-course perspective as a means of tracking the development of the person through his or her lifetime to determine the quality of life at different stages. Subjects were asked to chart their life stages in terms of subjective perception of the quality of their lives up to the present and into the future. Results indicate that although the future generally is perceived as holding more promise than the past, respondents see a peak in life satisfaction occurring between the ages of 50 and 70, followed by a continuing decline.

The most fully developed of these quantitative studies is the work of Clausen. In longitudinal studies of persons of different ages, respondents were instructed to reconstruct the high and low points of their lives in terms of self-perceived morale (Clausen, 1972). Noting that major highs and lows appear to be associated with role transitions, he also observes that the effects of one transition may carry over to another. Thus, the perception of past events tends to influence present evaluations.

Although the results of Clausen's research are important for the perspective proposed by this chapter, of greater interest is his conceptual development of life-course determinants. He views the life course as the result of a number of influences, biological and psychological as well as sociological. These determinants fall into four categories: (a) personal resources, (b) sources of support, (c) availability of opportunities, and (d) investments of individual effort (Clausen, 1972). It is important to note that even those resources that are predominantly biological or psychological are still defined and carried out within the context of a group. These factors contribute to the shaping of role transitions and their timing. As is readily apparent, each of them is either part of, or can be affected by, the social context. They also vary from group to group and are particularly differentiated when groups are dissimilar in regard to culture and language.

Utilizing this perspective, ethnic group membership is thus seen as a major shaping force in the development of the life course and the perceptions that persons have of that life course. The model presented in Figure 2-1 modifies the basic framework developed by Clausen (1972) and applies it to the process of aging within the context of an ethnic group. Although Clausen and others mention ethnicity as a variable that affects the life course, no one thus far has elaborated on the impact of ethnic group membership on role transitions.

The model shown in Figure 2-1 illustrates the relationship between individual, group, and cultural factors in defining the life-course process. Individual biological and psychological characteristics are at the core and are shaped and defined by the social context of the ethnic group that serves as the immediate reference group for the person. Additionally, the ethnic group is more or less influenced by the cultural norms of the host society, depending on the amount of contact with the ethnic group and its individual members. Typically, because of the accumulated effects of assimilation, the influence of the wider society will be greater on younger rather than older members of ethnic groups.

The timing of life-change events within the ethnic group, and the role transitions that accompany them, will vary according to group values and norms. Biological and psychological characteristics such

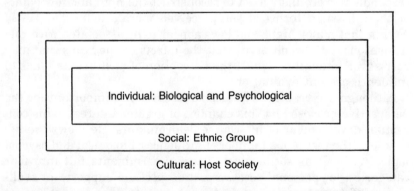

FIGURE 2-1. Characteristics affecting the life course of ethnic elderly.

as sex, age, stature, capacities, and drives become important as socially defined variables. In addition, the individual differences in these variables create dissimilar patterns of life-course development for persons even within the same group. When cross-cultural differences are taken into consideration, the process becomes more complex. This complexity is heightened when one ethnic group is located within the context of the other, as is the case with the typical ethnic group in the host-country setting.

This "problem" of assimilation or accommodation has been discussed by others (Holzberg, 1982; Rosenthal, 1986). Further difficulties emerge, however, when second- and third-generation persons follow a different timetable of life events from that of their foreign-born parents. Of course, because of social change this phenomenon applies to all cross-generational relations, but it is particularly disrupting when the two generations are using different cultural norms for a life-course model.

Another critical factor in the life-course process is the timing of these events (Hagestad & Neugarten, 1985). It is essential to know when these life-change events take place in the personal history of the individual. Early or late entrance into one significant role tends to have "carry-over" effect on the timing of subsequent roles. For example, early entrance into the occupational role shortens childhood and forces the person into adult responsibilities at an early age. Many ethnic elders bemoan a "lost childhood" because of the necessity to provide income for the family. This is especially true of eldest siblings. Delayed marriage provides another illustration. Later marriage results in an older age at birth of first child, and it causes entrance into the grandparent role to be postponed as well. Clausen's (1972) study points out that marriage and birth of first child were identified by both men and women as high points of early adulthood. It is easy to see that the delay of such important roles in one's life will have serious consequences regarding one's self-concept and overall status within the group.

There is also an interesting tendency for those individuals who are "off-time" in one life event to get back "on-time" in the next (Neugarten & Datan, 1973). Persons whose entrance into a life stage has been either delayed or accelerated will generally experience pressures to conform to group norms. More often their response will be not only to come into line with the expectations of their group but to get back "on time" in the next life change event so as to eliminate further sanctions.

To the extent that the ethnic group closely monitors the passage of individuals from one life stage to another it becomes a significant determiner of when these events take place. Analysis of data by Braun and Sweet (1984) from both the United States and Canada indicates the existence of such passages and the fact that they vary cross-culturally. They further conclude that "these results lend support to the sociologist's view that attitudes [regarding these passages] are formed by 'generational events' which occur during the teenage years and that these attitudes *remain fairly stable for the remainder of one's life*" (p. 173, emphasis added). This does not preclude change over a person's lifetime, but it does emphasize that persons socialized into ethnic groups at an early age, especially those who are foreign-born, will very likely continue to follow the dictates of that group regarding life-event passages into their old age.

Individual Characteristics Affecting the Life Course

Biological Factors

Although the norms and values that govern the individual in response to the life course are specific to the group of orientation, individual characteristics can cause variation in perception and performance. For example, sex determines the demands placed on one in regard to social roles and role transitions. All societies place unequal expectations and rewards on persons depending on their sex. Although these differences can be considered under gender roles as dictated by the group, it should also be noted that at the biological level sex differences contribute to survival rates and the propensity to engage in certain family and other roles (Simmons, 1945).

Similarly, stature and health factors contribute to the social roles that are open to the individual and can vary depending on the level of societal development and the emphasis placed on such characteristics. Personal size and strength are generally regarded much more favorably in underdeveloped rather than in modern societies. Cross-cultural studies reveal that in all societies social roles, and the entrance and exit from them, are affected by individual physical abilities. The emphasis on individual physical performance usually places the elderly in a disadvantageous position. This is particularly true of occupational roles, especially those that require exceptional strength or endurance.

In the premodern Inuit society of North America, during difficult periods for the group, elders who are no longer able to contribute materially or who are in poor health elect to stay behind when the group moves on. Although the decision is that of the elder, family and others in the group offer only token effort to dissuade them (Guemple, 1980). Modern societies are not quite as harsh, but they also demonstrate differential treatment of frail and ill elderly. In all societies and ethnic groups, role transitions are affected by physiological differences.

Psychological Factors

Psychological characteristics of the elderly also contribute to the shape of their personal life-course experience. The developmental perspective favored by many social gerontologists who hold a psychological orientation views these characteristics as the result of a combination of innate traits and the socialization process (Gould, 1978). What any particular group sees as useful traits, however, may vary from one culture to another. Intelligence, perfect pitch, or exceptional hand–eye coordination may be more or less valued depending on the level of societal development and its need for that particular ability. Gans (1962), in his classic study of a southern Italian community in Boston's West End, reports that their peer-group orientation curbed aspiration and caused derision toward those members who pursued self-interests and abilities. These restraints applied to the old as well as the young.

Drives recognized as acceptable for the young are often seen as unacceptable for the old. The sex drive is, of course, the most readily identified among those denied the elderly in most groups, but one could also add the need for food and drink. Because of their noncontributory economic position in most societies the elderly are fed last and are the first to suffer in times of famine. The various ways in which ethnic groups deal with these basic drives of the elderly structures their behavior. For example, many groups restrict the sexual behavior of all widows, including the elderly. The sex drive is presumed to be lost, or at least dulled, in the transition from married to widowed status.

Ethnicity also plays a part in the development of certain personality characteristics and attitudes that are manifested in the development of temperament and coping mechanisms displayed by the individual. McGoldrick (1982) discusses Irish reserve as contrasted with Greek suspiciousness and Jewish analyzing as characteristics to be aware of when providing therapy in ethnic family settings. These characteristics become internalized by the individual and are the recognizable, outward mannerisms that are utilized in dealing with life-change events.

For example, the southern Italian ideal characteristics for both men and women, and the ramifications for dealing with life, are expounded on by Gambino (1974). From early childhood males are taught the traits that are summarized by the term *pazienza* (patience). This is not stoicism or fatalism; it is the ideal of being in command of one's own life, of inner control of outward emotions. Women are expected to embrace those characteristics described by the term *serietà* (seriousness). The woman's role is to anchor the family and to be the solid foundation of love and concern on which it rests. From an early age young girls are expected not to be caught up in frivolous or meaningless activities; they are expected to be learning and honing those skills that will prepare them for their future role. For many career-oriented second- and third-generation women this also means that work activities outside the home that interfere with duties as a wife and mother are frowned on by those of an older generation.

Social Factors: The Ethnic Group

Sociological Characteristics

As is evident from the foregoing discussion, social memberships are extremely important in developing personal characteristics that affect the life course. The group delineates and defines the broader sociological characteristics such as age, gender, status, and cohort, which are then overlaid on the personal, individual characteristics to develop a particular set of roles. The socialization process makes it impossible to separate specific personal characteristics from those that are general to the group. However, for the purposes of analysis a distinction is made here between the basic biological and psychological characteristics of the person and the norms, values, and other structural mechanisms of the group that serve to regulate attitudes and behavior (Hagestad & Neugarten, 1985).

For example, the attribution of old age by gender is measured by Neugarten, Moore, and Lowe (1965) in their classic article on age norms. Utilizing a sample of young as well as older respondents, they record perceptions regarding the age at which both men and women are considered "old." Regardless of respondent age, women are consistently viewed as reaching old age sooner than men. This study, done with a U.S. sample is an interesting contrast to the Inuit perception reported by Guemple (1980). Among the Inuit a man is defined as old at about 50 years of age, when he is no longer able to hunt on a full-time basis, whereas women are not considered old until 60 or so. Tasks allocated to women are generally more varied and less strenuous, which allows them to be considered as contributing adults for a longer period of time.

Research conducted on older Mexican Americans shows that the majority of the sample responded that old age begins at or below age 60, with 45% indicating that it begins between 50 and 55 (Crouch, 1972). Another study relates perception of aging to occupation, stating that upper-class executives see themselves as maturing at 50, whereas working-class men identify this time as the beginning of old age (Leake, 1962).

Differentials in sex role expectations have been identified in American society as a "double standard of aging" that defines older women as less sexually desirable than their male counterparts (Sontag, 1975). Lewis and Butler (1972) also discuss this phenomenon, which allows, and even commends, older men engaging in liaisons with younger women, whereas older women are viewed as depraved for showing an interest in younger men. Differences have also been found in the levels of sociability and its effect on well-being for elderly men and women (Barresi, Ferraro, & Hobey, 1984).

These attitudes can also be seen cross-culturally in a study of Mediterranean women (Cool & McCabe, 1983). It was found that although advancing age neutralizes older women as sex objects, it also liberates them from certain restraints in behavior that would not be "seemly" for a younger woman. Older women are not only regarded differently but are also allowed in many instances to express opinions and assertions that would be completely tabooed for younger women and for younger men as well. Before menopause Lebanese women influence male honor through sexual behavior; afterward they influence both men and younger women by what they say about them in the community (Cool & McCabe, 1983). In general, elder Corsican and Lebanese women follow the same patterns of sex role reversal reported by a number of authors (Guttmann, 1976; Kerkhoff, 1966; Lowenthal, Thurner, & Chiriboga, 1975). The increasing power of women as they age results in a greater sense of control and confidence in their roles in the family and the society when compared to men (Guttmann, 1976). This sex role differentiation among elders, which exists in various societies, is carried over to relationships in ethnic groups in the United States.

Social class differences in the timing of life-course events among elderly persons have also been identified (Neugarten & Hagestad, 1976). Relationships exist between the timing of life-change events and median age for both genders. Such events as completion of schooling, leaving home, marriage, birth of first child, and so on are all experienced at an older age by persons of higher social class characteristics. These differences can also vary between race and cohort groups, as found in a study of Black and White family patterns (Uhlenberg, 1974).

Role Transitions

Ethnic group characteristics identified in Figure 2-1 deal with the ways in which values and norms associated with social aging are regarded in the group. These values and norms, as well as age-related roles and role transitions, are unique to the group and affect the succession of life-change events for the elderly. Role transitions for ethnic elderly are related to group norms and can vary widely depending on the specific allocation and content of age-related roles. Social roles that are most frequently allocated to persons in the latter part of the life course concern family and occupational status. More specifically, these roles deal with parental and grandparental activities, widowhood, and retirement.

Grandparent Role. The transition to the grandparent role in American society is generally not a very significant life-change event for most persons. The absence of a clearly defined grandparent role causes this role to vary widely among individuals, as indicated by previous research (Neugarten & Weinstein, 1964). Although this role is obviously not one of great importance for American society, the literature in ethnicity and aging reveals that the grandparent role is more salient in various ethnic groups (Cohler & Grunebaum, 1981; McGoldrick, et al., 1982).

For example, the traditional structure of the Native American family includes the involvement of three generations and multiple parental functions, which are shared by uncles and aunts as well as grandparents (Attneave, 1982). Grandparents often act as surrogate parents while parents engage in work activities outside the home. For children, this arrangement creates ties to several parental figures, including aunts and uncles. Although this pattern is not usually found in the more modern, urban, Native American family, it has created a carry-over of attitudes toward the extended family that influence intergenerational relations in a positive manner. Similar influences are identified among present-day Black and Hispanic families (Rosenthal, 1986).

The effect of these patterns on life-course transitions of elderly persons in ethnic groups, such as those illustrated above, stands in contrast to those reported in studies of the larger society (Kahana &

Kahana, 1971). The general picture that emerges is one that sees the transition from parental to grandparental role as more meaningful and satisfying for those elderly ethnics who have been socialized in a more supportive family environment.

Widowhood. The death of a spouse has been judged as the most stressful change event that can occur in a person's life (Holmes & Rahe, 1967). Because of the lower life expectancy among ethnic groups, as compared to the larger society, it is more likely that ethnic elders will become widowed at an earlier age. This phenomenon is also affected by the typically lower-social-class status found among ethnic elders.

The experience of widowhood, however, will be affected by the degree of integration of the elderly person within the group. In those ethnic groups that provide for a close and protective role for family members, the widowed person finds solace and comfort. There may be, however, a negative side to this cohesive treatment: the widow may experience restrictions on activities as well.

These restrictions are mostly experienced by women and are quite common in those patriarchal societies characterized by the extensive rights of men over women (Lopata, 1973). It is quite usual within these groups to find women required to wear clothing to indicate their widowhood status and continued mourning. In the Portuguese culture the widow is expected to wear black clothing for the remainder of her life and not to remarry (Moitoza, 1982). It is interesting to note that similar mourning restrictions applied to widowers need only be observed for one year.

Widows in such groups may also find their activities closely monitored by other group members to prevent behavior that might be considered unseemly for their status or disrespectful to the memory of the deceased spouse. Welts (1982) reports that whereas Greek widows are held "blameless" for their status and are thus treated respectfully, they are expected not to remarry, out of respect for and loyalty to the deceased husband. Many of these traditional attitudes are also applied by ethnic elders to younger widowed group members, causing a great deal of consternation within both cohorts. These beliefs can also create problems for service providers. For example, activities directors at senior centers that serve some of the more traditional ethnic groups, such as Italians or Greeks, report that widows complain that dancing or games where men and women have physical contact are not "proper" activities for widows.

There is, however, another possible consequence of widowhood in ethnic groups. In her study of Black and lower-class women in

Chicago, many of whom were members of ethnic groups, Lopata (1973) found that widowhood brought some women expressed feelings of relief. For these widows the death of a spouse brought escape from a domineering husband and a sense of independence and release from burdensome responsibilities. A more recent study (Morgan, 1976) also reports that much of the low morale expressed by lower-social-status widows can be attributed to factors such as financial problems or poor health rather than mourning for a lost spouse.

Retirement. Changes in the life course brought about by retirement or cessation of work constitute another major life-change event experienced by most elders. This event is experienced in ethnic groups as well as in the wider society, but the manner in which it occurs and thus the effect it has on group members varies. The involvement of elders in the production process is essential for their continued maintenance of valued exchange resources (Dowd, 1981). More traditional groups, with dependence on agricultural or pastoral economies, offer the elderly more of an opportunity for continued engagement in productive activity at one level or another. More modern industrial economies, however, generally deprive the aged of the work role.

Within ethnic groups, as in others, the work role serves the function of defining one's worth and status (Barresi, 1974). Typically, elders find their status devalued as they are no longer able to contribute valued work activity. This transition in work role not only lowers the status of the elderly, in many groups it also serves to identify the onset of old age. As noted earlier, the Inuit and Mexican Americans use the cessation of work to define the person as old. It is interesting to note that persons in both groups typically engage in strenuous work activity, which tends to hasten the loss of the work role.

The cessation or reduction of the work role and its corresponding losses in status alter the social status and relationships of ethnic elderly. The meaning of work may vary from group to group depending on the degree of internalization of the "work ethic" into group norms. For British-American elderly, work is the main vehicle for both companionship and competition. It also serves as an outlet for both intimacy and aggression. In comparison with the more supportive experiences of Chinese and Jewish elderly males, the loss of the work role is devastating to the typical "workaholic" British male (McGill & Pearce, 1982).

Another aspect to consider when dealing with work role and ethnicity is the degree of integration of ethnic group members into the economy of the wider society. A review of demographic characteristics of minority elderly in the United States reveals that all of the major ethnic groups (except Native Americans) have an overrepresentation of men over 65 years of age in the labor force (Fujii, 1980). The reverse is true for elderly ethnic women.

These figures are reflective of the pattern of underemployment (holding low-paying jobs) typical of most ethnic elderly (Davis, 1976). Their lack of skills and education bars them from high-paying jobs with pension plans and other desirable benefits. The combination of low pay and minimal pension and social security benefits compels many ethnic elderly to continue to work beyond normal retirement age. Thus, the retirement experience may be one that many ethnic elderly either do not share or one that is considerably different from that of other elders in the society.

Cultural Factors: The Host Society

The group dimension of the model in Figure 2-1 concerns the integration of the individual into the ethnic group; the cultural dimension pertains to the integration of the ethnic group into the larger or host culture. This "fit" between ethnic group and host culture affects the life-course transitions of the individual in a number of ways. The greater the degree of separation between the ethnic group and the host culture, the more difficulty ethnic group members have with those life-change events that bring them into contact with segments of the host culture such as work and retirement.

An additional consideration in regard to the relationship between the ethnic group and the host culture is what Trela and Sokolovsky (1979) refer to as cultural distinctiveness. They explain that some ethnic groups are more, and some are less, distinct from the larger society in terms of cultural values, norms, and related social patterns. In addition, ethnic groups differentiate in regard to their attachment to those cultural dimensions that make them distinct from the host culture. Three areas in which this cultural distinctiveness is particularly salient to life-course transitions are language, cultural values and beliefs, and relationships with family and friends.

Language

The proper use of language provides an impetus for integration into the host culture by ethnic group members. The greater the fluency in the language of the wider society, the more likely that ethnic group members, and indeed the entire group itself, will be integrated into the host culture. Language is at once a part of and the means of transmission of the culture. It incorporates the values, beliefs, and even the imagery of the culture as it facilitates thought and shapes the way in which persons view the world around them, as described in the linguistic relativity hypothesis (Sapir, 1929; Whorf, 1956). This hypothesis holds that speakers of a given language interpret the world through the unique grammatical forms and categories that their language provides, and the language they speak predisposes them to particular interpretations of reality.

Language problems, therefore, not only create difficulty in communication but can also restrict the ability of the individual to conceptualize. An understanding of such categories as time, tense, space, and person depend entirely on the manner in which one's language facilitates concept formation (Whorf, 1956). Translation, no matter how accurate, will simply not provide the non-native speaker with the same view of the world. Social reality is constructed, and language is the raw material from which that reality is fabricated. The use of the rules and patterns of one language to construct an everyday world not only creates a different world from the one viewed through other languages but also restrains the ability to conceptualize that world (Berger & Luckman, 1966). An illustration is Whorf's (1956) description of the lack of a future tense in the language of the Hopi Indian.

The language problem can be further exacerbated when the ethnic and host culture languages stem from entirely different linguistic traditions, as is the case with Oriental ethnic groups in Western host societies. Ethnic groups that are closer in language and tradition to the host culture have fewer difficulties in assimilation and in generally partaking in the everyday worl' that it defines.

The inability to communicate in the language of the host culture directly affects the members of the ethnic group in their life-course transitions by restricting access to work, education, social services, and other institutions. The greater the language barrier, the more isolated the group is and unable to participate in services provided in the wider society. Consider the typical profile of Chinese elderly in the United States as "urban residents, living alone, with little formal education, unable to speak English, and poor without knowing how to obtain services" (Fujii, 1980, p. 273).

Values and Beliefs

The degree of polarization between ethnic and host cultures is determined to a great extent by the amount of continuity or discontinuity in basic values and beliefs between the two groups. In many instances the value systems of the two groups are at odds and therefore require the person to make choices between "old" and "new" ways. Belief systems that are particularly salient to the life-course process and have a profound effect on the life of the individual are those in the areas of religion, family, and work.

A review of the impact of values and attitudes of the elderly on life-course transitions identifies such central values as morality, filial piety, and productivity (Tornstam, 1982). The level of belief held by the elderly person, as well as the beliefs of those around him or her, can result in differential life-course patterns. The social values of an ethnic group and the institutional foundations on which such beliefs are structured determine not only the timing of life-course transitions but also the way in which those transitions are regarded.

Of particular importance for understanding the role of cultural values in life-course transitions is the disjunction between value systems that hold to the Protestant ethic and its associated beliefs regarding productivity and the worth of the individual. Groups that observe the value of filial piety find their views in conflict with more modern materialistic cultures, which place emphasis on independence and individuality (Lenzer, 1961). Oriental ethnic groups in the United States are especially affected (Fujii, 1980).

Other values that can vitally affect the life course are those that deal with basic philosophies of life. The Iranian family in the United States has been described as possessing a deeply seated hedonism. This is expressed in their poetry and literature and has become ingrained in their way of life. Iranians are characterized as living for the present, with their greatest concern being to extract the most from it. Planning is unnecessary because the future is uncertain (Jalali, 1982).

Life-course orientation in such a group is more present- than future-oriented, and life-course stages tend to be less rigid. Iranians, like Sicilians, have a long political history of mistrust and cynicism toward authority, which leads to closer relationships to family and friends, and a sense of fatalism that leads the individual to believe in less control over the direction of his or her life (Gambino, 1974; Jalali, 1982).

Family and Friends

Relationships with family and friends provide another dimension of ethnic group culture that varies considerably from group to group and can critically affect life-course transitions. These relationships include intergenerational as well as peer group associations and can lie anywhere on a range of intimacy from close to distant. The socialization and level of support provided by these relationships direct and sustain the person through entrance and exit of such late-life-course transitions as grandparenthood, widowhood, remarriage, and retirement.

Much has been written on the ethnic family and support levels, and recent works have concluded that many of the differences between groups can be accounted for by socioeconomic levels (Rosenthal, 1986). It has also been suggested that the pattern of filial obligation is stronger among younger and middle-aged adults than among elders in some ethnic groups (Fandetti & Gelfand, 1976). However, differences still exist between older and younger ethnic group members, especially those at lower socioeconomic levels. These differences are further supported by traditional values, and ethnic groups such as Italian or Polish continue to show closer family relations and support than do Scandinavian Americans, for example (Woehrer, 1978).

Groups such as Japanese, Italians, and Mexicans display lineal family relationships, in which position and status within the family is dependent on age and sex. Male parental authority in these groups is absolute, and intergenerational relationships are strictly defined and rigidly observed. This pattern stands in marked contrast to ethnic groups in which the collateral form of relationship prevails. In this latter type the relationship between siblings, and even between children and parents, is more egalitarian. Black and Irish-American families are more likely to follow the collateral form, which is more typically "American" than ethnic (Greeley, 1972). As ethnic groups become more assimilated, the relationships between generations tend to become more collateral, thereby changing the nature of support system expectations, as defined by both elders and their younger kin. These differential expectations lead to strain and conflict in intergenerational relations, especially when offspring become upwardly mobile.

Those ethnic groups with traditionally closer family relationships tend to be less open to seeking support from persons or groups outside the family. Relatives tend to be one's best friends, and there is less involvement with social organizations than with kin groups (Gambino, 1974; Gans, 1962). Friends are chosen with great care, and those who are admitted into intimate relationships are usually made into near-kin by becoming a child's godparent or confirmation sponsor or by involvement in some other equally meaningful family life-course event.

These near-kin are added to the list of closely related persons who serve the individual in time of need. However, there may be a negative side to the reliance on close family and friendship relations. In times of need those persons who have never become integrated into the host culture may experience problems when family members are not readily available because of death or mobility (Woehrer, 1978). In contrast, individuals who have learned to utilize social services and other formal organizations to assist in life-course transitions may be better off in the long run.

Conclusion

The purpose of theoretical formulations in science is to provide insight into the workings of the everyday world as we find it, not as we wish it were. This chapter places emphasis on the life-course perspective in ethnic aging and the importance of the mechanisms of the life-course process in the development of an individual's history within the larger historical event of the group. Thus, it acknowledges the dynamics of change as it occurs in both the person and the group and the many factors that affect both individual and group history.

An understanding of the life-course perspective is essential for a more complete comprehension of the process of social aging. Circumstance and timing are variables that contribute greatly to the occurrence and sequence of events that govern roles and their impact on both the person and the society. Ethnicity is also a major factor influencing the life course and should therefore be included as a central variable when attempting to explain, understand, and predict behavioral issues regarding the elderly. Because of the influence of the group on the individual, the salience of the ethnicity variable is evident in the many ways in which it impinges on life-course components, whether they are physiological, social, or cultural. These three components are integrated and have interrelated effects on one another.

Although there are many facets of the life course that impact on later life, the most salient center on family and work activities. These basic institutional structures provide the foundation for the dominant controls over the individual's development. This developmental process is structured within the context of individual characteristics and group norms. Progression through successive life change events is grounded in the reality of one's unique personal characteristics and group memberships. By focusing on central roles within the most salient of group memberships, the life-course perspective brings attention to the core components of personal and social development. The added dimension of temporal sequence and the dynamics of social change allow this approach to be attuned to the realities of social aging. It is imperative that not only gerontological researchers but also policymakers and service providers be aware of the necessity of approaching the unique world of the elderly ethnic from a perspective that furnishes a broad level of understanding of the factors involved. The life-course perspective not only supplies the necessary breadth for such a level of comprehension; at the same time it opens new vistas that other approaches fail to penetrate.

3

Ethnicity and Lifetimes: Self-Concepts and Situational Contexts of Ethnic Identity in Late Life

Mark Luborsky and Robert L. Rubinstein

Ethnicity has often been discussed in at least three ways: as the product of historical and cultural group identities (Handlin, 1973); as part of an individual's self-concept and self-identity (Rosenberg, 1981); and as these two in relation, the interaction of individual and group identities over time (Barth, 1969). Certainly, patterns of ethnic behavior may be thought of as a fundamental orientation to living common to individuals who share historical and cultural circumstances. However, ethnicity may also be thought of as situational. Ethnic thoughts and behaviors, conscious and unconscious, may be produced, heightened, or diminished in situations of both ethnic contrast and complementarity.

One such situation is the life course and its component life stages and key events (Frank, 1984). Hypothetically, as has been proposed by Erikson (1968), if each life stage is characterized by central existential or developmental issues concerning "identity" and if ethnicity is a key component of identity, then ethnicity must in some way meaningfully intertwine with the occurrence of life stages and key events. As a person moves through various life stages, he or she may enter settings that call for aspects of ethnic identity to emerge or be submerged (Myerhoff, 1978). Such situations and key events may include school, dating, work, marriage, child raising, neighborhood life, friendships, and, in late life, retirement, widowhood, and the subjectively defined onset of old age. Along this line, Kastenbaum (1979) has hypothesized that ethnicity may be "resurgent" in late life, possibly in response to a separation from the public sphere. Psychodynamic and developmental aspects of ethnicity have received little attention. There is increasing awareness, however, of the role of ethnicity in such events in several ways. First, ethnicity shapes individual identity and self-conception. Second, ethnicity can influence the dominant values and modes of communication of ethnic individuals (McGoldrick, Pearce, & Giordano, 1982). Third, ethnic values and modes of communication can influence how individuals typically relate to one another, either through what is spoken of and how or what is left out and how. And, fourth, as we point out, ethnicity is a popular language of family function (Friedman, 1982). People do not "naturally" know about depth psychology but may speak of many important relational behaviors, especially in regard to the family, through a language of ethnicity.

The life course does not exist in a vacuum. Each part of a lifetime is experienced in a social, cultural, and historical context (Hareven, 1978), which greatly shapes and is shaped by the objective and subjective realities of life. Thus, although it is possible to talk, theoretically, about ethnicity, it is not in fact possible to separate the experience of ethnicity and ethnic identity from concrete historical moments.

Similarly, it would be short-sighted to treat the ethnic identity of elderly individuals as if it exists solely with reference to feelings of ethnicity at the moment. Or, put another way, it is likely that current ethnic identity has been distilled through past ethnic experiences. Thus, if it is true that a present-day sense of identity is constructed from a lifetime of experiences, this should be true of ethnic identity as well.

The purpose of this chapter is to examine ethnicity as a life-course phenomenon and to show how it operates similarly for different groups. In a sense, then, this chapter is not about three discrete ethnic groups but about ethnicity as a social and individual process that may exist regardless of the particular group in question. We further suggest that ethnic identity as viewed from late life draws some of its substance from lifelong ethnic concerns in two ways. First, past experiences relating to ethnic identity serve as salient complements, contrasts, or settings to present-day ethnic identity. Second, there is evidence that each person's identity in late life is organized thematically (Kaufman, 1981) and is constructed from a lifetime of varied experiences. As has been pointed out by those who write about the life review, retrospectivity is purposeful and concerns issues of identity at the present (Butler, 1963).

Ethnicity and Older Widowers

In this chapter we report on data being gathered in a study of Jewish, Irish, and Italian men, aged 65 and older, widowed 2 to 8 years, after a long-term marriage. The study is being conducted at the Philadelphia Geriatric Center. The focus of the study is on life reorganization by ethnically identified older widowers after the initial bereavement period has passed. Issues of identity reformulation, changes in health and activity patterns, ethnic identity, and lingering attachment to the deceased spouse are central to the study. Ethnicity is operationalized here both as self-identification as Irish, Italian, or Jewish (to screen those who answered ads for men with these "backgrounds") and as lineal symmetry (that both parents were of the same ethnic group). The generation of immigration was not a concern for sample selection. Here we will discuss findings from the initial phase of the research in which we are interviewing 15 widowers from each of the three ethnic groups.

We adopted two strategies in measuring ethnicity. One was to develop a short instrument that focused on behavioral and psychological aspects of ethnicity so as to compare briefly what seemed to be salient indicators of ethnicity as they had been noted in the literature and in our own experience. The second was to develop a series of open-ended questions about the meaning of ethnicity and allow sufficient time for their discussion in the context of a multiple-session, in-depth-interview format.

It is apparent from the responses to questions about ethnicity, identity, and personal beliefs that, although questions of ethnic identity can in some sense be answered with reference to the present day, men in the sample often discuss ethnic identities and their meanings with reference to past events. Let us give a number of brief examples.

Mr. Donnell, aged 76, had been widowed about 3 years. When he phoned in to participate in the study, we assumed his name was Irish but learned it had originally been Doniletti. His Italian ethnic identity was a source of conflict to him. In the interviews he described an early life that featured family strife, conflict, and brutality as well as warm memories of the aunt who raised him. Mr. Donnell's upbringing was reflected in lifelong conflicts about his ethnic identity. On the one hand, he did many things typical of Italian-American elderly in Philadelphia: he lived in an Italian neighborhood, attended church in an Italian parish, married an Italian woman, and had close affinal relations. Most of his acquaintances and significant others on a social network profile were Italians.

On the other hand, his response to a question about the meaning to him of his Italian identity prompted a vigorous discussion of how the Italians were "the worst" ethnic group, this anchored by several stories of how Italians had caused difficulties for him in several employment situations. The rejection of his heritage was played out in other domains. For example, in his 40s he suffered a mental and physical crisis that, among other things, led to a psychologically based stomach disorder. He ceased eating Italian foods, which his wife loved to prepare and eat, and substituted bland American foods, which he processed in a blender and drank. Additionally, his wife's death, 3 years before the interviews, led to a further redefinition of the life-course situation influencing his ethnic identity. After his wife died, he was able to disentangle himself from his Italian in-laws; for his taste, they were too concerned with being "Italian." He was now quite isolated. This latest synthesis about the meaning of his Italian identity—a pulling away from it—was in fact one in a series of lifelong conflicts and resolutions. His current ethnic feeling was thus influenced by an important life-span event (widowhood) compounded by long-standing conflicts.

Whereas Mr. Donnell pulled away from his ethnic heritage, another informant, Mr. Goldberg, drew closer to it. Mr. Goldberg, aged 73, had been widowed for 3 years. A Jew, he made a distinction between Judaism as an ethnic identity and as a religion. Although hardly religious, he had spent much of his life acting on a number of deeply held moral convictions about the need for equality and democracy. He noted that although he was an atheist he felt very much a Jew. Because of his personal concern for social welfare and reform he felt that, although he was not Jewish in a religious sense, he fit well within a Jewish tradition of prophetic protest.

He received a large settlement from his wife's insurance policy and spent a good deal of the money lavishly outfitting a woodworking shop in his basement. His wife was Catholic, and when they married, he reported, he and his wife agreed never to discuss religion in the home. He felt that they had kept to this policy. Mr. Goldberg had three daughters, two of whom "practice no religion" and one who had become very involved in Judaism.

A year to the day after his wife's death, Mr. Goldberg was awakened by sharp chest pains. Fearing a heart attack, he was hospitalized for tests, which found nothing. Eventually, one doctor asked him how he felt toward his deceased wife. He told the doctor of many unresolved feelings: guilt about having treated his wife poorly and fear of estrangement from his daughters. The doctor encouraged him to talk with them about his feelings, which he did.

At one point his religious daughter told him that some of the woodwork in her synagogue needed repair, and she put him in touch with her rabbi. He did the work there and was also able to engage the rabbi in conversations about religion. This represented a reconnection of sorts with Judaism as a religious system. Mr. Goldberg also noted that his wife's death enabled him to appreciate more actively the Jewish religion and cultural tradition. He attributed this change to now being free of the pact with his wife not to discuss religious matters. He also felt that the change had to do with his own aging and an increased concern with his place in the world.

Life-Course Concerns

The ethnic groups represented here each have distinctive cultural practices and world views. Nevertheless, despite such differences, which pertain to both the behavioral content and world view of members of each group, we suggest that developmentally, on the level of the individual, ethnicity has similar moral meanings and tactical applications for the older men we interviewed.

Reflecting on how ethnicity is built from episodes and experiences over a lifetime, we suggest that for the older men in the sample the meaning of ethnicity is related to four intertwined life-course concerns. First, the meaning of ethnicity in late life derives from issues of life-span development and family history. Second, ethnic identity derives meaning from the historical settings and circumstances during which key events are experienced. Third, current-day ethnic identity is situationally evoked depending on the needs and goals of individuals. Fourth, past ethnic identity and experiences continue to be reworked as raw material for current-day ethnic meaning. We will discuss each of these points in turn.

The Meaning of Ethnicity in Late Life Derives from Issues of Life Span Development and Family History

That the meaning of ethnicity derives from issues of life-span development and family history was quite apparent in the material collected from many of our informants. At one level ethnicity represents continuity, but it is possible to view analytically statements of ethnic identity as a shorthand by which informants express themes of personal development, differentiation, individuation, and identity regarding family as well as intrapsychic and interpersonal conflict. Key points along the developmental cycle may be infused with aspects of family meaning embodied as ethnic traits, practices, and beliefs.

We became concerned with the possibility that informants were framing ethnicity as a language for discourse on two related issues: family relations and developmental events. Instilling ethnic knowledge of practices and conceptions of self are accomplished in dyadic filial relationships. Moreover, whatever involvement an ethnic individual has in a larger ethnic community, a particular stance on ethnic beliefs and practices is likely to be part of a family's tradition. An individual's subjective sense of identity and attitudes toward his or her ethnicity are enmeshed with those toward parental figures.

Let us briefly consider here some aspects of ethnicity as a language of family relations. Ethnicity has often been operationalized as a unitary thing but in two ways. First, it has been portrayed—for example, in quantitative research—as an independent variable that will wholly or partially explain something about a person. The thinking here is that if a person is known to be an X, his behavior becomes understandable. Second, the unitary conception of ethnicity is found in its conception as a feeling of "we-ness" and a commitment to a community that produces "typical" behaviors or actions. In either version of this unitary view, ethnicity may be said to emerge as a "solid" property of persons and communities. Yet, in contrast, ethnicity has also been portrayed as "fluid" in two ways. First, it has been seen as a set of differences between generations consequent to processes of immigration, acculturation, and generational succession. Second, it has been viewed as a set of differences in what constitutes core or "acceptable" ethnic behavior by individuals. For example, minimally, if persons A and B display the very same ethnic behaviors, but in addition person B enacts many nonethnic behaviors and A does not, who is "more ethnic"? And, of course, further complications in defining the degree of ethnicity will ensue when two individuals do not enact the same behaviors.

Thus, in its fluid sense ethnicity may serve as a foil for intergenerational issues in its role as an arena that overlaps, but is analytically distinct from, family process and filial concerns. For example, key developmental issues of individuation and the establishment of individual identity may be conceptualized as both family and ethnic problems for the individual. We would suggest, as many have, that issues of personal identity are lifelong, and we are therefore suggesting that issues of ethnic identity are also lifelong. Ethnic traditions not only afford the individual a sense of continuity with a nationality, family, or heritage but also provide one language for the expression of conflict and the need for redefinition at any moment in life. When one's cultural heritage and concommitant bundle of values and identities may be difficult to accept during certain periods of life, another package of values and identities may be acceptable and substitutable. This makes even more complex Kastenbaum's (1979) conceptualization of ethnicity as lineage, behavior, and self-conception in that both self-conception and behavior may change periodically.

It would seem that both the fluid and the solid perspectives represent distinctive manifestations of the same phenomenon, and in fact "ethnicity" may constructively be thought of as having these two forms. In the solid form ethnicity is transgenerational, enduring, communal, and positive, and ethnic identity is stable. The fluid form has as its focus each generation and therefore the fact that, within each generation, individuals must make their own way, supplant the older generation, and in a some sense turn against them by adapting new values and deriving core experiences from new situations.

This way of discussing ethnicity bears a striking resemblance to issues of, on the one hand, differentiation, separation, and individuation in the family and, on the other, the continued integration, participation in, and attachment to the family. We learn to be both apart from and a part of our families. As a consequence, we might conclude that one important function of ethnicity is as a distinctive language for an intra- and interfamily dialogue about issues such as attachment, community, individuation, separation, and relationships. In a sense, ethnicity is a language of parent–child relationships.

Some of these issues are apparent in the case of one informant, Mr. Silver, a vital, 90-year-old Jewish émigré from Poland via England who was often loath to talk about personal feelings in our interviews. At key points in his life course his Jewish identity was heightened or diminished, and influenced by particular events, forming a foundation for both individuation and integration. Such key points occurred at the onset of adulthood, at marriage, at retirement, and at widowhood.

The outlines of his life were reviewed in a life history interview we conducted. He went to public school in England; in the evenings he studied for his bar mitzvah at the Hebrew school (*Cheder*). He noted happily that during one of the school terms his mother was the teacher. He viewed his father with no fond memories as a stern, distant man. As a Jew in England he experienced "lots of harassment and bad treatment; you were considered less than a person." When at age 14 he started selling newspapers, he bought his mother a single fresh peach weekly, a luxury that cost more than a third of his pay. Within 2 years he was fired for refusing to work on Yom Kippur. After a bleak year of unemployment he emigrated to America as his older brother had. During the interview he made the unsolicited comment that "the hardest thing in my whole life was leaving my mother." This statement was surprising in the force of its emotionality because, throughout five interviews, he consistently failed to describe any inner feelings or affect states, even when prompted.

On the boat he shared a cabin with a non-Jew. Mr. Silver feared revealing his religious identity and "being treated as less than a person," so he removed his *tfillin* (ritual cloths) and hid them under his mattress for the trip. He reported that he forgot to retrieve them from under the mattress in the cabin when he arrived in America. Further, he did not buy a new set once here. Moreover, he failed to attend temple for several years after arriving, but he started regular observances when his mother emigrated to America 6 years later. At age 33 he married and joined the reformed temple his wife attended. He explained the shift by saying that he read Hebrew well but could not translate it, and so he never really knew what was being said. He therefore entered an Americanized contemporary tradition, leaving behind the orthodoxy of his childhood and his mother. In addition, he gave up observing traditional Friday night practices of candle lighting and wine blessing. He was chastised by more orthodox friends for not knowing Hebrew, but he regarded them contemptuously, he said, because he attended temple each week and they did not. After his children were born, he was too busy working to become very active in the Jewish community, he reported. But upon retirement at age 76, he immersed himself in Jewish organizations and received many awards of recognition for his work.

At age 83 he became a widower. Now, he noted, he only dates "Jewish girls" and lives in a predominantly Jewish apartment complex. He said that he retains a strong attachment to his wife, wearing her Star of David pin on his jacket lapel and kissing her picture each night and morning on the way in and out of the bedroom. After remarking on his lifelong and childhood experiences of feeling harassed as a Jew, he said he now has only Jewish friends.

In summary, it appears that, at key moments when consolidating a new identity—as a young adult, an immigrant to America, husband and father, retiree and widower—his sense of Jewishness emerges distinctively and serves in part as a means of differentiation, integration, and identity formation and maintenance.

A number of postures are available in respect to ethnicity and self over the life course. Working through tensions about one's ethnic identity may be a mechanism for working through the relationship of a person to his family. Alternatively, one may seemingly accept family relations but reject an ethnic heritage and in so doing reject ethnic values. Thus, ethnic values and practices may become a vehicle for externalizing and objectifying aspects of subjective experience that a person is unable or unwilling to confront directly within the family or community.

Ethnic Identity Derives Meaning from the Historical Settings and Circumstances During Which Key Events are Experienced

We will discuss two sorts of such key events here. The first is the creation of a general meaning for ethnicity as a cultural category in society. The second relates to specific events occurring within and influencing the life spans of informants.

One of the most important circumstances has been the changing public climate and meaning of ethnicity in society at large. Ethnic festivals common today suggest that there may now be a generic ethnicity in the folk sociology of identity. This identity is viewed as a part of each citizen's social identity as an individual in America and above and beyond membership in an ethnic family. Such a view of ethnicity contrasts with the other popular notion of ethnicity disappearing in a melting pot.

Among the men we interviewed, ethnicity was regarded as an inherent part of everyone and conceptualized as family background, traditions, and group characteristics, defined in terms of the nationality of immigrant ancestors. Ethnic identity provides members with an affiliation in a particular group of people who share similar "roots." Such a sense of generic ethnicity has been enhanced by its commercialization and its use as a favored expressive entity in the public realm, such as in television news stories and international day festivals.

However, in response to the particular question "Who is most and who is least ethnic in your family?" informants often phrased replies in terms of a continuum spanning from "traditional" to "Americanized." More Italian and Irish than Jewish men, for example, answered in terms of who was most traditional in the old country ways and who was the most Americanized in spending habits, language, cuisine, or education. Persons classed as most ethnic were categorized as still retaining knowledge of family relationships, distant relatives, special foods, holidays, and proper observances, and often as living in the old neighborhood.

There have been specific changes in the meaning of being Italian, Irish, or Jewish across the life span of the informants. Changes have been focused around the meaning of co-experienced events, such as the Depression, World War II, and labor union movements, as well as particular events that seem to pertain more to one group than to another, such as the Holocaust, troubles in northern Ireland, or the fact that Italy was the enemy in World War II. These aspects of ethnic identity again reinforce the importance of attuning analysis of ethnicity to the interplay between individual experiences, historical times, developmental phases, and current situational factors. It is important to note that the awareness of distinctions between ethnic groups has never been uniform during the lives of our older informants but rather has alternated with periods in which there has been a heightened sense of ethnic blurring.

Several of the older Italian men, for example, reported incidents in the 1920s and 1930s in which they suffered at the hands of the Irish. Mr. Donnell, mentioned above, could "pass" as Irish because of his name, although he is Italian. As a young man he worked on vegetable farms in southern New Jersey and benefited from his fictitious ethnicity in the hierarchical organization of the farms: English were owners, Irish were managers, and Italians were field pickers. Mr. Passo, an Italian, spent much of his childhood in a Catholic orphanage run by nuns who were of Irish descent, and he suffered, he felt, because they tended to favor the Irish orphans. Both men view the Roosevelt administration and World War II as the time at which these sharp ethnic distinctions began to wane. It is clear that for both men certain eras affected ethnic definition and that, at the current time, the historicity of ethnic experiences serves as backdrop for their ethnic identity.

Current-Day Ethnic Identity is Situationally Evoked

That current-day ethnic identity is situationally evoked among the older widowers we have interviewed should be clear from the discussion above. Yet this too is somewhat paradoxical and is best understood, we feel, in light of a conceptualization of ethnicity as both solid and fluid. Ethnic identity should be continuous, constant, and community-reinforced, not only as an attribute of personhood, like gender, but also as a product of popularized ethnicity. However, among the older men in the sample, important situations evoked reconsideration of ethnicity. These included the need to reorganize their lives after the death of a spouse and the onset of aspects of a subjectively defined old age. Such tasks may engender, for example, a desire to forge a sense of continuity with one's past or one's "people" or, conversely a withdrawal of sorts. The former may be interpreted in part as a projection of the desired continuity with one's departed spouse into a larger system of shared substance.

Mr. DiAngelo exemplifies these dimensions. Italian born, at 2 years of age he and his mother joined his father, who had already emigrated to Philadelphia. They shared a house with other members of his father's family in the Italian neighborhood and led a "traditional" Italian home life. Family life was described as paramount. His father and brothers ran a clothes-making business. His Italian identity and lack of formal education at that time limited his employment prospects. He spoke of being harassed by non-Italians at school and elsewhere. He framed accounts of his life history by aligning himself with his father, who early on admonished him "above all else you care for the family you bring into the world." He described a major goal throughout life as to give all to his family and children and to provide them with a "good" (i.e., Catholic) education. Although it was his role to earn the money, his wife managed it and prepared and distributed food among family members following traditional patterns of Italian commensalism.

Although he continues to grieve for his wife, Mr. DiAngelo attributes learning to manage his grief equally to the need to set a good example for his children and grandchildren and to the desire to live for his wife to see how the grandchildren turn out. Nowadays he has invested himself with the role of preparing and distributing traditional Italian foods to his two daughters and their families, his sister, and his 94-year-old mother. In this fashion he has taken on aspects of his deceased wife's family role, which also was in part a way of vivifying his attachment to her: "My wife's family ran a restaurant. She learned cooking there, and I learned from her." He frequently receives orders from sons-in-law and grandchildren for special dishes and desserts. He makes weekly trips to the old Italian neighborhoods to buy fresh Italian breads and pasta for his daughters' families who live in the suburbs. In brief, the Italian family culinary heritage and patterns of exchange provide him with outlets and materials for building a new identity, both as an Italian and as a widower.

Mr. DiAngelo described himself as "the black sheep of the family," referring to his English-language abilities, job, and residence. He described his father as very strict about defending the family's Italian name, speaking only Italian at home, and not becoming

Americanized. His brothers, sisters, and relatives who worked in the clothing factory all spoke Italian at work and at home. Mr. DiAngelo broke with his family when he did not join the family business. At age 14, when he left school, he took a job as a metal-worker, an occupation he would retain throughout his life. The predominant language was English wherever he worked. He gave this as the reason for his weaker grasp of Italian. Contrasting the generations and at the same time identifying himself with his mother, he depicted himself as "just like, but the opposite of my mother. She spoke Italian only but could understand English. I speak English but understand Italian." He was among the first in his family to move out to the suburbs; his mother and sister still live in the old neighborhood.

But he also regarded being a black sheep in a positive light. He believed he was specially able to care for his wider kin because of the new (among tailors) skills in metalwork and construction. Repeatedly during the interviews he stressed that the whole family depended on him to do things around the house that they, as garment workers, could not do. He installed concrete patios, built fences, and did minor electrical repairs, among other tasks, which saved them from having to hire an outside contractor. In part, he regarded himself as having taken a step away from the traditional ways of life and skills of his natal land, becoming skilled for life in America.

Another example shows how current-day ethnic identity is situationally evoked. Mr. O'Connor, aged 77 years and widowed 3 years, was devastated by the loss of his wife and "was pretty bad off for a year, year and a half after she died." After her death he sold their Florida condominium and moved back to Philadelphia, where they had lived for many years. The property sale, his wife's savings, and insurance benefits left him with more than $100,000. He enjoyed giving most of it away: $15,000 to each of three sisters, $1,500 to each of 20 nieces and nephews, $1,000 to each of 18 cousins.

He got the idea for this distribution, he said, from his mother's uncle, who, arriving from Ireland in the 1840s, settled in the Midwest, became wealthy, and gave members of his own family substantial sums of money in a similar manner. During a trip to Ireland, Mr. O'Connor returned to his mother's hometown and found the cemetary of his mother's family, where the grave stones were inscribed with a note that they were provided by his mother's uncle from "Indiana, USA." This was a satisfying link in a circle of identity for him.

Past Ethnic Experiences Continue to be Reworked as Raw Material for Present Day Ethnic Meaning

Our fourth point in examining ethnicity as a lifetime phenomenon is that past ethnic identity and experiences continue to be reworked as raw materials for current-day ethnic meaning. By this we mean that the construction of ethnic identity by individuals across their life span is not immutably fixed in youth or young adulthood. Rather, the personal meanings of ethnicity are important materials for reworking notions of the self and social identities in later life. Further, the ethnic experiences of youth and adulthood are reinterpreted over the life course. Whereas we previously described how ethnic identity can be rejected or elaborated in part as a language for familial issues, it is also necessary to consider there may be a different set of meanings attributed to reembracing or rejecting dimensions of one's ethnic identity in later life. This can be illustrated in the case of Mr. Green.

Mr. Green, a 66-year-old widower, was born in America 4 years after his parents emigrated in 1914 from Russia. He considers himself to be very Jewish. A difficult birth left him with only partial use of his left hand. As a child he worked hard at therapy to overcome the disability. He reported with satisfaction how he refused to accept his disability. Rather than becoming dependent, as a youth he took up woodworking, to his parents' chagrin. His ability to do woodwork was a personal symbol throughout his life of his being able to overcome adversity and to thrive despite limitations.

Two years after his wife's death Mr. Green moved into a converted garage attached to his daughter's house. He would not date other women, noting "that part of my life is over," and he had not relinquished his grief or disposed of his wife's personal belongings. His current-day life revolves around family and religious activities. He helps care for his two preschool grandsons and is proud of them. An accomplished woodworker, he teaches crafts at a senior center 2 days a week. He also actively attends religious services.

His fondest memories as a child were walking to and from temple with his grandfather, who was a respected religious teacher who prepared boys for their bar mitzvahs. When his grandfather died, his father took over those same duties in the community. His grandfather, and later his father, gave him several prayer books for the various holidays and commentaries on the Torah. He cherished these not only for the memories they evoked but also because they allowed him to carry on traditions of the Jewish people and the roles of his paternal ancestors.

He built a special bookcase to keep the collection of old prayer books. In addition, he taught the Hebrew alphabet to his grandson. Before his marriage he was "not too observant." Once married, however, he joined the temple's men's club and served as secretary for several years. He was most active when his children were growing up and became less active as they got older. However, after his wife's death he increased involvement by attending morning and evening services and serving as an usher. Traditional mourning practices, including attendance at the temple, provided him with a framework for daily actions at a time when he "did things automatically without feeling or thought for a long time." He reported feeling closer to his Jewish faith since his wife's death, wanting to participate even more. Fifteen months after his wife died he made his first trip to Israel and was preparing for a second trip at the time of our interviews.

The synagogue is valued by him now as a community, as well as a religious center. In order to cope with his wife's death, he said, he "buried myself in woodworking to avoid sitting and thinking of her." Nowadays "people ask for advice for fixing things. I now do repairs on the chairs for the *bimah*" [raised area at the front of the temple]. About a year after his wife's death he noted that the temple's wooden chairs and the children's jungle gym were in bad condition, and he spent many satisfying hours rebuilding them. He makes special wood pointers used for reading from the Torah during services. He presented his nephew with a specially carved pointer for reading the Torah during his bar mitzvah. Several of the religious objects he makes are in use by Jewish people around the United States and in Israel.

After his wife died, Mr. Green closed that part of his life and sought to fulfill his needs for intimacy within his daughter's family. He revitalized his Jewish identity and his role as a religious teacher, following the path of his father and grandfather. The dynamics of his life reorganization included combining woodworking skills, Judaic religious practices, and a Green family role for older men. The older men instill in children Jewish knowledge in preparation for adulthood. Woodworking carried, for Mr. Green, a vigorous sense of his lifelong tenacity at overcoming adversity, epitomized and acted out through his craft, despite a partially disabled arm. Woodworking is an instrumental activity by means of which he keeps busy and meets people, and it is also a personal model, developed in his youth, of how to overcome disability, which he has applied to today's challenge of adapting to being a widower.

He is combining these elements of life experience, Judaism, and family roles for older men in religious training to work out a new synthesis of his identity and life.

Broader Significance

To close, we would like to indicate how our approach and data may be relevant to other ethnic groups, and also their bearing on the field of ethnicity and aging.

Our approach in using the concept of lifetime ethnicity suggests, first, dimensions that may be common to many ethnic groups. These were illustrated here with cases from three different ethnic groups. The data suggest that, for each group, ethnicity intertwines with life stage and that the personal meanings and social experiences of ethnic identity continue to be salient and mutable in late life. Yet many other questions remain. We examined three Caucasian ethnic groups. We suspect that the mutability of ethnic identity seen among these groups might not be duplicated among minority, non-White ethnic groups, the social meaning of whose ethnicity is less amenable to so much individual redefinition. Thus, some differences may be revealed by applying that concept to ethnic minorities. Differences may suggest limitations or alterations to the concept. The concept poses a second interesting question. Ethnic identity would appear to be "fixed" within the person and redefined at different points according to an internal ethnic cycle across people's lifetimes. The relationship of a particular ethnic identity cycle to other life-course cycles and developmental tasks may differently shape individuals' attraction to or distancing from their own ethnic identities. Such questions need to be addressed in new studies.

These concerns lead to considerations for the field in general. Ethnicity is a basic variable traditionally used in social science research. Our data suggest that we must be more sensitive to its construction and relevance because it may be neither unchanging nor carrying the same meaning from one group to another. Rather, ethnicity may also be fluid and may operate at several levels. Our approach suggests that ethnicity should be viewed not just in terms of its specific content but also as a vessel that facilitates public expression of subjective experience and meanings. Thus, the cases of late-life ethnic experiences we presented suggest that ethnicity also serves to foster transformation and reworking of new symbolic meanings (Peacock, 1968) or to revitalize and intensify traditional values and meanings. In summary, the approach and data outlined above suggest that studies of ethnicity and aging need to consider ethnicity and ethnic identity as both a stable variable and as a vehicle by which an individual creatively transforms or revitalizes social identity and self. More fundamentally, the approach presented in this paper may help to overcome a limitation inherent in much previous work by providing a concept for more clearly understanding the psychodynamic and developmental aspects of ethnicity in life-course perspective.

4

Issues of Conceptual Discourse in Ethnic Research and Practice

Elena Bastida

In 1979 Bengtson examined some recurrent problems and some emerging potentials in the conduct of research on ethnicity and aging. Among the recurrent problems singled out by Bengtson were "problems in concepts and theoretical relevance" faced by social scientists, policymakers, and practitioners "as they attempt to consider more adequately the complex interplay between ethnicity and aging."

It is the objective of this chapter to identify and illustrate some critical problems of conceptual relevance to the study of ethnicity and aging and to discuss some recently collected data on the subject. It should be noted that the present discussion is limited to cultural systems of meaning and their shared interpretations, and it therefore excludes other important dimensions of ethnicity such as differential placement in terms of stratification and race, a sense of peoplehood, and the like. Moreover, emphasis will be given to the significance of conceptual relevance in the empirical world of the practitioner and policymaker. All too often, issues of conceptual relevance are dismissed by practitioners as too abstract or irrelevant to the everyday practical issues of the real world. However, the ensuing discussion will attempt to illustrate the serious consequences brought about by applying the inappropriate terminology to everyday life situations and cases faced by policymakers and practitioners.

Conceptual Development

Theories are built from concepts. Concepts denote phenomena; in so
doing, they isolate features of the world that are considered for the
moment at hand important (Hempel, 1952). Familiar gerontological
concepts include, for example, adjustment, life satisfaction, coping,
and disengagement. Each of these terms is a concept that embraces
aspects of the sociopsychological world considered essential for a
particular purpose. Thus, concepts that are useful in building theory
have a special characteristic: they strive to communicate a uniform meaning to all those who use them (Turner, 1986). In social
gerontology, expression of concepts is based on conventional language rather than on technical or more "neutral" language, such as
the symbols of mathematics. Hence, the verbal symbols used to label
phenomena not only must be precisely defined but should convey a
universal meaning.

Emphasis is given here to the conceptual choice of terminology
used to denote observable phenomena among ethnic groups and,
for our purposes, the ethnic aged. Caution should be employed
when using terms to which a non-neutral conventional meaning is
attached, e.g., pessimistic, fatalistic, paranoid. Even if the researcher painstakingly avoids any type of negative connotation in
the technical definition of the concept, the term itself warrants a
judgmental appraisal.

Social Definitions of Aging

Bengtson (1979) suggests that perhaps the most basic philosophical
assumption common to those who consider ethnicity crucial to understanding contemporary aging relates to the importance of social
definitions of age and aging in contrast to chronological or biological
parameters. Social definitions of age and aging, however, must be
understood within the larger context of a shared social reality. As
Bengtson observes, shared definitions of situations vary according
to location in the social system, "especially in terms of broader
systems of meaning provided by cultural interpretations of normative events such as growing old." Analysis of perceptions of aging
and the way such perceptions vary across social strata such as
ethnic subcultures is of considerable importance in understanding
the phenomenology of aging. Therefore, "the basic constructs of
interest to gerontologists (time and aging) may have quite different
meaning for one group of humans in contrast to another" (Bengtson,
1979). It is precisely the importance of understanding cultural sys-

tems of meaning and basic constructs such as time and aging that concern us here, as this subject is directly related to gerontologists who seek to expand the understanding of the phenomenology of aging across cultural, subcultural, and social strata. These researchers are hindered in their efforts by the lack of an adequate conceptual framework to denote and isolate observable phenomena and to transmit their meaning correctly.

In short, the study of subcultural variations in aging has been jeopardized by the fact that it aroused consistent gerontological inquiry only 20 or 30 years after social gerontological research examining dominant aging patterns had been firmly established within the social sciences. Hence, researchers investigating subcultural patterns of aging found an already developed, even if fragmentary, conceptual terminology at their disposal. Concepts such as life satisfaction, adjustment, adaptation, well-being, and the like, and their respective definitions and operationalizations, were then applied to the study of cultural and subcultural aging patterns. Moreover, because social gerontology is the offspring of the more established social sciences, other terms were borrowed from anthropology, sociology, and psychology to isolate and denote cultural features that were deemed important to the study of ethnicity and aging for the moment at hand. Thus, such terms as "fatalistic," "passive," "familistic," "present- or past-oriented" became incorporated into the conceptual terminology and discourse of ethnic aging research.

Paradigmatic Orientation and Ethnic Research

Given the multidisciplinary nature of ethnic research in general and particularly the ethnic aged, it is not surprising to find conflicting tensions in orientation and methodologies that ultimately obstruct and confound conceptual terminology in this area. For example, anthropological ethnography generally relies on a form of knowledge building based on interpretation of individual cases and careful translation across cases to make controlled comparisons, whereas psychologists and sociologists are concerned with finding culture-specific instances of universal values and statistical analyses. Finally, researchers delving into ethnic aging research from a policy or practice perspective are interested in methodologies that will allow them expeditiously to identify and assess the problems of these groups so that remedies to alleviate them may be proposed and implemented. Underlying these different approaches are different assumptions about knowledge of human behavior and what can be legitimately regarded as knowledge.

Although these differences prevail, researchers in the field of ethnic aging increasingly combine methodologies that, in our opinion, represent a creative dialectic in cross-cultural and subcultural studies that advances and revivifies the subject. However, caution must be exercised when indiscriminately extrapolating and applying the conceptual terminology developed in one discipline to another. For example, in an ethnographic work in which the term "fatalistic" is employed to denote and isolate features of an observed phenomenon, the definition accompanying the term will be a lengthy one usually supported by the researcher's extensive fieldwork.

The ethnographer masters the local language, spends many months, even years, in the field, and he or she concentrates on translation and interpretation of meaning. When the same term is abruptly extrapolated from its original content and context and used to examine or explain findings from a large social survey, much of the original definition is unfortunately lost, and one is left with a fragmented understanding, if that, of the original term. For example, Mirowsky and Ross (1983) conducted a community mental health survey of 463 persons living in El Paso, Texas, and Juarez, Mexico. Their findings indicated that "belief in external control" was directly associated with Mexican heritage. Moreover, belief in external control interacts with low socioeconomic status to produce mistrust, which in turn is the main factor associated with paranoia. These findings, we believe, as reported by the authors, must be handled critically and with caution, for the authors did not spend any time with respondents, were not conversant in Spanish, and did not reveal an in-depth understanding of Mexican culture in their writings. But let us take this point further in terms of practice. Let us assume that a Southwest-border service provider to the aging reads about these findings in the *American Sociological Review*. Is he or she then to assume that most or all of his/her Mexican clients are mistrustful and likely to become (or are already) paranoid? Indeed, some very dangerous implications can be drawn from this type of analysis. Hence, tensions in paradigmatic orientation lead to confusing applications of conceptual terminology that can have serious implications for the understanding of ethnic behavior. More important, the inaccurate application of terminology can lead the service provider or practitioner to the incorrect identification of a case or client, which can result in the wrong diagnosis and undesirable human cost.

Other tensions characterize paradigmatic orientations in ethnic aging research. Ethnography and surveys sharply pose these differences. The former is qualitative and concerned principally with the problem of validity. The latter is quantitative and concerned primarily with the problems of reliability and replicability.

In short, conceptual development in ethnic aging theory and research is still jeopardized by the slow development of conceptual terminology to denote empirical phenomena. This slow development is partially accounted for by the interdisciplinary nature of gerontology in general and ethnic research in particular. Problems of paradigmatic tensions in world views, methodologies, and theoretical assumptions are at the core of this lack of appropriate conceptual terminology and discourse in ethnic aging theory and research. But is this conceptual problem really critical to our understanding of aging? If so, how critical is it? In what remains of this chapter, we will posit answers to the above questions by examining this abstract theoretical problem against the background of our empirical data on fatalism. For the purpose of illustrating the conceptual problem at hand, we will limit discussion to the conceptual notion of fatalism and derivative concepts such as pessimism and mistrust, which have been frequently and consistently used to characterize ethnic aged populations.

Fatalism or Realism: Who Does the Labeling?

We suggest that the behavioral sciences in general remain bedeviled by a language problem. A single concept—fatalism—refers to different phenomena, ranging from the belief that the details of one's life have been traced out in advance (fate), as the ancient Mayas, many Native American cultures, and other cultures throughout the world believed, to a disbelief in one's power to control his or her own destiny, to a protective mechanism that shelters older ethnic persons from severe depression and anxiety (Varghese & Medinger, 1979). Some investigators have extrapolated from data derived from small samples to speculate about general cultural "fatalistic" characteristics for given ethnic groups. Others, on the contrary, have chosen to ignore culture altogether and have emphasized sociostructural situations in their analysis of fatalism. Such problems in studying the sociopsychological characteristics of a given population or across several populations are, in part, the products of language. We insist on denoting certain features of the empirical world according to a previously established terminology regardless of their appropriateness to the data. This, indeed, as we see it, is a critical epistemological problem at the core of ethnic aging research and obviously one of paradigmatic orientation.

Empirical data collected on this subject (Bastida, 1987) reveal that isolating certain features of the empirical world and choosing a particular term to denote such features is closely related to the predominant construction of reality uncritically accepted by the investigator. This, of course, has been the persistent argument of sociologists of knowledge since Mannheim (1936) and Schutz (1973) and more recently by Berger and Luckmann (1967). Thus, it is our contention that the indiscriminate use of the term "fatalism" as applied to some populations of ethnic aged is the result of early- and mid-20th-century Anglo-American and northern European construction of reality, which had become so predominant among social scientists in those days that it was accepted uncritically as an obvious standard by which all else was to be measured and judged. From a phenomenology-of-aging perspective, this is a particularly critical issue to the cross-cultural study of aging because such aberrant notions in denoting empirical phenomena appear to remain unquestioned in our search for objective indicators of the various sociopsychological dimensions associated with aging and death.

Based on our reading of the various research studies examining fatalism among various subpopulations (Clark & Anderson, 1967; Hsieh, Shybut, & Lotsof, 1969; Joe, 1971; Justin, 1970; Lefcourt, 1966, 1976; Lefcourt & Ladwig, 1966; Lessing, 1969; Madsen, 1964; Saunders, 1954; Scott & Phelan, 1969; Strickland, 1971), we isolated the persistent feature associated with fatalism as one related to locus of control. In light of the conclusions reached by Varghese and Medinger (1979)—fatalism not necessarily defined in terms of detrimental consequences but rather viewed as an adaptive response to stress for those faced with circumstances that reduce their capacity to cope directly with the stressor—we decided to label such empirical occurrences as "realistic" rather than "fatalistic" in formulating our empirical research question. In order to pursue its investigation we chose not to define the concept as one of "coping" but rather as an element of the group's social construction of reality.

The empirical question of whether either of these two conceptual definitions—of fatalism and of realism—characterize the sociopsychological attitudes of an ethnic elderly group has been examined by the author (Bastida, 1987). It was investigated in a study of elderly Hispanic Americans that included all three major subpopulations of Hispanics—mainly, Mexican American, Puerto Rican, and Cuban.

Fatalism, Realism and Hispanic Americans

Studying Fatalism

Data were derived from a triangulation of methods that included extensive fieldwork among all three groups of elderly and the administration of a structured interview schedule containing open and closed questions. Through content analysis, responses to open-ended questions were quantified. A three-member panel representing each of the subgroups under study read all open-ended answers, helped to develop the criteria employed in the content analysis, and evaluated one another's interpretations.

Early in this process it became apparent that qualifying statements were made regarding the necessity to be realistic about one's age. Thus, we began to assess systematically the use of realistic qualifiers by carefully annotating them on the interview schedule alongside the question that elicited the comment. Questions eliciting such "realistic" qualifiers included self age identification and self-assessment of health, aging, family matters, and death. Based on the broad range of diverse life experiences that respondents qualified by alluding to the term "realistic," we suggest that this emphasis on realism is an important element among this population's construction of reality in general and aging in particular.

One hundred sixty respondents were randomly selected from a list of 412 eligible participants. Eligibility, determined by the research design, required participants to be 55 years old or over, of either Mexican, Puerto Rican, or Cuban origin, and noninstitutionalized. Participants lived in predominantly Hispanic communities, and Spanish was their dominant language.

Structured interviews lasted for approximately 2 hours. Each participant was questioned about perceptions of aging, family relationships, and the meaning of death. Basic demographic characteristics were elicited from all respondents. Finally, extensive fieldwork was conducted for a period of 18 months for at least 5 hours a day.

Of the 160 men and women over 55 years old, 65 were of Mexican, 42 of Puerto Rican, and 53 of Cuban origin; 101 were women and 59 were men. The age range was 55 to 84; the median age was 66. More than half (N = 90) were not high school graduates, and only 18 had completed more than 16 years of school. Family income ranged from $200 to $1,180 per month.

Attitudinal Responses to Realism

Extensive content analysis of all open-ended responses indicated that 69% of the men and 83% of the women used realistic qualifiers when responding to open-ended questions. Furthermore, even when responding to close-ended questions, 66% of the men and 84% of the women relied on realistic qualifiers when elaborating on reasons behind their choices. A realistic qualifier is defined here as a direct reference to the word *realistic* as used within a given respondent's statement. The following are typical statements alluding to realistic qualifiers:

> Look at my wrinkled face and hands. I am an old man. How can you ask otherwise? When you get old, it's better to be realistic about it [a 72-year-old male respondent].

> What were you expecting me to choose with these old bones? I cannot fantasize about my years but must face reality [a 66-year-old female respondent].

> I can't hide it; there is too much white hair; I must be realistic about my age [a 65-year-old male respondent].

> What do these wrinkles tell you? Well, I'm old and must be realistic about it [a 76-year-old female respondent].

Findings indicate that reference to realism as manifested by respondents when commenting on their perceptions of aging did not seem to have a negative adjustment to aging. This suggests the plausibility of our earlier definition of realism as a cultural dimension exacerbated to some extent by the situational circumstances of life. This hypothetical definition needs further investigation over several large cohorts because we do not know to what extent that emphasis on realism may be considered as a modal cultural response.

At this point we are simply exploring the conceptual validity of the term. What appears to be clear, however, is that the presence of a realistic attitude does not seem to affect the aging experience of this population adversely. We would like to cite below a rather extreme statement that illustrates this point, using death as a realistic qualifier. The following are the comments of a 68-year-old woman when asked about her perceptions of her aging experience:

Of course, we get older by the day, and every year that goes by means a closer step to the grave. But though I know this to be the case, I do not let it disturb me. My life is a peaceful and relatively happy one. To the extent that life can be happy I feel rather content and satisfied with mine. My aging experience has not been a bad one.

Regardless of socioeconomic class—and we did have at least 18 professionals in our sample, including physicians, attorneys, accountants, former elected officials (not necessarily among the 18 with professional degrees), managers and division directors, and small business owners (e.g., restaurants, beauty shops, delicatessens)—we found that realistic attitudes toward different life experiences were selectively and not randomly applied to all life experiences. If we were to refer to realism along the already established definition for fatalism as one of perception of life events from an external locus of control, then it is important to note that respondents were well aware of which types of experiences were internally controllable and which were not. For example, they alluded to realism on occasions such as the biological and chronological experience of aging. In their opinion—and this opinion was voiced over and over again throughout each of the 160 interviews—there was nothing they could do about getting older. Interestingly, most did not like getting old nor did they want to get old, contrary to many traditional views about aging. However, it is precisely at this point in life when, according to our respondents, one must be realistic about aging. "Nothing that one can do can successfully lie to the clock" was expressed by a 73-year-old Cuban physician. "The clock keeps moving," he went on to say. "Only fools think they can stop it."

It must be noted at this point that one detects a cultural interpretation of a normative event in the physician's observation. This type of normative interpretation was observed not only in the physician's comments but in the observations of many others, ranging from some who were very well educated to others with less than 6 years of formal schooling. Morever, being realistic about one's age significantly affected self-assessments of health, concerns about age, age identification, and comments on the possibility of remarriage. Hence, being realistic about one's life experiences, we suggest, is a major dimension underlying all aspects of these older people's lives. A realistic attitude, however, is selectively applied to those areas of life that they have learned to experience as being beyond their internal locus of control. In general, such learned experiences are acquired either through shared cultural modal expectation, through the adversities of structural discrimination (the latter may be more appropriate to segments of minority populations severely discriminated against), or through the adversities of limited resources in general (the latter may be more appropriate to lower-income elderly not discriminated against). Such acceptance does not seem to us to be fatalistic but a rather genuine appraisal of their potential and limitations. In fact, Varghese and Modinger (1979) support our suggestion when they observe: "One reason that fatalism is no longer closely associated with poor adjustment in situations of high constraint is that it is *realistic* [emphasis ours] to develop a generalized expectancy for external control of reinforcement in environments that severely restrict the instrumental behavior of those living within." Our data, however, do not support the authors' argument on the extent to which the environment must be severe in order to develop a realistic generalized expectancy.

We suggest that there is a need for more precise conceptual terminology to facilitate discourse among researchers. Such terminology may be helpful in avoiding the problematic conceptual and methodological issues arising in this type of investigation, in which distinct cultural characteristics and adverse socioeconomic conditions may frequently interact with one another. Perhaps a first step in this direction is to broaden our knowledge of the social construction of reality and aging of the population under study so that more precise statements may be made about the influences of culture and structure.

Implications for Ethnicity and Aging

Research Implications

There are direct serious consequences for research when investigative discourse and efforts are hampered by either a lack of terminology through which to denote empirical phenomena or the extrapolation of concepts that inadequately denote and define phenomena. Attention has been given here to illustrating how the term "fatalism" may be inappropriately employed to denote empirical phenomena that may be more appropriately denoted and defined by other terms. A further step in this direction is the serious ramifications of indiscriminately using a term not precisely defined for a given population or populations in a large survey research cutting across a diversity of cultures or subcultures. For example, we do not find rigorous attempts by cross-cultural survey researchers to take additional steps to ascertain whether the use of a concept to denote a given empirical phenomenon in one culture denotes the identical empirical phenomenon in another. This is a critical issue of conceptual validity that transcends the adequacy of a questionnaire translation, usually the extent to which cross-cultural researchers consider the issue of validity and reliability.

Epistemological concern should exhort ethnic researchers to develop universal conceptual categories through which to denote empirical phenomena and transmit their meaning; however, these categories should indeed be truly universal and thus applicable across culturally diverse groups (Palmore, 1983). To propose that the conceptual categories developed within one cultural orientation at one point in time are universal is ethnocentric, if not irresponsible. Perhaps it is advisable, given the rudimentary and fragmentary conceptual framework available to the researcher on ethnicity and aging at present, to concentrate less on representativeness and reliability and more on conceptual validity. How valid are our measuring scales when applied to other populations? Does the concept of "life satisfaction" denote and isolate the same empirical features among one group of elderly as it does for another and yet another? Should greater attention be given at this time to improving our conceptual terminology? These are serious questions that deserve the careful attention of investigators whose careers have been dedicated to exploring ethnicity and aging.

Practice Implications

Throughout this discussion we have emphasized the grave consequences for practice brought about by the incorrect application of conceptual terminology to persons or situations. This is an important issue deserving serious attention. Service providers and policymakers are usually uncertain in their approach to ethnic populations, especially when those populations are old. This situation is not necessarily improved by bringing in providers from the same ethnic groups. Younger ethnic providers are very likely to have learned the same conceptual categories and labels as nonethnic providers because they were educated in the same institutions of higher education. As a young Jewish social worker recently noted at a workshop on ethnicity: "I am most successful in working with the Jewish elderly when I set aside many of the techniques I have learned and I just try to understand their lives and experiences."

Among the less educated service providers, issues of value-laden terminology are even more critical in terms of human cost. This problem is even more pervasive in rural areas where service providers and members of advisory and decision-making boards and councils are more parochial in their shared definition of social reality and less understanding of cultural differences. The author (Bastida, 1983), in her study of urban-rural differences in accessibility to services and resource utilization, found this attitude to be all too pervasive in the small communities in which the lives of the ethnic elderly unfolded. In the many situations observed by the author, local nonethnic service providers acted somewhat suspiciously toward the ethnic elderly and referred to them as "they" rather than "our elderly," as was often the case when referring to the nonethnic elderly. In this case the ethnic elderly were also members of minority groups; thus, they represented a markedly visible segment of these small communities. But let us assume that our more parochial service provider or advisory board member becomes familiar with findings that allude to fatalism, low optimism, mistrust, or paranoia among members of a given ethnic group with whom he or she deals in some decision-making position: how will these reported findings influence his or her behavior toward such clients in need? What happens if a diagnosis is required? Clearly, these are serious questions that deserve careful scientific and ethical considerations by researchers delving into the subject of ethnicity and aging.

Future Directions

It is our hope that this chapter will serve to stimulate new theoretical and conceptual formulations in the relation of cultural systems of meaning and aging. A number of old questions that have produced great discussion over the years have simply been left aside. Hence, our discussion has not focused on questions of double, triple, or quadruple jeopardy as these affect the minority ethnic elderly. Nor have we sought to offer a descriptive account of one group's cultural patterns of aging. Finally, no attempt has been made to determine commonalities and varieties of the aging experience for various populations. Questions and issues such as these, as important as they are, have been replaced here by several newer concerns.

First, the questions raised in this chapter address significant issues of discourse (terminology), methodology, and interpretation in research on ethnicity and aging. Emphasis is given to the need for a sustained analysis of systems of meaning and discourse. An interpretive model is encouraged as a first step in researching culturally different elderly. The interpretation model, we propose, should focus not only on lay interpretations and perceptions of aging but also on our own social science discourse in terms of which we view and analyze the discourse of members of other ethnic groups. It is our belief that an interpretive analysis offers important directions for research in the field.

Second, by stressing the interpretive model, we are not discouraging larger-scale social surveys. But in our opinion the large-scale social survey approach generates meaningful and significant knowledge only after a careful conceptual foundation has been established and validated. This chapter reflects the growing awareness of the limitations inherent in any single methodological approach to studying ethnicity and aging.

Third, this chapter poses the challenge of bridging paradigmatic orientations. The subject of ethnicity and aging is neither a simple reflection of structural disadvantages and limited resources nor a culturally constructed phenomenon free of structural and psychological constraints. The subject of ethnicity and aging is of such interest to behavioral scientists and policymakers alike because it provides a prime opportunity for exploration of the interaction of culture and structure. We believe this interaction will remain at the center of attention and that future research will begin with some of the questions raised by its investigation. Indeed, we think a core contemporary concern of cross-cultural studies and behavioral science research generally is the way to measure meaning so as to be able to study its relationship to social behavior.

Finally, we believe that studies of the type suggested here will have a variety of direct applications. Enormous investments are being made in research and demonstration projects based on minority-ethnic aging. These approaches need to be examined critically in light of adequate terminology and interpretation. Not only does the validity of conceptual categories require critical attention in terms of theory and research, but the issue of applicability and diagnosis as it relates to practice also needs to be opened to analysis. The various assessments and evaluations of the needs of ethnic clients, or the diagnoses of patients' disorders and representations of disorders using already established categories and explanatory forms, need to be critically examined. Together the questions and issues raised here argue for a rethinking of the relationships among culture, aging, and structure of the models used to conceive and denote such relationships, the methods used to study the relationships, and the way paradigmatic disciplinary orientations influence scientific discourse and our search for knowledge and understanding.

5

Explorations in Ethnic Identity, Oldness, and Continuity

Milada Disman

The present state of the art does not provide for a scientific grasp of ethnicity; to date, we do not have a single empirical study in North American gerontology that attempts to analyze and conceptualize this phenomenon. In contemporary gerontological literature, ethnicity is not treated as a topic in itself but only as a more or less significant variable (Gelfand & Kutzik, 1979). North American gerontologists tend not to define "ethnicity"; when they do, they customarily employ the term solely to categorize their sample. Thus, a delimited population (e.g., Italians in a particular city) is usually surveyed within established gerontological categories (e.g., morale, service utilization). Furthermore, the lack of a clear conceptualization of ethnicity implies the lack of analytical attention to the *meaning* of ethnicity for members of a population thus designated.

Most North American gerontological studies analyze the segment of the elderly population defined as "ethnics" with absolute disregard for the experience of ethnicity. Specifically, almost nothing is known about the experience of being an old immigrant in Canada. Recent Canadian critiques of the neglect of aging and ethnicity (Crawford, 1980; Zay, 1978) have called for new sociological research aimed at clarifying the interrelation of selected variables within established gerontological categories, such as life satisfaction and morale. Yet the heterogeneity of aged people (Areba et al., 1971; Atchley, 1971; Crawford, 1980), and immigrants in particular (Wictorowicz, 1980; Zay, 1978), should also suggest a methodology that utilizes the data of individual experience. A need for research on the experience of ethnicity has been voiced by Marshall (1978–1979, 1980), who calls for studying the perceptions of aging held by the aged themselves, and by Gerber (1983) who found that "ethnic variety only serves to complicate the interpretive task" and called for "additional in-depth research into the experiential world of these ethnically distinct elderly individuals" (p. 77).

This chapter addresses this concern by focusing on ethnic identity as it is experienced and attending to concrete manifestations of ethnic identity in individuals' lives.

Conducting Life Histories

The life-history interviews reported here were the primary method of data collection, supplemented by other qualitative techniques, including mental maps and statements on domestic possessions. Each participant was asked to draw a sketch (mental map) of childhood surroundings, as remembered, and another sketch of personally significant places in contemporary Toronto. Domestic possessions are understood to be any objects present in the dwelling and owned by a respondent. The purpose of these questions was to discern emotional ties with particular objects and the meaning that they had for their owners. The data from these three methods were found to be mutually supportive. The people interviewed were born within and outside Canada and presently live in Toronto as senior citizens.

The use of reminiscence for telling one's life history is different from the more usual gerontological approach, which tends to focus on the therapeutic value of reminiscence, in the sense of Butler's life review (1963), or to ascribe an orientation toward the past as characteristic of old age (Kaminsky, 1978; Liton & Olstein, 1969).

Life history is defined here in terms of how a person interprets his or her life at a particular point in time (Gefro, 1980–1981). The utilization of life history as a source of information about the life of the aged person is a fairly recent innovation (Lieberman & Tobin, 1983). This trend may be perceived as a shift from treating the elderly as subjects to seeing them more as equal partners in interaction with social scientists.

Following the strategies for qualitative research outlined by Glaser and Strauss (1967, 1978), an attempt was made systematically to generate theory from the data collected. Their grounded theory approach includes the notion of theoretical sampling as opposed to representative sampling. Following this strategy, the size of the theoretical sample is not predetermined but develops in the process of joint collection, coding, and analysis of data. The accepted strategy is to constantly modify the interview style, location, and interviewees in order to keep following up new ideas (Glaser, 1978). The size of the sample is determined by "theoretical saturation," that is, by achieving a stage at which no new properties of the categories are emerging. Groups for comparison are chosen as they are needed rather than prior to beginning the research. It seemed that a fruitful step for theorizing on ethnicity would be to interview Canadian-born elderly persons as well as individuals born abroad; the comparison was expected to highlight manifestations of ethnic identity.

Forty-four in-depth interviews were conducted with the following groups: 20 elderly people living in the community, 11 residents of homes for aged, 5 residents of nursing homes, and 8 caregivers in institutional settings. Four so-called ethnic shelters—Jewish, Italian, Chinese, and Ukrainian homes for the aged—one additional nursing home, and one home for the aged were visited.

The interviewees were born in 15 different countries, and ranged in age from 58 to 92 years. They had obtained between 6 and 16 years of education, and their length of residence in Canada varied between 5 and 88 years. Those living in the community were found in many different circumstances: living alone, living with a spouse or child, and living in houses, in apartments, and in buildings restricted to seniors. Twenty-four elderly women and 12 men participated; five couples are included in this total. The respondents were selected by a snowball technique in which one interviewee directs a researcher to the next potential respondent. Six female and two male caregivers who expressed interest in the research were also interviewed.

In a semistructured life-history interview, the topics to be covered usually emerged naturally in the flow of the conversation, and only occasionally were prompting and guidance needed. A checklist was developed with orientation points for the interview. If an interviewee introduced a theme that was thought worthy of pursuit, questions related to this theme would be included in subsequent interviews. Some areas of interest were discarded as the respondents' answers and spontaneous accounts sharpened the interviewer's perception of what was most important for the interviewees themselves and relevant to the project. Staff members willingly participated as translators.

Because most interviewees appeared inhibited in front of a tape recorder, the interview content was written down verbatim. An average interview lasted 2 hours. The content of the interviews was coded, and major themes were identified. Analysis of the interviews revealed four major themes: ethnic identity, oldness, continuity, the ethnic self. An understanding of these themes provides a better understanding of the meaning of ethnicity for older ethnic individuals.

Exploring Ethnic Identity

Exploration 1: Manifestations of Ethnic Identity

The obvious places to find manifestations of ethnicity among the elderly are the so-called ethnic shelters. The research was conducted in three such shelters, homes for Chinese, Italian, and Ukrainian elderly. In these Toronto homes, the "external" aspects of ethnicity (Isajiw, 1981), such as use of first language, traditional food and decor, presence of artifacts, were immediately obvious to the observer. An interesting question, however, is to what degree the less tangible features of ethnic identity, such as attitudes and images, are recognized by someone from another background.

A person from another culture visiting these homes would probably perceive ethnicity in terms of difference. A person from the same background, who also knows about the mainstream culture, would have the advantage of a deeper understanding of the setting. Since managers of the three ethnic homes were from the same culture as their residents, they became my valued informants on less tangible aspects of ethnicity.

Even with the assistance of these informants, there were some problems in understanding the backgrounds of my interviewees. For example, during my interview with residents of the Chinese home, I realized that no matter what I asked, the individuality of an interviewee seemed to be escaping me. The manager explained that the question of individuality is alien to a Chinese person: "Confucius taught that we are not individuals; we are subjects of a country, members of a clan, members of a family. However, these residents do have a personal attitude, but they will not reveal it to an outsider; they are very reserved." Thus, they will not say what their personal attitude is partly because they are unable to and partly because they do not choose to reveal the self.

In all three homes, residents share a sense of history. The manager of the Ukrainian home pointed out indirectly the notion of ethnicity as a basis for being happy there when she said, "You wouldn't be happy in this place unless you know history," and explained that by this she meant a shared understanding, perhaps a shared experience, of history, foods, and language.

In interviews with elderly immigrants living in the community, the persistence of ethnic identity was manifested in a number of ways, including stated preferences for traditional foods, extensive use of the mother tongue, and friendship and information networks from the same background. These manifestations of ethnic identity conform to research findings on "the typical tradition-bound ethnic group member" (Anderson & Frideres, 1981, p. 37). This was true even among those who had come to Canada as youths. For example, a woman who emigrated from Russia at 5 years of age related that her closest friend in Montreal is Russian.

Another interviewee, who came to Canada from England at 6 years of age, said, "I am still an Englishman." His wife, who came here at the age of 23, comments: "He is more English than I am; he buys everything English; he thinks English. Every week he gets his three English papers. . . . He is in England all the time!"

An effort to probe this interest in ethnic identity on the part of a person who could easily have been identified only as Canadian produced a clear reason: "It started in the thirties when we bought a radio; I liked band music from England. Then I took their magazine called *Listener*. That's how I became interested in those programs. Then I read more and more, and then I realize it's something to be proud of, to be English."

In addition to their direct reflections on the enduring importance of ethnicity in their lives, the respondents' perceptions of various situations or objects brought their cultural backgrounds into focus. An Italian woman who emigrated to Winnipeg after World War II expressed no regrets about moving to Canada, although she missed Italy. She spoke no English and had no friends because people from southern Italy and northern Italy are different; she and her husband were northerners, and the other Italians in Winnipeg were from the south. These regional differences were also cited as the reason why she could not remarry after her husband's death in 1948.

The perception of the environment may also reveal an enduring ethnic identity: "You see, this house is really very much like an English house. You have a front door, and the bedrooms are upstairs." The wife of the older man with a strong attachment to England remarked: "If he could live in Virginia, he would like it there." The husband added, "It is very much like England—green."

For some of the respondents, persisting ethnicity appeared to function as a source of identity and also as a coping resource. The latter was most aptly expressed by a woman from Britain. She traced her stubborn refusal to give in—to her physical infirmities and grief from other losses—to her ethnic identity: "As we British are fond of saying: What we have, we hold. . . . Never say die, never give up."

Exploration 2: The Elusive Quality of Oldness

Matthews (1979) explored various definitions of self as presented to her by older women and identified their refusal to see themselves as old as a coping mechanism, serving to maintain a sense of self-identity, and as a refusal of stigmatization.

The life histories revealed few people who, without hesitation, would define themselves as old. The exceptions were residents of the Chinese home; an acceptance of old age seems to be embedded in Chinese culture. Other interviewees stated that they were not old, or rather, perhaps they were in number of years but not in any other respect. On the other hand, a distinction was made between age in years and "old behavior": "He is old—not in years; he is eighty-three—but in behavior, oh, he is old; he could be a hundred and ten." Some remarks hint at people who made use of being chronologically old: "Years mean nothing. . . . They take advantage of their years and act old." To act old for these respondents means "not to hurry, not to go anywhere." Other statements suggested that "old" has something to do with orientation toward the past rather than toward the future: Possibly, "oldness" calls to attention "being" rather than "becoming." The dynamics of past endeavors are frozen, and instead of planning for tomorrows, all that is left are yesterdays.

At this point in my research it seemed appropriate to ask, when is one old? A woman in a nursing home asked how she was selected for the interview. She was extremely pleased after I told her that the nurses selected her: "They must think that I have still my marbles together." It seems that she was not sure if "oldness" is happening to her.

Respondents were asked when a person is considered old. Replies were: "when losing your marbles" (Mrs. C.); "talk too much" (Mrs. B.); "lose interest; it is in your attitude" (Mr. P.). Other statements seem to suggest that oldness is something that happens to you if you are not careful enough. These examples illustrate what I call the elusive quality of oldness.

Matthews (1979) argues that refusing the label "old" is a strategy for the protection of self. This research suggests that such a refusal is also an expression of an individual's endeavor to preserve continuity. Oldness seems to be understood as a time of loss of control, as an identity crisis. It appears that the primary concern of elderly people is the threat to continuity in their lives. The notion of oldness provides such a threat.

Thus, many interviewees refused to view themselves as old and pointed at someone else, physically or mentally deteriorating, as being old. An elderly man recalls a confused woman encountered in the lobby: "That one, remember her? She doesn't know where she is. . . . One would say she is old." An 83-year-old woman says: "Old people are the ones I see around; I think they are here."

A striving for continuity can be seen in the interactions of the institutionalized elderly in terms of their former roles, illustrated here by two upper-class British women: When Mrs. F. first came, Mrs. K. thought they could be friends. She went to Mrs. F.'s door at 11 a.m. and knocked. Mrs. F. opened her door and said: "I am not receiving today." Mrs. K. responded: "I didn't think you would, but I just wanted to say hello to you."

The threat of oldness as loss of control is interpreted by the elderly as occurring in two distinct areas: loss of control over one's mind and loss of control over one's body. Control over one's mind is more important than physical ailments one may not be able to control. Mrs. B., although concerned about mental deterioration, is quite cheerful about her partial loss of sight.

Age is not always an issue; sometimes the threat to continuity is attenuated by other factors or accepted (as in the Chinese example). Oldness is also not threatening when it does not seem to challenge continuity. For example, a 92-year-old musician, still practicing, said without regret that he was very old. On the phone he told me: "Please, speak slowly to me. I am very old and I do not hear very well." In the interview he expressed his hope that he will be able to practice his music as long as he lives. When identity is not challenged because continuity is maintained in other areas, oldness can be accepted.

Exploration 3: Continuity as a Challenge of Aging

The life histories enabled ethnicity to be viewed in the context of immigrants' lives. Life history provides us with a sense of a person. In the life histories as pictures of selfhood, several selves clearly emerge. These selves are presented in a hierarchy that represents a person's identity. Within this hierarchy, the dominant self is clearly identifiable. This notion refers to the primary aspect around which a person's identity has been organized This "dominant self" can be illustrated by examining the excerpted notes of one life-history account.

The Story of Mr. P. Over lunch, Mr. P. spent more than an hour reminiscing about his career, giving the names of bosses and talking about his financial successes. (He always remembered the exact amount of money involved.) He also recalled his closeness to his brother, who died in World War I. After lunch I asked him about how and when he got married. He said, "It's a long story" and continued to recall his business successes. It did not seem to me that he refused to discuss his marriage; rather, he preferred to speak about what he considered important. After I insisted, he told me that he went back to Scotland and married a girl from his hometown. There was no comment on courting or on what she was like except to say that after she came here, she was very homesick and went back often. Later they returned every 2 years. He recalled buying his first house; again he knew its exact price and how much he sold it for. When he came home and told his wife that he had bought a house, she was only worried that there would be no money for her trips home. Speaking of himself as a son, brother, friend, and husband, but most of all as a successful financier, he is obviously presenting the latter as his dominant self.

Some of those interviewed were able to continue enacting what they presented as their dominant self. These people appeared to be the happiest in the sample. For example, some women for whom motherhood was of primary importance were now living as grandmothers with an adult child's family. They felt loved, respected, and truly needed. I also met a couple who treasured above all their relationship with their grandchildren. Soon after their son emigrated to Canada with his family, they were asked to emigrate; the grandchildren refused to eat until grandma and grandpa could come to Canada.

Most of my informants, however, experienced some discontinuity of selves. The importance of a particular discontinuity was clearly related to whether it touched the dominant self. For example, Mr. B. presented his dominant self as being a "family man." For him, retirement posed no threat of major discontinuity. He claimed that in some ways it was a relief because he used to worry too much about his work. On the other hand, from his life history and what I could observe about his relationship with his wife, her loss would be a major disruption to his life.

It appears then that not every change is perceived as a threat to continuity, only a change that is regarded as a loss. Thus, oldness does not pose a threat to continuity when continuity is provided for the dominant self. The "family man" saw 65 as an ideal age; he would like to be that age again.

The notion of continuity of the dominant self deserves further research and has implications for some of our taken-for-granted knowledge about the elderly. For example, the wisdom of viewing all life events as a stable hierarchy of stressors (Holmes & Rahe, 1967) can be questioned, as it seems that life events as stressors merit different ratings of importance according to an individual's hierarchy of selves.

Exploration 4: The Ethnic Self and the Hierarchy

In life histories, ethnicity finds a place in the hierarchy of selves, but it is not necessarily central. For purposes of present explorations, the focus is on only the external features of ethnic identity as representing ethnic selves. Ethnicity in its external manifestations—language, food, and artifacts—is readily observable by an outsider, but these aspects are also easily identified by the person presenting the life history. Internal aspects of ethnicity, such as values and attitudes, tend to permeate other selves. For example, the way a person goes about being a grandparent can be influenced by cultural understandings of familial responsibilities.

External features of ethnicity are the aspects consciously cultivated or rejected in a different culture; they are also consequential for my interviewees because admissions are made to ethnic homes for the aged on the basis of the cultivation of such visible traits as language and food.

Life histories of the elderly immigrants contain many references to ethnic selves in terms of external attributes. For example, a Dutch couple referred first to these attributes and then commented on the desirability of an ethnic shelter. The husband said that at home they speak Dutch, and they are also members of a Dutch senior citizens club. They keep up some customs, especially concerning food. Their closest friends are Dutch. He would not object to living in an old age home if it were for the Dutch. Ethnicity is viewed then by many older people as a resource, the continuity of which is desirable. Ethnicity in its external features was addressed by the immigrants as a phenomenon of long standing in their lives; in fact, ethnicity represented continuity.

Interestingly, however, a few life histories presented ethnicity as disruptive of continuity. For example, a second-generation Italian woman now lives in the Italian home, although her ethnic background was not a major part of her earlier life. For her, the Italian home offers not continuity but alienation. She has "nothing in common" with the women there, and she resents them for not knowing or not speaking English. She is not used to the Italian diet and resents eating so much pasta. Another example of ethnicity versus continuity is a Jewish woman who did not want to go to the "right" ethnic home. She had lived for some years in Italy, spoke the language, and had lived in an Italian neighborhood in Toronto; she chose the Italian home.

On the basis of these findings, it is proposed that ethnicity matters in later years only to the degree that it has been important to that person throughout his or her life. It now appears that ethnicity becomes an issue if there is a threat to the continuity of the ethnic self. Such a threat is meaningful if, and only if, the ethnic self was in earlier years consistently high in a hierarchy of selves. For example, we can see that the lack of an ethnic shelter is experienced as a problem only by those immigrants for whom ethnicity has been important throughout their lives in North America.

This finding differs from current beliefs about ethnicity as an identity that the "elderly can turn on and off as needed" (Holzberg, 1982, p. 254). It also refutes the notion of an automatic resurgence of ethnicity in later years after a middle-age period in which ethnicity was less important (Kastenbaum, 1979). However, further empirical research based on the recognition of the multidimensionality of ethnicity is needed. Such an inquiry might unite the seemingly contradictory findings in a more sophisticated theory of ethnicity and its importance in later years. Ethnicity now seems to be only one possible resource for providing continuity of self. In this exploratory study, the immigrants brought up the notion of continuity as a much broader issue than that of ethnicity. Consequently, the study included in the theoretical sample informants born in Canada.

The inclusion of Canadian-born respondents in the sample puts ethnicity in a new perspective; one of the salient features of ethnicity is an emotional affinity with the country of origin. However, there was no discernible difference between yearning for a country of origin and longing for a childhood place in Canada. Recollections of a childhood in a Canadian hometown were as emotionally charged as, say, recollections of childhood years on a farm in Holland. (The situation will differ if an immigrant arrived here late in life.) These and similar observations make it very obvious that ethnicity applies to each one of us. Thus, an analytic view of ethnicity brings into focus ethnicity as embedded in personal history.

In addressing the meaning of ethnicity in their lives, the responses of elderly immigrants point to external and internal features of ethnic identity. The interviewees tended to define "oldness" in terms of an identity crisis, refusing the chronological perspective. An acceptance of oldness was found to be either embedded in a particular culture or to occur in instances in which age posed no threat to continuity of the dominant self.

In the life histories, the ethnic self appears to be but one in a hierarchy of selves. It suggests that ethnicity is relevant in later years only to the degree that it mattered to that person throughout his or her life. This implies that an "ethnic shelter" may not be appreciated by a person who emigrated to Canada early in life and was enriched by living in our multicultural environment. Therefore, ethnicity becomes one of several possible resources for continuity in elderly immigrants' lives.

If we are all ethnics, is there a need for "ethnic gerontology" as Holzberg (1982, p. 254) has called it? I believe there is. We need to analyze the transformation of cultural traits on this continent, to examine changes in values and attitude, and to clarify the meaning of ethnicity for various immigrant generations. Life history is a powerful tool that may help us achieve some of these goals. Explorations in ethnic identity, oldness, and continuity seem to suggest that there might be commonalities among various ethnic groups. A systematic analysis along ethnic lines would point to similarities and differences.

Ethnic gerontology also has a potential for changing our practice. If we understand aging as a cumulative process, one of the tasks of society is to help people maintain continuity in their lives. Institutions should take this as a goal, understanding that environments have to fit the needs of the residents.

We should look for ways to create conditions supporting continuity in the lives of the aged, in the community and in institutions. Presently, the latter are planned for residents' physical well-being, and activities are geared to an expectation of physical and mental infirmity. The unhappiest residents are those who deviate from these expected levels. For example, residents in need of medical attention but mobile and with alert minds will not participate in activities organized for people with impaired memories. Residents have a different notion of oldness than that held by those around them. With the goal of supporting continuity, the life history could serve as a sensitive method of assessing the needs of the elderly accepted into an institutional setting.

Finally, ethnicity, a North American invention, is currently used to depict "otherness." Analytical attention to ethnicity as experienced may help to dispel the underlying connotation of ethnicity as a social stigma.

Part II

Research and the Ethnic Dimensions of Aging

As the chapters in Part I illustrate, theory development often rests on a research base. In the following chapters the authors utilize a variety of research approaches in their analyses. Some of the chapters utilize familiar research approaches with specific ethnic groups, whereas others utilize large data sets to compare across ethnic groups. The ethnic groups studied also vary in their establishment within North American society. They range from recent immigrants groups such as the Hmong to long-established groups (Jews, Blacks, Finns, Japanese).

For recent arrivals the most important issues may be those related to adjustment in a new and, in many ways, alien environment. The environment may be alien not only in climate, in basic features of everyday life such as transportation, or in physical setting (e.g., urban rather than rural) but also in culture.

Immigration to a new environment always involves both losses and gains. In a host environment that is alien in culture and physical structure of daily life, the losses may be more apparent than the gains. This sense of loss is clear in Hayes's work with the Hmong, a group that he notes had no choice but to depart their long-established ancestral homes in

Laos. The overwhelming losses in both possessions and culture causes Hayes to adopt a pessimistic outlook about the future integration of this group of ethnic elderly into American society. From a more positive perspective it is possible to argue that integration of the Hmong into American society will occur among the children of the present elderly.

For groups that are long established in North America, the issue may not be one of integration into the United States or Canada but rather the maintenance of a distinct ethnic culture. Kart attempts to trace the role of the elderly in preserving religious commitment among Jews. In contrast to the Hmong, Jews in the United States and Canada come from urban backgrounds, have technological skills, and have attained high social mobility.

Noting the absence of adequate research into the relationship of religion and age, Kart finds stronger religious commitment among older Jews, particularly women, than among their younger peers. There thus appears to be a nexus among age, gender, and religion that needs further exploring. Kart is unable to determine the extent to which religious commitment increases among Jewish women as they grow older. Kart is also unable to determine the extent to which the maintenance of a Jewish identity is related to the maintenance of religious commitment. Separating the effects of religious affiliation and commitment from ethnic identity is difficult. This is true not only among religiously based ethnic groups, such as Jews or Mormons, but also among groups such as Italians, Poles, and Irish that have strong links with the Catholic church.

As is the case with Jews, the Amish are a group whose ethnic identity has a religious base. In contrast to Jews, however, the Amish have remained apart from mainstream North American society. As Brubaker and Michael note in their chapter on this fascinating group, the separateness of the Amish from the majority society is based on their interpretation of the Bible. Separateness has also enabled the Amish to retain their distinct ethnic culture, a culture relatively unknown to the general public.

In the Amish culture, family members remain in close geographic proximity. This proximity is clearly an enabling factor in the assistance provided by family members to older relatives. Perhaps most important, note Brubaker and Michael, is "the unwavering feeling of familism permeating the generational relationships that provides support for the older members of the Amish family." This emphasis on family is bolstered by the ethnic community. The community is prepared to step in if family assistance is insufficient and ensure that older individuals can live out their lives in the Amish community.

In Chapter 9, Stoller examines a group of ethnic elderly who have moved from their original communities. Her chapter illustrates how shared ethnic identity can be a positive factor in later years. Examining Finnish Americans now living in Florida, she notes that "shared ethnicity can partially compensate for lack of kin in the support networks of first- and second-generation ethnics in sunbelt retirement communities". This finding may be of some comfort to families worriedly witnessing the movement of their older relatives to communities far away from close relatives. It is also interesting to note that the Finnish community examined by Stoller was not native to Florida but rather represented a transplantation of Finns from other communities in the United States and Canada. Among first- and second-generation ethnic group members, it thus appears possible for ethnic identification to survive geographic migration. Continued longitudinal research is required before we can know the extent to which the exchanges found by Stoller will be maintained among future cohorts of older Finns.

Lubben and Becerra provide us with a better understanding of some of the factors that determine the degree of exchange and support within specific ethnic groups. Examining a large data base comparing Black, Mexican, and Chinese elderly, they note differentials in specific assistance in a number of important tangible areas, such as household chores and transportation. On the basis of their statistical analyses, they conclude that "the closer one's tie to traditional culture, the greater the parent–child supportive behavior." Among their sample, however, individuals close to traditional culture also suffered from a number of deficits that made support necessary. These deficits include a lack of fluency in English and limited socioeconomic resources. Lubben and Becerra thus raise the fundamental question of the relationship of class and mobility to the maintenance of ethnic traditions. Again, we need to support ongoing research that can follow individuals from a variety of ethnic groups. This longitudinal research will provide an understanding of the factors that affect the retention of ethnically based traditions of social support.

One fruitful approach to studying the maintenance of ethnic identity among older individuals is an examination of the extent to which they allocate their time to activities related to the ethnic culture. Ujimoto undertakes this type of analysis among older Japanese Canadians in Chapter 11.

Rather than studying the whole complex of time allocation among older Japanese, Ujimoto focuses on the organizational activities of a sample drawn from four major Canadian cities. Although cross-sectional in nature, his study fortunately includes first- and second-generation older Japanese Canadians. The data reveal a strong commitment to organizational membership and less of a commitment to organizational participation. Participation was weakest among second-generation Japanese Canadians. The extent to which ethnic organizations can serve as a bulwark for maintaining ethnic traditions and important roles for the older person is thus brought into question by this research. Continued membership in Japanese organizations because of a sense of obligation may not provide the needed sense of well-being among older Japanese provided by the retention of traditional roles in the family. Ujimoto's focus on time budgeting is an important step in providing data on role *enactment* among older members of various ethnic groups.

The research in Part II thus illustrates the complex interrelationships of socioeconomic, demographic, and cultural forces, as well as individual factors, in the web of ethnicity and aging. The historical patterns of particular ethnic groups, the opportunities and constraints placed on them by the environment, and the power of the traditional ethnic culture are all variables that must be brought into any equation that attempts to predict the future importance of ethnicity in the aging process.

6

Two Worlds in Conflict: The Elderly Hmong in the United States*

Christopher L. Hayes

In April 1975, the U.S. government made the decision to end all military involvement in Southeast Asia. This decision marked the beginning of the largest influx of refugees into the United States in recent history (Murase, 1982). The latest figures indicate that well over 600,000 refugees from Vietnam, Cambodia, and Laos have been resettled in the United States, with California having the largest number (Office of Refugee Resettlement, 1981).

Among these refugees are some 60,000 Hmong, a group previously living in the mountains of Laos. Although studies of Vietnamese and Cambodian refugees are increasingly found in the literature, little attention has been accorded the Hmong. In addition, there is a lack of understanding as to what comprises the experience of older Hmong and whether these elderly have adjusted to the new culture.

Literature on refugee behavior (Haines, Rutherford, & Thomas, 1981; Stein, 1980) often fails to identify the unique concerns of elderly members within the incoming group. Assimilation models that generalize about all members of a group entering a new culture (Eisenstadt, 1954; Gordon, 1964) provide little understanding of generational differences within the population. However, there is evidence that the acculturation process generates intense conflict within the family structure. For example, Sue and Morishima

*The author wishes to express special thanks to Dr. Richard Kalish of Antioch College, Yellow Springs, Ohio, for his mentoring role in this research effort.

(1982) found that exposure to a multicultural environment often creates value conflicts between parents and children.

This chapter addresses the experience of older Hmong in Laos, during relocation, and in the United States. Because this country is quickly becoming a haven for different refugee and immigrant groups, the study of the elderly within these populations has critical policy and direct-service implications. Attention will be given to making several comparisons between the experience of elderly Hmong and other Indochinese refugee groups.

Methodology

To gain a grasp of the experience of the older Hmong the qualitative and open-ended research strategies that remain the core of anthropological inquiry (Glaser and Strauss, 1967; Patton, 1980; Pelto and Pelto, 1978) were utilized. The first phase of the study, conducted in Long Beach, California, involved informal interviews with refugee resettlement counselors, Hmong community leaders, and the elder Hmong to gain an initial understanding of their relocation experience. These interviews were supplemented with the mapping and review of anthropological field reports, newspapers, and government reports. The goal of Phase 1 was to gain an initial picture of experience of the older Hmong from a variety of different perspectives, which could be explored in depth in Phase 2 described below.

With the assistance of a Hmong interpreter, 19 elders and their families living in the greater Los Angeles area were interviewed on two separate occasions. It is critical to point out that the elders interviewed in this study ranged in age from 40 to 78 years. Within Hmong culture a person is designated "older" at a far earlier age than in Western culture. The focus of the interviews involved six areas of inquiry: (a) life in Laos, (b) the Hmong view of old age, (c) the position of the elderly in the existing family structure, (d) intergenerational conflict, (e) the relationship of the older Hmong to social service providers, and (f) the extent of assimilation and acculturation into mainstream American society.

Content analysis was utilized to determine common themes of experience among the older Hmong. To ensure that conclusions reflect accurately that experience, the Long Beach Hmong Association leadership (which contained elders) reviewed the findings. This review provided an opportunity to clarify and add depth to the understandings reached in this study.

Life in Laos and Relocation

The Hmong Clan and Household

In Hmong culture, the patrilineal clan system is the basic social, economic, political, and religious unit. At birth a child automatically becomes a member of the clan of his or her father. The 20 clans in Hmong society are organized around the principles of reciprocity, friendship, and mutual assistance (Department of the Army, 1970).

The most important aspect within the clan is the extended family. It usually includes all individuals who share the immediate paternal grandparents, along with all of the in-laws. The extended family is to a large extent self-sufficient in terms of providing its own leader, religious figure, musician, blacksmith, and marriage negotiator (Vang, 1981). Everyone who belongs to the same clan is treated as a brother or sister (Whitmore, 1979).

The importance of the extended family structure to the Hmong individual cannot be overemphasized. The family is a property-sharing group in which the interests of its individual members are qualified by the interests of the whole. The material property of the entire family includes the house, paddyfields, animals, and common food stock. A Hmong person is never viewed as an individual; rather, he is always part of a family. When an individual makes a decision, he takes the family into consideration. There are economic, social, political, and emotional benefits in being a member of an extended family, and there are constraints placed on individuals who do not conform (Vang, 1981).

The Hmong household can contain as many as 35 members living under one roof. Great emphasis is placed on raising large families, which is equated with prosperity and security. Older Hmong parents remain in the same household through their old age and are cared for by their children. Vang (1981) notes:

> It is extremely rare for an aged couple to occupy a separate household since such is looked down upon in Hmong society. It is viewed as a disgrace on the part of the children. In Laos, old people seem to have a role set out for them, that is to look after the young children and guard the house. (p. 86)

Order and Authority in the Hmong Household and Community

Both Geddes (1976) and Barney (1967) note that order and authority in the Hmong household are maintained by respect for age and tempered by recognition of capacity. Through kinship terminology, birth-order titles, and the attitudes encouraged in the children, respect for age is constantly reinforced. In Hmong culture, brothers respect their older brothers, sons respect their fathers, and nephews respect their father's brothers, in order of their seniority of birth.

Within the Hmong village, the oldest male of each clan sits on a governing council that handles general disputes, dissolution of a marriage, or problems between clans. Heinbach (1983) witnessed several gatherings of a Hmong tribal council that operates by a majority consensus. In Laos the elders, in cooperation with each other, act as the "justice department."

Besides the village chief, both male and female elderly experience a high degree of status within the village. This is described by Barney (1967):

> The Hmong place high value on old age. In their conception, anyone of old age should have respect. This is reflected in the titles by which people of older generations are customarily addressed. A stranger is impressed by the manners and poise that a young Hmong boy will demonstrate when he is along. Among his elders, he is just one of a group in the presence of the respected elders. The writer has often observed the great care and attention which an entire village shows to elderly people, and the measure of pride displayed when he was introduced to these aged Hmong. (p. 44)

Relocation from Laos

To appreciate fully the experience of the older Hmong, we must look at the reasons why they left their country. Unquestionably, all of the older Hmong interviewed felt that they had no choice about departing. First, they feared that if they stayed in Laos, the Communists would kill them. Many also stated that they could not bear watching their farms being seized. In addition, 12 of 19 elders indicated that their sons' families were tied to the CIA; and because the sons were fleeing, the elders had no choice but to follow. The elder Hmong did not want to be left alone in old age without the family surrounding them.

The despair and boredom experienced in the refugee resettlement camps in Thailand were particularly difficult for the older Hmong to accept. Two younger Hmong informants described several instances in which elders committed suicide due to the inability to return to Laos and search for missing relatives. These conditions were difficult for the younger Hmong as well.

During their stay in the refugee camps, the Hmong believed that they would be resettled in one large group, rather like an Indian reservation. It was a major blow to the older Hmong when they were informed that, by relocating in the United States, they would be living in a city surrounded by strangers and that they would eventually have to become assimilated into American society (Bliatout, 1979). Many older Hmong simply wanted to find a field or farm where they could continue the life-style they had known. In addition, several Hmong interviewed for the study stated that their older relatives refused to come to the United States because they had two wives, and polygamy is not allowed here.

The majority of the older Hmong interviewed in the study stated that, when the final arrangements were being made for relocation to the United States, they were shocked to learn about American housing standards. The elders had a difficult time understanding why a house or apartment with two bedrooms was not suitable for a family of ten because in Laos a family would often share one bedroom (Barney, 1967). As one older Hmong recalled, "When I found out that some of my children would not live with me, life stopped." The problems of accepting living arrangements in the United States were greatly compounded when Hmong families were separated because of the different geographical locations of American sponsors and social service agencies (Bliatout, 1979; Thao, 1982).

Characteristics of the Older Hmong

Education

None of the older Hmong interviewed for this study had had any formal education in Laos. This is consistent with the finding that 92% of all adult Hmong had had less than a high school education in Laos (Baldwin, 1982), and the younger Hmong were more likely to have had classroom experience. In the refugee camps in Thailand the adult education classes were especially distressing to the older Hmong. They felt that they could not learn new skills and knowledge, and they regarded the instructors as leading to the circumvention of traditional roles while assisting in the training of the young (Bliatout, 1979).

According to several younger Hmong Association leaders, the elderly are unaccustomed to sitting in a classroom, and they find that learning English is an "impossible task." The Long Beach Hmong Association, which sponsors a class in English as a Second Language (ESL) on weekends, does not have any Hmong over the age of 40 enrolled. In Laos the first Hmong did not even enter school until after World War II, and even then classes were greatly disrupted by war. In fact, the Hmong did not have a written language until two decades ago, and few elderly can write their language today.

The Changing Hmong Family Structure

Relocation from Laos has created a variety of changes within the family structure. Because of economic problems faced by the family, younger Hmong wives are working in low-paying jobs. Often, younger Hmong men have experienced the loss of some authority, prestige, and self-confidence through dependence on government assistance and the wife's income-producing status. Reportedly, this has resulted in marital difficulties between husband and wife, and traditionally, the elder within the family would mediate all family problems. According to Vang (1981), the Hmong have utilized a strict traditional procedure in Laos concerning domestic problems. The husband and wife must first obtain counsel from the family elder. If the elder cannot resolve the problems, the next step is to go to the clan leader. After this, the problem can be handled further by the village chief and mayor of the town.

A strong concern found among 11 of the elder Hmong was the fear that an escalating divorce rate was the result of increasing education and freedom for Hmong women. In addition, two younger Hmong in the study felt that the elders were no longer capable of mediating disturbances between husband and wife because "they are not in touch with the American way."

According to the Long Beach Hmong Association leadership, parents of school-age children have approached them with dismay about their diminished authority. The leaders feel assured that Hmong children still respect the ultimate authority of their parents and believe that the aging father "is always right," but this may perhaps be an ideal that does not reflect the actual interaction between certain parents and their quickly acculturating children. According to Pao Yang, a Hmong officer:

There is a major problem in the parents' wanting to control the younger ones. They are afraid the children will forget the customs of our people. In Laos, the eldest son and the older father held the power in the family. Now, the son holds the power and will just listen to the father. (Interview notes)

The Hmong family can be conservatively characterized as having great flexibility, adaptability, and resourcefulness in coping with their new surroundings. One critical element of the Hmong family structure that is continuing in this country is the mutually supportive kinship system. An example of this, observed in Long Beach, is family lending pools, in which each member contributes a small amount monthly and in return is able to withdraw funds to buy items such as a refrigerator, other household appliances, and the like. No interest is charged, and the borrower pays back the money when able.

Despite all of the obstacles, the Hmong *are* attempting to understand American life-styles, customs, and institutions. Especially difficult for the Hmong to comprehend are the rules and regulations that determine welfare benefits. As new knowledge is gathered, it is shared among family members to add to the accumulating understanding about this strange environment, and in this way the family acts as a mutually supportive educational catalyst.

The Role of the Older Hmong within the Family

Younger Hmong family members, who were interviewed with the elders, spoke of great concern about the situation of the older Hmong. Eleven younger Hmong interviewed felt that one of the biggest problems facing the family was the unhappiness and lack of adjustment of the elders. The issues discussed below represent the perceptions of many of these younger family members.

Principally, all of those voicing concern felt that the elderly need to learn English and that, according to the elderly, this is difficult, if not impossible, to accomplish. In seven situations, younger children have had to either skip school or attempt to leave work early to assist their parents at the welfare office. One Hmong family recalled that the elders' welfare benefits were cut off because of the inability of a younger family member to obtain permission to get off work early. One younger Hmong stated: "Without the young, our old people would be lost." It should be emphasized that the younger Hmong assist the elders without question, but the difficulties of the elders affect the family as a whole.

A second major concern voiced by all younger Hmong family members is the relative inactivity of their older parents. The majority of family members felt that because the elders cannot live on a farm or continue some familiar skill, they tend to "dwell on the past," mourning those who were killed or left behind during the relocation. During several interviews, Hmong family members attempted to rephrase questions directed to the elder when they felt the response would require discussing painful memories. One distinct observation made during several interviews was the apparent emotional shielding that goes on between younger family members and elders. As one younger Hmong stated; "We protect our elderly from bad news and thoughts."

The role of the older Hmong within the family has been restricted severely since arriving from Laos. In all but two interviews with the elders, they spoke primarily of no longer feeling "useful" within the household. The role of the elder within the traditional household was that of teaching, looking after the children, raising animals and vegetables, coordinating domestic activities, and guarding the house (Vang, 1981). These responsibilities underwent an abrupt transformation upon their arrival in the United States. The continuation of these roles is particularly problematic for those elders living in urban areas.

In discussing with the elders what they did around the apartment during a normal day, all of the older men stated that they spent most of the time with little to do. After exploring this further, it was found that they felt restricted because they cannot read an American newspaper or operate the appliances around the apartment. For example, 12 older Hmong stated that they were unable to operate the stove or dishwasher; nor could they regulate the heat.

All of the older women in the study felt that their major role in the household was supervising and playing with the children. This appears to be a continuation of the role performed in Laos. During many of the interviews, it was difficult to keep the women seated long enough to complete the interview without having them get up to perform a task for a child. The child care provided by older women has been a great asset to the younger husband and wife, who are both frequently seeking employment or attending school. In fact, younger parents need the elders to supervise the children to a much greater extent now than they did in Laos.

Relocation and Loss

Loss of Possessions

A repeated theme in each interview was the loss of possessions in relocating. The elders expressed the idea that security in old age was obtained through both family support and one's accumulated objects that had cultural significance. As Barney (1967) notes, possessions such as horses, tools, guns, and musical instruments were passed down from generation to generation, and their maintenance was often delegated to the elder. In particular, the elder in Hmong society played a vital role by teaching children how to use farm equipment, weave baskets, and build homes (Geddes, 1976). Many elders also spoke of missing their animals, which played a critical role in their economy and religious life. Chickens, goats, pigs, buffalo, and cattle were found in almost all Hmong villages (Barney, 1967).

Tied closely to the loss of possessions was the feeling that no ownership of present belongings existed. For example, 14 older Hmong mentioned that because they have to rent, they cannot view the rental as a home, and there is great concern over breaking anything in the apartment.

Loss of Mobility

In Laos, every household had at least one horse, which was used for traveling and transporting materials (Barney, 1967). All of the elders in the study spoke of being restricted to the apartment because of a lack of transportation. None of the elders interviewed owned a car, and riding a city bus alone without a younger family member was extremely difficult because of the inability to read bus schedules, communicate with the driver, and use city maps. To compound the problem, the older Hmong are unable to walk within their own community because they cannot read the street signs. Family members explained that their parents became disoriented when walking in the city "because everything looks the same." The following example characterizes the problems associated with the loss of mobility:

Ly Nhia is a 73-year-old Hmong who has lived in Long Beach for the last three years with his son's family. When he first arrived, he tried to walk around the neighborhood, but would often get lost. He stated that since speaking English was not possible, he had problems asking people to direct him back to his house. Finally, his son told him not to walk outside any more. Nhia misses walking outside because it helped him with his boredom. But, the biggest problem is that he cannot visit his friends because his son works during the day and cannot take him out with the car. (Interview notes)

For many of the older Hmong, being confined to an apartment is equated with a loss of personal freedom and independence. According to Long Beach Hmong officials, next to the language barriers, they view transportation as one of the biggest problems facing their elderly. Of concern to both Hmong officials and elders alike is the fact that a lack of mobility affects socialization. In a positive vein, several Hmong families stated that they attempt to take their elders on short trips and accompany them shopping whenever possible.

Changing Customs

To fully grasp the world view of the older Hmong today, one must appreciate the traditional customs of this culture and their current transformations. In every interview with the elders, it was clearly apparent that they were experiencing tremendous emotional loss due to the modifications or elimination of customs that had previously been passed down for hundreds of years. As mentioned before, it was the elders within Hmong society who were the guardians of the customs that governed all aspects of social, political, and religious life in Laos (Geddes, 1976). Two specific customs were identified as undergoing radical changes—marriage customs and birthing practices.

In traditional Hmong society marriage between a man and a woman can be negotiated only through a go-between (*may kong*), who is usually the eldest brother or paternal uncle of the groom (Barney, 1967). The go-between will carry on all negotiations with the girl's parents, including arrangement of the bride price. After the marriage has been negotiated, the go-between ensures that the customs are followed throughout the wedding celebration.

In six of the interviews with the elder Hmong, it became evident that they are concerned that some younger Hmong no longer use go-betweens nor pay the bride price. The elders feel that the traditional marriage customs ensure that they have some input concerning the future of their sons or daughters. Several older clan leaders spoke of not understanding why some of the younger Hmong want to alter this custom when it has been used for so many generations to wed the Hmong. Other older Hmong felt that shortening the traditional marriage feast from 4 days to just 1 day does an injustice to the clans. One elder stated, "The marriage feast was long in order to get to know the other clan. This was important."

Birthing practices have also undergone a radical change. In Laos the birth of a child is a family affair in which all members play a vital role (Geddes, 1976; Potter & Whirin, 1982). According to traditional custom, about 1 month before the child is due, the husband's parents instruct the wife in childbirth procedures, including the rules governing taboos. According to Geddes (1976), the grandparents must purchase a soul for the child, usually by burning "spirit-money," a form of Hmong currency. Also, the wife is instructed not to touch or swallow anything cold during the last 4 weeks of pregnancy because it would affect the baby adversely.

The majority of the older Hmong interviewed in the study stated that the role they play in the delivery of a child has radically changed. Specifically, they felt that American doctors were interfering with their traditional role of instructing the mother concerning childbirth. In many cases, the doctor's recommendations contradicted what the elder felt was in the best interests of the mother. For example, one elder spoke of her daughter's being told by her doctor that she could eat anything throughout her pregnancy. However, in Hmong custom the mother's diet is regulated closely, and certain foods are forbidden. An additional problem mentioned by the elders is that hospital regulations do not allow the presence of anyone except the husband in the delivery room. This further diminishes the elders' traditional presence and role during the birth of a child.

Loss of Religious Customs

The Hmong's relocation from Laos has greatly affected their religious belief system, and many elders have abandoned or questioned the validity of their faith. To appreciate this change, a detailed description of the Hmong religion is discussed by Scott (1982):

> The traditional Hmong religion is comprised essentially of three interrelated elements: animism, ancestor worship, and shamanism. According to this religious view, most events in the world, both human and otherwise, were ultimately governed by a variety of supernatural agents. Spirits (dab) were pervasive in the environment, those of a familiar or "tame" nature (dab nyeg) residing in houses, parts of the village, and cultivated fields, and those of a dubious or "wild" nature (dab gua) existing in certain trees, rivers, rocks, caves, and animals of the forest, as well as in a metaphysical realm mirroring that of the living. Providing an extension of human society in this transcendant realm were the ancestral spirits (dab txwokoob), who, together with the spirits, had to be appeased with offerings (txi dab) if the conditions of life over which they held sway were to remain favorable to the people. (p. 65)

Eleven older Hmong stated that they were no longer able to practice their faith because of an inability to conduct religious ceremonies. All of them stated that it is impossible to find an appropriate outdoor place within the city where offerings can be burned and the site left undisturbed. According to several elders, traditionally they would construct an olive box and place within it the blood of an animal, paper money, incense, eggs, and rice. They would burn it on New Year's Day, at the birth of a child, or on the last day of the harvest. Now, because city ordinances restrict outdoor fires, they can no longer practice this custom.

Further restricting the practice of religious ceremonies for the Hmong is the inability to perform these ceremonies without a public outcry. First, even if the Hmong were able to obtain the sacrificial animals, mainly chickens and pigs, it would be awkward to perform the ceremonies in an apartment complex. Second, the Hmong believe that the loud chanting and playing of instruments that accompany the ceremonies need to be done outdoors to invoke the spirits, and this would draw complaints from neighbors. One older Hmong explained that his family tried to sacrifice a chicken to bless the apartment where *sier klang* (the protective house spirit) resides. When neighbors heard the noise of the fowl being killed, they called police.

Loss of Status

The most disturbing impact of the relocation on the older Hmong is their perception that they have lost important status. As seen in previous sections, old age and respect in Hmong culture are closely tied to meaningful roles. The elders would often make statements such as, "The children do not ask me about customs;" "I receive a lot of respect within my family, but not from younger Hmong. I have no dignity because I can't do anything for myself, and I can't help my family."

The loss of status and respect that the older Hmong are experiencing can be analyzed on several levels. First, the Hmong family still provides the elders with respect for their station in life even though the elder does not have a clear-cut role. Second, it seems clear that the elders are looking to the family unit for a definition of their roles, functions, and responsibilities and for a sense of usefulness.

Closely tied to this issue of respect is the transformation that has occurred with the honor name, or "old name," as the elders refer to it. According to some elders, they have had to drop the use of the name because it is confusing to Americans. In some situations the elder is known by one name within the family and by another in the community. Some elders reported feeling troubled about this; others say it is no problem.

In exploring further this loss of status among the elders, I came across a disturbing finding. Although it was difficult to get the elders to discuss it in front of family members, they are deeply concerned that they will eventually be placed in nursing homes. In Laos, of course, they would age and die while living with family members.

Mental Health Status of the Older Hmong

The Hmong interpret mental health from a different perspective compared to Western society. The term *mental health* is often confused with mental illness or being crazy *(veu)*. From the Hmong perspective one is either crazy, or one is not. It is clearly a black-or-white definition. In Laos, when a person was deemed *veu*, a shaman would be summoned to burn incense, pray to the spirits, and sacrifice two chickens on the person's behalf (Murase, 1982).

Possibly because of the stigma attached to being *veu*, none of the elders admitted to being depressed. However, a majority of the elders interviewed described symptoms often related to depression: inability to sleep, poor appetite, prolonged sadness, and agitation. In addition, younger Hmong family members characterized their older parents as "living in the past" and "continually crying."

To verify my perception concerning depression among those interviewed, I asked the Long Beach Hmong Association leadership how many elders in their community suffered from the symptoms identified above. According to the leadership, 90% of their elders were experiencing those symptoms on a regular basis. This high percentage was also confirmed by several Long Beach Public Health nurses who see elders at the clinic for mandatory vaccinations. In addition, when the Association leadership attempted to survey what the needs of their elders were at a recent meeting, such responses as "I simply am waiting to die" and "my life is over" were frequent.

The impact of the relocation on the mental status of all elderly Southeast Asian refugees was apparent in a presentation delivered by a Vietnamese elder at a Southeast Asian Mental Health conference at Chapman College, Orange, California, on July 16, 1983:

Being refugees, the most one can say about them is they're uprooted in the full sense of the term. How have they taken root again on this new land? The response is just negative.

While the young people have tried to adjust to the new environment in order to make a living for themselves and their children, the elderly have been experiencing the most tragic trauma they have ever known, and feel cut off from the past as well as from the present and a future they are unable to help shape as they wish. This is a source of frustration and stress in both mental and physical senses.

Of the past, which has penetrated and constituted the fabric of their lives, the elders have remembrances and nostalgia for all things lost . . . country, children, brothers, sisters, friends, many dead or in refugee camps until now. These memories of the past are so insistent that they have become a haunting.

I have personally experienced this kind of torment, which prevented me from sleeping well for three years, with the past reappearing in my mind as if on a movie screen. To free myself of this haunting, I finally wrote down all my memories, and this acted as a relief valve for me. But what a terrible thing for all those who cannot write. They just keep crying—as my wife does—with the resurrected images of the lost things, images which they cherish more with each remembrance, far back to their young age, to the maternal home.

The culture shock which you know that all the refugees have to experience is particularly acute with the elderly because of the language barriers and lack of communication with people all around. It would help them somehow if they could go out to see and talk to some rare friends. But transportation problems are insoluble to them.

This culture shock has become a gap between generations, between elders and youngsters, between grandparents and grandchildren, even between parents and children, because of the fast westernization of the young, generating many kinds of conflicts in behavior. A great many families have been split again in this country because of the job problems which drive the children away from their parents, leaving them walled with their loneliness. (Interview notes)

It is important to reiterate a point here. The majority of Hmong family members interviewed in this study are at a total loss concerning how to handle their elders' mental health problems. In many ways, family members convey a feeling of being in a double bind. They cannot increase their elders' outside activities because of the elders' limited understanding of English, lack of transportation, and fear of crime. However, outside activities could provide assistance in coping with the depression. Also, they are unable to restore the traditional roles that elders had in Laos and that provided a high level of status. The predicament in which the family finds itself is new to them.

According to various families interviewed, the family unit traditionally was the primary resource in the management of mental health. This differs from the Western world, which relies on resources outside the family for mental health services. One younger Hmong recalled the story of an elder in the family who refused to eat for weeks after the loss of her husband. The family intervened by having each member take turns feeding her forcibly and encouraging her. It cannot be overemphasized that illness suffered by an individual, whether physical or mental, is viewed as a family affair.

Throughout this study there was no evidence that any of the elders had obtained any counseling from external mental health resources. Also, family members conveyed strong reservations about bringing their parent to a counselor. There was a limited understanding of the role of a mental health professional in helping to deal with mental health problems. It is important to note that during a 4-year period, from 1978 to 1982, the largest counseling program for older adults in Orange County (Project PACE) did not see one older Hmong for treatment, even though Orange County has the highest population of Indochinese refugees per capita in the nation (Baldwin, 1982).

All of the elders interviewed wanted to return to Laos. This is similar to Baldwin's (1982) survey, which found that 84% of the Hmong wanted to return to their country. The highest percentage of those wanting to return was in the over-age-55 group. They realize, however, that for political reasons their desire to return is unrealistic. Attached to this desire to return is one to regain what has been lost in the relocation.

Social Services and the Older Hmong

Throughout the course of this study no services targeted for the older Hmong could be identified except public assistance support through welfare. Two findings stand out as critical in addressing the social service needs of the older Hmong. First, personnel in the network of services for the aging are largely unaware of the problems and concerns of this group. No training has been conducted by the Area Agencies on Aging to sensitize service providers regarding ways to target resources, conduct outreach, and interface with Hmong leadership to assess the elders' needs. The aging network is clearly at a loss to know how Western models of service can be shaped to address this group of elders.

Second, the elder Hmong in this study do not understand how the welfare or social service system operates or how benefits are provided. Institutions and services such as senior centers, nutrition sites, or homebound meals are foreign to the elder Hmong. In many instances they do not understand the purpose of the entities or why the family cannot provide the same benefits. Though the Hmong leadership recognizes that such services would provide help for their elderly, there is great skepticism that any elders would accept willingly services outside the family.

A growing realization within the Hmong leadership is that the community must begin addressing the socialization and cultural needs of their elderly. The Long Beach Hmong Association is developing plans to start a Hmong senior center, which would include appropriate ethnic food, music, and activities.

Comparison with Other Indochinese Elderly Refugee Groups

Having lost a variety of social, cultural, and familial roles, elderly refugees from Vietnam, Cambodia, and Laos find adjustment in the United States very difficult. Each of these Indochinese societies traditionally has provided for their aged significant roles that are difficult to maintain in urban settings within the United States. There are preliminary indications that all three elderly groups are suffering from high levels of depression because of their current situation (Westermeyer, 1985).

Although little research has been done to compare experiences between elderly Indochinese refugee groups, it is the author's observation that the elderly Hmong face the greatest difficulty in adjusting to their new culture. Several factors make their adjustment more problematic than that of Vietnamese or Cambodian elderly.

First, in comparison to Vietnam and Cambodia, the country of Laos is a technologically backward society. For the majority of Hmong, modern technology (television sets, stoves, heating appliances, and so forth) fills them with uncertainty and fear. In contrast, the Vietnamese elderly, having been exposed to modern technology to a greater degree because of U.S. involvement in Vietnam, have had an easier time adjusting to our material world. It could be surmised that the Vietnamese elderly may be able to function more independently and utilize less family assistance in negotiating what are perceived as barriers by the Hmong. Certainly, research needs to be conducted to validate this observation.

Second, the elder Hmong have few skills outside of farming and related activities. This poses particular problems in developing new roles and occupations for the elder Hmong in urban areas. Elderly Vietnamese and Cambodians, because of their involvement in businesses and nonfarming activities, may have an easier time establishing employment-related roles.

Summary

This article has attempted to present as complete a picture as possible, within the space constraints, of the refugee experience of older Hmong in the United States. Without question, the older Hmong have experienced serious upheaval and deterioration of traditional roles, customs, and life-style. One cannot help but question how the aged Hmong will fare in ensuing years.

From this author's perspective, the ability of the older Hmong to assimilate into American culture looks bleak at best. Obviously, the transplanted Hmong family structure will need to provide the majority of assistance for these aged. Certainly, there is no indication that younger family members are abandoning their traditional role of caring for older members.

At this time there is a great need to provide culturally appropriate services for the older Hmong refugee and the existing family. Attention needs to be directed to developing models that provide linkages between the network for the aging and the Hmong community.

7

Age and Religious Commitment in the American–Jewish Community

Cary S. Kart

The element of religion distinguishes Jews from other ethnic groups defined largely by national origin and/or language; consequently, Jews may be considered to constitute a religioethnic group (Gelfand & Olsen, 1979; Kahana & Kahana, 1984). This chapter assesses the relationship between age and religious commitment in the American Jewish community. It begins with a review of the literature on the relationship between age and religious commitment, though such studies generally have not distinguished among individuals of different religious affiliation.

Writing almost 15 years ago, Heenan (1972) described the literature on religion and aging as "empirical lacunae." Have things changed since then? Though the literature on death and dying has grown dramatically in the last decade or so, empirical research on the religious attitudes and behavior of older people is still relatively scarce. One explanation for the scarcity of such research is that this aspect of older life is taken for granted: Elders are consistently portrayed as both more superstitious and more religious than younger people, and the assumption is that the religious role of old people remains strong and enduring (Hess & Markson, 1980; Orbach, 1961).

The scarcity of research on religion and aging may also have roots in methodological concerns. First, most research in social gerontology is cross-sectional in design. Thus, it is difficult to disentangle age, cohort, and period effects on a wide variety of behaviors and attitudes, including religious behavior and attitudes (Maddox, 1979). Second, certain concepts are difficult to define in the area of religion. What constitutes a religious individual? And how should religiosity be measured: church or synagogue attendance or engagement in private devotional activities?

Third, though religious groups "differ in terms of the amount of participation and interest demanded of their adherents, the degree of organization they possess and the opportunities they offer for the individual to achieve his or her goals" (Atchley, 1980; p. 331), there seems to be a general insensitivity within the field of gerontology toward the need to distinguish among religious groups. Thus, what few studies there are make no basic attempt to separate Protestants, Catholics, and Jews, and further subdivision among these groups is even more rare (Crandall, 1980). A recent review of the measures used in studies of age and religiosity indicates that most are Christian and church-oriented (Payne, 1982).

Insensitivity toward religious diversity among the aged may simply be an extension of the development of the broader field of social gerontology. Only recently has recognition of the ethnic and racial diversity present in the aging experience begun to rub off on the field. In the early 1970s, Moore (1971) could argue that most of what we have come to learn of aging stems from studies of "middle-majority Anglos." Similarly, Kastenbaum (1971) characterized the great majority of studies carried out on aged whites as follows: "Any resemblance to the aging non-Caucasian is accidental and unintentional." Students of religion and aging may be in a position to paraphrase these gerontologists: Most of what we have come to learn of aging and religion stems from studies of middle-majority Christians; any resemblance to the aging non-Christian may be accidental and unintentional.

Age and Religious Commitment

Just what do we know about how age affects religious behavior and/or commitment? Bahr (1970) analyzed prior research in this area and suggested that the relationship between aging and church attendance be interpreted with reference to four distinct models: traditional, lifetime stability, family life cycle, and progressive disengagement. According to the *traditional* model, there is a sharp decline in religious activity during young adulthood. Beyond age 35, this model posits a steady increase in church activity until old age. The *lifetime stability* model alleges that aging and church attendance or religious activity are not related. One interpretation of this model is made by Lazerwitz (1962). He suggests that "perhaps church attendance is based upon patterns established fairly early in life and subject to little (if any) change with aging."

A third model derives from the view that stage of *family life cycle* is related to religious participation. In general, family life cycle seems to be a euphemism for presence or absence of children. According to this model, when children are young and tied to the home, parental involvement in religious services peaks; with children no longer in the home, regularity of religious participation falls off. The *progressive disengagement* model is tied to the disengagement theory of aging. From the perspective of this theory, aging is seen as "an inevitable mutual withdrawal or disengagement," resulting in decreased interaction between the aging person and others in his or her social systems (Cumming & Henry, 1961). Applied to participation in religious activities, the theory suggests a model of decline following middle age.

Bahr's own interviews with more than 600 men from three distinctive socioeconomic strata (skid row, urban lower class, and urban middle class) show substantial religious disaffiliation during adult life in all three groups; the progressive disengagement model is most congruent with the pattern of church attendance reported by his respondents. With advancing age, church attendance is increasingly less important as a source of voluntary affiliation among both well-to-do and poor men (Bahr, 1970).

Wingrove and Alston (1974) have argued that support for each of Bahr's four models varies by the type of sample and methodology used and the year of the data collection. Applying cohort analysis to data collected by the Gallup Poll between 1939 and 1969, these authors found that while church attendance appears related to age, no consistent support for any one of the four models was provided. Each cohort was found to show its own church attendance pattern. Gender and social environment seemed to have greater impact on church attendance than did age.

Criticism of these and other studies of the relationship between age and religious behavior often centers on the fact that researchers have too narrowly conceptualized religiosity in terms of attendance and/or participation in formal religious organizations. As Mindel and Vaughn (1978) point out, the role of "religious person" encompasses more than simple participation in a religious organization and may include private or nonorganizational religious behavior. Some even suggest that with aging these more private and nonorganizational religious expressions increase in importance (Moberg,

1972). Stark (1968) found that greater piety among the elderly compared to the young was manifested in the reported frequency of praying.

Employing a small sample of elderly from central Missouri, Mindel and Vaughn (1978) observed that although a majority did not attend religious services frequently, a majority of sample members were nonorganizationally religious "very often." For the purposes of this study, examples of nonorganizational religious activity included engaging in individual or family prayer and listening to religious music or religious services on the radio or television.

Analyzing data from a large sample of Washington State residents, Finney and Lee (1976) found that age had a small, positive influence on private devotional practices but no effect on four other dimensions of religious commitment: belief, ritual, knowledge, and experience (Glock, 1962; Glock & Stark, 1965; Stark & Glock, 1968). Finney and Lee (1976) suggest that older people may tend to employ religion as a means of reducing or alleviating anxieties, and they point to the small effect of age on several dimensions of religious commitment as indicative of the need "to raise questions about recent thought in both social gerontology and the sociology of religion."

Age and Religious Commitment among American Jews

Historical Background

Concerns about the loss of religious commitment or identification have been present in the American Jewish community since the first Jewish immigrants came to these shores. In part, the initial concern may have occurred because many of the first immigrants were less than religiously orthodox. Despite colonial America's reputation as a land of religious tolerance, immigrating Jews' primary concern was freedom to engage in commercial trade. As Hershkowitz (1976) has written, "Their business was for the most part business. They struggled harder for the right to trade than for the right to have a burial ground or a synagogue" (p. 12).

Kart and Engler (1985) content-analyzed the wills of aged colonial Jews in New York state between 1704 and 1799. They found Jewish testators to be well integrated into the mainstream of non-Jewish society. However, assimilation, for all of its benefits, created pressures for colonial Jews. Cultural integration threatened their *Yehudishkeit,* their Jewishness. Formal and informal religious sanctions were employed to combat the negative effects of assimilation without actually preventing it. Daniels (1977) has described how Shearith Israel, the colonial New York synagogue, controlled the behavior of its followers through tight jurisdiction over the only consecrated Jewish burial site, approval of marriage partners, and regulation of dietary laws. In return for accepting its religious control, Shearith Israel was instrumental in fostering unity among Jews and providing essential communal services. Ritual foods were supplied, the poor were supported, and burial grounds were well tended. Although testator piety is difficult to gauge, Kart and Engler (1985) report that the synagogue was important to many. About one-third of the testators made some bequest to the synagogue, and several others contributed to the "poor of the Jewish nation." In a number of wills, testators made clear specification of a desire to "be buryed [sic] in our Jewish burying ground in said New York among my friends and relations and according to the Jewish Custom."

The 20th century has brought increased concerns about Jewish identification, in part, perhaps, exacerbated by a demographic imperative. After all, by the end of the 18th century there were only about 1,200 Jews in America. As a result of high rates of net immigration from Eastern Europe and natural increase, the Jewish population in the United States increased to over 1 million by the turn of the 20th century and to over 4 million by the mid-1920s. By 1950 the American Jewish population numbered approximately 5 million—an almost 100-fold increase in a century (Goldscheider, 1982; Goldstein, 1981).

As Goldscheider (1986) rightly points out, Jewish immigrants who arrived in the United States around the turn of the 20th century did not, for the most part, transplant the world of their origins. These Jews came largely from eastern European backgrounds and may have had more in common with other peasants from eastern Europe than they did with the more educated and cultured German-Jewish immigrants who came to America in the mid-1800s (Gelfand & Olsen, 1979). Eastern European Jews had been subjected to great hostility and oppression in their homeland. Many faced laws that prevented them from owning property; others experienced pogroms. Shtetl life was precarious, yet conflict with non-Jews helped maintain Jewish identity and solidarity. America was another matter. As Dimont (1978) describes it, "As they stepped off their boats, they were swallowed into the vastness of America" (p. 164). Yet as we know, the great social processes of the 20th century—industrialization, urbanization, secularization—worked their ways on these Jews. Virtually every indicator reveals how Jews became modern, secular, and American by the 1980s.

From 1900 to the beginning of World War I, about 1.5 million eastern European Jews came to the shores of America. Yet those who constitute the majority of "old-old" Jews in America today were an odd lot, hardly homogeneous in terms of their life histories. Mixed among them were "provincial Hasidim, arrogant Maskilim, scornful socialists, hopeful Zionists, emancipated intellectuals" (Dimont, 1978, p. 161). And those Jews who came after them, many among today's "young-old" and "old-old" were different still. The threat of Nazism and the experience of the Holocaust continues to cast a shadow over the lives of these Jews, even today.

A Current Assessment

Demographic information currently available on the American-Jewish population shows that it is older than the general U.S. population. Approximately 12.5% of the Jewish population is 65 years of age or older; 43% of Jews are over age 50 versus 39% for the general U.S. population (Kahana & Kahana, 1984). Data available on younger age cohorts suggest that the American-Jewish population will continue to age at a faster pace than the total U.S. population.

Lazerwitz and Harrison (1979) have pointed to the importance of denominational preference among American Jews. Such preference reflects historical changes in the American-Jewish community and influences the value systems and interaction patterns of individual Jews. Using data from the National Jewish Population Survey (NJPS), including 5,790 household interviews completed during 1970 and 1971, Lazerwitz and Harrison present the following pattern of denominational identification among American Jews affiliated with a synagogue: 14% identified with Orthodoxy, 49% with Conservative Judaism, 34% with Reform Judaism, and 3% indicated no preference. Among those without a synagogue membership, 7% preferred Orthodoxy, 35% preferred Conservative Judaism, 33% preferred Reform Judaism, and 25% had no preference.

Orthodox Jews generally adhere to traditional religious values and practices. Conservative Judaism is tradition-minded in terms of adherence to religious values but in practice shows more flexibility than Orthodoxy in the demands it places on its members. Reform Judaism is the least traditional of the three denominations. Elderly Jews are found disproportionately in the more traditional branches of Judaism; more than one-third of the members of Orthodox synagogues are 60 years of age or over, and more than one-half are foreign-born (Lazerwitz & Harrison, 1979). The Reform and Conservative denominations are distinctive in their high percentage of married synagogue members with children under 16 years in the household; in both cases, 57% of the membership is so constituted (Lazerwitz & Harrison, 1979).

What is the significance of historical background and denominational preference for religious identification among Jews in America? Conflicting views abound about the religious commitment or identification of American Jews today. On the one hand, pessimists describe continued decline across the generations in the performance of traditional ritual practices such as frequent worship, dietary law observances, and Sabbath candle lighting. They see this continued decline across the generations leading to the virtual disintegration or assimilation of the American Jewish community (e.g., Hertzberg, 1979). Optimists, on the other hand, employ what may loosely be characterized as a "stabilization theory," in which they imply that the trend toward declining religious observance can be expected to halt among fourth-generation American Jews (e.g., Sklare & Greenblum, 1979).

Pessimists and optimists both may be incorrect. Cohen (1983) asserts that generation-by-generation changes in religious and ethnic behavior can be nonlinear and offsetting. He argues that straight-line theories provide an inadequate guide to the effects of acculturation and assimilation. For example, he reports that second-generation American Jews observe fewer religious rituals and are a bit less likely to belong to a synagogue than are members of the first generation, but they are considerably more likely to contribute to Jewish charities and to belong to other kinds of Jewish organizations. Further, the changes in religious behavior that occur across generations are not at all uniform. The generation-by-generation reduction in observance of some rituals, such as lighting Sabbath candles and keeping a kosher home, is accompanied by a generation-by-generation increase in observance of others—in particular, attending a Passover Seder and lighting Chanukah candles.

Perhaps, though, both pessimists and optimists are correct. Kart, Palmer, and Flaschner (1986) found support for both of these apparently contradictory views in their study of age and religiosity in Toledo, Ohio. For men in this midwestern community, no statistically significant age differences could be observed on an array of organizational and individual measures of religious commitment, including such items as whether dietary laws are observed, ritual prayers for the deceased are said, and mezuzahs are placed on doorposts. This is in contrast to Orbach's (1961) report, more than 25 years ago, from the Detroit Area Study that Jewish men showed increased synagogue attendance with age. In Toledo only the number of Jewish organizational memberships showed age-related differences. Older men are much more likely to hold multiple memberships in Jewish voluntary associations or organizations. In general, such results might be considered supportive of the stabilization theory.

Women in this study provide a different picture. Statistically significant age differences can be observed on a number of organizational and individual measures of religiosity, including synagogue attendance and the use of mezuzahs on the doorposts of the home. In all cases, older women show stronger religious commitment than do younger women. Only on a single scale made up of two items—observance of dietary laws and lighting of Sabbath candles—do Kart and his colleagues (1986) report no apparent age differences. The results for women seem supportive of a disintegration or assimilation theory and are consistent with those reported by Lebowitz (1973) for the Portland, Oregon, Jewish community. In this study, interviews with heads of households revealed quantitative and qualitative differences in the direction of decreased religious identification on the part of younger generations.

Goldscheider (1986) has written of the multiple bases of cohesion in the American-Jewish community. Generational continuity in religious affiliation and religious identification is one of these bases. The notion of generational continuity implies a high level of consensus between and among generations in life-style, interests, kin networks, economic linkages, values, and norms (Goldscheider, 1986). Kart, Palmer, and Flaschner (1986) suggest from their data on Jews in a midwestern community that the process or pattern of generational continuity may be different for men and women, though perhaps it simply proceeds (recedes) at different rates for men and for women.

This should come as no surprise to students of change in women's role participation in America. Societal attitudes toward those roles appropriate to women have undergone great transformation in the post–World War II period. These attitudinal changes have manifested themselves in changing marriage, family formation, and divorce patterns, as well as in increased participation by women in the labor force. This post–World War II "modernization" of American women has only very recently begun to affect the position of women within the context of institutional Judaism. Cynthia Ozick has argued that the exclusion of women from Jewish religious life and learning has involved "a loss numerically greater than a hundred pogroms" and was "culturally and intellectually more debilitating than a century of autos-da-fé" (quoted in Silberman, 1985).

In summarizing his work on the Boston Jewish community, Gold-scheider (1986) indicates that there are no clear relationships be-tween educational level and religiosity or between other social class indicators and Jewishness. Hence, he concludes, "neither the attain-ment of high levels of education nor upward mobility can be viewed as a 'threat' to Jewish continuity" (p. 182). Kart, Palmer, and Flaschner (1986) report a different relationship between educa-tional level and religiosity in their sample of Jews in Toledo, Ohio. When controls for education were employed for women on the relationship between Jewish organizational membership and age, and between subjective evaluation of religious intensity (do you consider yourself a strong Jew or not?) and age, a case of specifica-tion was observed. That is, among women with the most education, the generation or age gap in religious commitment was also the greatest. Aged women (64 years of age and older) with a college degree and beyond showed stronger religious commitment on these measures than comparably educated women less than 45 years of age. Younger women with less education are much more like their comparably educated mothers and grandmothers in terms of religious values than are highly educated young women.

One explanation for the low level of religious commitment exhib-ited by younger women relative to older women in the study by Kart and his colleagues (1986) has to do with the conflict between a secular world accepting of changes in the roles women occupy and a religious world rooted in traditional roles played by women. In the face of such conflict, younger Jewish women may be choosing the modern or secular world at a higher rate than have their mothers and grandmothers. And this appears especially to be the case among the most educated women.

Summary and Conclusion

Although it may be difficult today to describe accurately the litera-ture on religion and aging as "empirical lacunae," empirical re-search is still scarce. This is especially the case for non-Christian religious groups. Perhaps in the future the relationship between age, aging, and religious commitment will be grist for the research mills of social gerontologists. Methodological emphases should be placed on measures that distinguish between organizational and individual devotional aspects of religiosity and on research designs that allow for teasing out age, period, and cohort effects on religious identification and commitment. Comparative studies across different religious groups in America would seem to be especially useful.

Concerns about the loss of religious commitment or identification have been present in the American Jewish community since the first Jewish immigrants came to these shores. The 20th century has brought increased concern because of the high rates of net immigration from eastern Europe and natural population increase. Life in the "old country," the immigration experience itself, the threat of Nazism, and the experience of the Holocaust are but a few of the factors that must be superimposed on the Americanization process in order to understand differences in religious identification and commitment by age among American Jews.

Denominational preference influences the value systems and interaction patterns of individual Jews. Elderly Jews are found disproportionately in the more traditional branches of Judaism; more than one-third of the members of Orthodox synagogues in America are 60 years of age and over. Reform and Conservative denominations are distinguished by the high percentage of congregants who are married and have young children at home.

Two contradictory views of the relationship between age and religious observance among American Jews have received empirical support. The assimilationist view posits a continued decline across the generations, leading to virtual disintegration in the American-Jewish community. The stabilization view sees a halt among young Jews in the decline in religious observance. Kart, Palmer, and Flaschner's (1986) study of a midwestern Jewish community provides evidence supportive of both views. Similarity in patterns of religious observance between young and old males in this community provides support for the stabilization view. Women show a different pattern, suggesting support for an assimilationist view. On a variety of indicators, young women show less religious observance than do older women. Lazerwitz and Harrison (1979) report that two-thirds of the members of Reform synagogues in America are women. They argue that these synagogues "appear to have greatest appeal for women because they deemphasize the traditional religious distinctions between the sexes and are thus closer to the current secular ideal of sexual equality" (p. 659). Future researchers of the American-Jewish experience will have to be especially sensitive to how gender affects the relationship between age and religious identification and/or commitment.

8

Amish Families in Later Life

Timothy H. Brubaker and Carol M. Michael

The Amish represent a small group of individuals who are religious-ly bound together. Their views on family life, old age, and inter-relationships with the dominant society are premised on their interpretations of the Bible. The ultimate authority in their social system is God, as defined by their religious leaders. Views of later life and support provided to older people are inextricably tied to religion.

Definitions of ethnicity provide several criteria for a group to be considered ethnic, and the Amish meet these requirements. Gordon (1964) defines an ethnic group as "any group which is defined or set off by race, religion, or national origin, or some combination of these categories" (p. 27). It is a group of people who have a sense of "peoplehood," of belonging. Further, an ethnic group has a shared social and cultural heritage that is unique and is transferred from one generation to another (Mindel & Habenstein, 1981). To the Amish, religion sets them apart from other groups and is an impor-tant part of their social and cultural heritage. Although religion is important to the Amish, the ethnic themes and ideals permeate their total way of life. Thus, following Cohen's (1981) definition of ethnicity, the Amish are an ethnic group within the United States.

There are three aspects of the Amish culture that suggest that they are an ethnic group within the United States. First, their separateness within the dominant culture is based on their in-terpretation of the Bible. They see themselves as a "peculiar peo-ple." Kephart (1982) notes that the Amish are peculiar because they "believe in a literal translation of the Bible and rely heavily on the statement, 'But ye are a chosen generation, a royal priesthood, a holy nation, a peculiar people' (1 Peter 2:9). Since they have been specifically chosen by God, the Amish take great pains to stay 'apart' from the world at large" (p. 51). The Amish are an ethnic group because they have chosen to be "peculiar," "separated from," or "set apart from" others within the dominant culture on the basis of their religion.

Second, their culture is unique as evidenced by their customs and social structure. The most obvious unique characteristic is their dress. Hostetler (1980) emphasizes the symbolic and unifying aspects of the unique dress of the Amish. For example, the hat worn by an Amishman is symbolic of membership within this ethnic group. At the same time, the hat "clarifies his age, sex and position within his society" (p. 234). Similarly, garb worn by Amish women signifies membership in this ethnic group and subordinate placement to men within the social structure (Schreiber, 1962).

Third, the Amish customs and culture are transferred from one generation to another. The Amish have been in the United States since at least 1737 and, with a few exceptions, seek to continue the same traditions and customs in the 1980s. The older generations are very important to the transfer of these traditions from one generation to another. One of the primary goals of the older Amish is to keep the younger generations in the Amish society (Markle & Pasco, 1977). Because their religious beliefs encourage respect for the older and past generations, it is not unexpected that there has been little change in the Amish culture during the last 250 years.

The Amish, as an ethnic group, provide an interesting group from which to view aging. Age is respected, and the family unit is strong. Their interactions are strongly buttressed by their religious beliefs, and becoming older is a natural, accepted sequence for individuals. In this chapter we will first define the Amish as an ethnic group and discuss their historical roots. The second section is an overview of the life of the older Amish. The ethnic themes related to the lives of older Amish will be outlined in the third section. And finally, the uniqueness of the lives of older Amish as compared to other ethnic groups is discussed.

Who Are the Amish?

The Old Order Amish are the most conservative followers of Jacob Ammann, a 17th-century Swiss Anabaptist who founded this faction within the Swiss Mennonite group in 1693 in Switzerland (Hostetler, 1980). As a result of severe persecution in Europe, the Amish began immigrating to the United States around 1737, settling first in eastern Pennsylvania. By the early 1800s, Amish groups had also settled in Ohio, New York, Delaware, Maryland, Indiana, and Illinois. Today, Amish live in 20 U.S. states; Ontario, Canada; Honduras; and Paraguay. Of the estimated 85,000 U.S. population, however, about 75% still live in rural areas of Pennsylvania, Ohio, and Indiana. The vast majority of these are Old Order Amish. Two of the largest settlements are in Lancaster County, Pennsylvania, and in Holmes County, Ohio (Foster, 1981).

Old Order Amish are characterized by strong religious beliefs that require separation from the world and rejection of modern technologies that they believe will adversely affect their families and communities. Old Order Amish are not permitted by the *Ordnung* (church rules) to own cars or tractors, use electricity in their homes for light or modern appliances, or own telephones or radios. They are distinguished by their simple, traditional ways of living, their plain dress and their Pennsylvania-Dutch dialect.

The Amish are an agrarian society; farming is still considered the ideal occupation. Although the majority of Amish still live and work on family farms, more recent studies have shown that in some areas only about half of the heads of Amish households are employed in farming on a full-time basis (Ericksen, Ericksen, & Hostetler, 1980). Many are engaged in trades and in small cottage industries. Some have taken traditional factory work out of economic necessity because the Amish population is rapidly expanding and the prices of available farmland are skyrocketing.

Amish believe in community self-sufficiency and care of their own. Consequently they have requested and received exemption from the U.S. Social Security system as citizens. They receive no governmental medical or welfare benefits and take out no insurance policies. If any type of financial aid is needed by an Amish family and immediate relatives cannot provide it, other families in the Amish community come to the assistance of the family (Hostetler, 1980).

The institution of central importance to the Amish is the family, the school and church being supplemental (Ericksen et al., 1980). The Amish live in extended family groups with as many as four generations living on the same property in adjoining houses. Marriage partners are chosen from within the Amish community, and marriage is for life; divorce is unheard of among the Amish. Family structure is patriarchal, with women having a secondary but economically crucial role.

Parenting is taken very seriously among the Amish. Amish parents carefully teach their children the traditional values of the society in the home and in the parochial schools that are provided. Because children are highly valued and are considered an economic asset, Amish families routinely have large numbers of children. The average number for Lancaster Amish is seven children per family (Ericksen & Leon, 1978).

The Life of the Older Amish

Elderly Amish continue to be loved, honored, and respected members of their community. Unlike the rest of society, in which the elderly are often separated from their families or communities, elderly Amish stay with their families until their death. When a father approaches retirement age and determines that one of his sons is ready to assume the management of the farm, he and his wife move to an adjoining "granddaddy house" on the same property, usually leaving the main house to the married son's family. Both grandparents, however, stay intimately involved in productive work (Schreiber, 1962). The grandfather remains an active participant and becomes a consultant to his son in the running of the farm. Gradually, responsibility for all major decisions is transferred to the son, yet the grandfather's opinion will always be sought and considered seriously.

The grandmother continues to be involved in the management of the extended family household. Though major decisions are transferred to the daughter-in-law, she continues to be directly involved in the daily care of family members, food preparation, production and preservation, cleaning, and other activities. In this way older Amish pass on their legacy to the next generation, decrease their involvement as their physical strength begins to diminish, and yet remain active and useful members of the family. The desired balance of involvement and independence is maintained with the establishment of separate living quarters. Three or more generations may be operating on the same property.

It is considered the duty of the older generation to help provide their children with the material resources they will need for their livelihood. Generally, this means that the father is expected to provide his sons with farmland. If a gift of his own land is not possible, he may purchase land for them or lend them the necessary money (Ericksen et al., 1980). The same principle applies to the Amish involved in cottage industries or trades. As new households are established, family and friends outfit the young couple with the furniture and other household articles needed.

Elderly Amish men continue to be valued in the religious life of the community. Serving as bishops, ministers, deacons, or general advisors in the church, their opinions on the interpretation of the Scripture and possible changes in the *Ordnung* are sought and respected, keeping them intimately involved in the group practices of their faith.

When the health of the elderly begins to fail, it is considered the responsibility of the family to provide whatever health care is needed. Expert medical care is sought, and hospitalization occurs as needed but rarely for extended periods.

Because the elderly live in an adjoining household on the farm, multiple family members usually are available to provide attention and care, though the primary responsibility falls on a daughter or daughter-in-law. When sons and daughters live on separate properties, they still may share care of older family members who are physically or mentally impaired. In such cases, the elderly person or couple may travel from household to household for monthly visits with the various sons or daughters in the family (Bryer, 1979).

Home care of the elderly with failing health may last from several months to periods as extended as 20 years (Bryer, 1979). Provision of this care is not perceived by the family as a burden but as a normal, expected part of life, and it is honored and valued as a needed learning experience.

Death is not feared among the Amish. In a community where religious beliefs and practice are strong it is viewed as a natural culmination to a valuable, productive life. As the terminally ill are generally cared for by the family, most Amish die at home. When death comes, the entire community immediately comes to the aid of the family. Certain families may be designated to provide for the immediate physical needs of the surviving family members and the deceased; all are there to provide emotional support. For at least a year following a death, a widow or widower continues life in the context of the extended family. Other family members help fill the space created by the missing spouse, helping reduce the emotional pain and loneliness that a death brings (Bryer, 1979).

Ethnic Themes of the Amish

Ethnicity includes cultural values that influence the everyday lives of the members of the ethnic group. There are several ethnic themes that influence the lives of older Amish. These themes include the propensity for large families, value of the family, respect for older people, view of women as caregivers within the family, and the value of being separate from the world. Each of these themes is discussed below.

Large Family Size

The demographics of the Amish indicate a small portion of elderly and a large group of younger people. Family size is one of the major reasons for the youthful demographic structure. The size of the Amish family provides a large number of persons to support the older members of an Amish family. Hostetler (1980) notes that "the Amish have large families, a low rate of infant mortality, increasing longevity and prohibitions against birth control. Thus they have experienced a much greater net population gain in recent years than have non-Amish people" (p. 101). Hostetler reports that seven is the average number of live births per Amish couple, and approximately 21% of Amish couples have ten or more children. Trends indicate that the family size of the Amish is increasing and that fewer Amish couples are childless.

In addition to producing large families, the Amish have been successful in keeping their children within the Amish group. Huntington (1981) reports that more than 90% of the grown children of Amish women interviewed in Pennsylvania have remained Amish. Consequently, the number of kin within an Amish family is very large and tends to be larger than the number within a non-Amish family.

The size of the family unit is important to the older Amish. Elderly Amish men and women have a large number of relatives with whom to interact. Kephart (1982) illustrates the extraordinary size of Amish families by reporting that an Amish widow, aged 89 years, died with 350 descendants, including seven children, and a 95-year-old Amish man was survived by 410 descendents. Huntington (1981) suggests that "the demographic structure of the Amish makes it relatively easy for the youthful population to carry the burden of supporting the aged; there are many productive young people to care for the relatively few old people" (p. 301).

Feelings of Familism

Without a sense of filial maturity or family responsibility, the sheer number of family members is not necessarily indicative of support for older persons. It is the unwavering feeling of familism permeating the generational relationships that provides support for the older members of the Amish family. An older Amish man or woman knows that there is a vital family who will provide support whenever necessary. If illness occurs and care needs to be provided, the family is there. If a spouse dies, the survivor is not alone. The family is there to provide emotional and practical support. There is little doubt that the concept of filial maturity (Blenkner, 1965) is realized in many ways within the Amish social structure.

An older Amish person's definition of family is broader than what is generally included in the dominant society's definition of family. Family, to an older Amish person, includes kin (primary and secondary) as well as other members of the Amish church within the locality. Although the nuclear family unit may include the initial persons to whom an older Amish person may turn, there is little reluctance to expect assistance from other church members. To the Amish, church members are family.

One example of the sense of familism occurs when an older Amish person enters the hospital. It is not uncommon for the hospitalized person to have a large number of visitors. The Amish elderly who experience health difficulties are often visited and supported by members of their family.

The sense of familism that is so strong among the Amish has penetrated the whole church community. If, in rare instances, a family member cannot provide assistance, church members feel a sense of responsibility. In many ways, the church members' feelings of responsibility are similar to feelings of familism. As Kephart (1981) notes, "There is a good deal of evidence to suggest that the Amish maintain what is perhaps the strongest and most stable family system in America" (p. 154). For the older Amish, the strength and stability of this family system are translated into support. This support seeks to meet the financial, physical, and socio-emotional needs of the elderly within the Amish community.

Congruent with their desire to be separate from the world, the Amish expect the family to provide support to the dependent elderly. The Amish do not expect support from nonfamilial groups. Indeed, government and other sources of outside support are strictly forbidden within the Amish community. The devout older Amish person does not receive Social Security, Medicare, or the benefits from other government-sponsored programs. They seek to provide for their needs through their families or church so that they can continue to be separate from the world. The strong sense of filial responsibility is reinforced by their religious beliefs to be a peculiar people, and young Amish are willing to care for their older, dependent members.

Respect for Elders

The Amish view the elderly with respect. Following the biblical command "to honor thy mother and father" (Exod. 20:12), the Amish hold older persons in high regard. The social structure of the family and community place older persons in an honored position. Within the family, the older persons are seen as wise and welcomed. Many times, the oldest male is an advisor on farming practices. Hostetler (1980) states that "respect for the elders . . . is even more pronounced with regard to mature Amish people. All age groups in both sexes revere parents, grandparents and great-grandparents" (p. 167).

The status assigned to older persons in the Amish community can be seen within the organization of the Amish church. The older men hold the authority and occupy places of honor at all church meetings (Schreiber, 1962). The older men are the elders who encourage the religious values and admonish the younger people to follow the church teachings. Therefore, Amish older people receive respect from younger generations and have authority to direct younger people on practical as well as religious matters.

The close relationship between older Amish and younger generations can be seen when the older Amish man discontinues farming and transfers the responsibility to a son. Within the Amish community, "old folks normally signify their retirement by moving into the grandfather house adjacent to the main farmhouse. . . . With retirement or semiretirement the role of the parents is modified, but still continues, for the old people remain physically and emotionally close to their children and grandchildren" (Huntington, 1981; pp. 315–316). The move to the "grandfather house" permits the younger generation an opportunity to be responsible for the farm while still receiving advice and direction from the older generation. There is no age for retirement. Rather, the elder Amish man decides to move to the grandfather house based on health and other family needs. When retirement occurs and the older Amish man moves into an "advisor" position, respect binds the generations together.

Another example of the importance of the family to older Amish relates to the strong intergenerational relationships. One frequent activity of older Amish men and women is visiting with family. They direct particular attention toward the grandchildren and great-grandchildren. After retirement, older Amish interact more frequently with the younger generations.

For Amish of all generations, "the final stages of life are characterized by integrity rather than despair. Amish attitudes and practices with respect to aging constitute a sound system of retirement" (Hostetler, 1980, p. 168). Regardless of their health, older Amish are held in an honored position. Consequently, later life is viewed with little regret and is seen by many as a special time to direct younger people in the ways of the church.

Women as Caregivers

The Amish social structure views the woman as the primary caregivers for older elderly. Women are expected to meet the expressed needs of the family. When an older person needs assistance, it is the wife, daughter, or daughter-in-law who is expected to provide physical assistance. Within the social structure of the Amish, it is understood that a son respects and has a close emotional tie to older parents. However, as the primary breadwinner, the son cannot become the primary caregiver for an older, dependent person. Hence, it is within the domain of the woman to provide care for the elderly.

The choice of which woman within a particular family will be the primary caregiver varies. Proximity to the dependent older person is related to who is expected to provide the care. For example, if the dependent older person and a son are living on a farm, the son's wife is expected to be the primary caregiver. Marital status is also a determining factor. If there is a daughter who has not married, she is expected to become the primary caregiver because she does not have the responsibility of caring for a husband or children.

One Amish family well known to the first author provides an illustration of the latter situation. The family lived on the farm where the children were born and raised. When the father could no longer perform the rigorous activities associated with farming, he, his wife, and two adult unmarried daughters moved into a smaller house located adjacent to the primary farmhouse. At this time the eldest son and his family moved into the larger farmhouse. As the parents aged and needed more assistance, the unmarried daughters became the primary caregivers. For several years their lives were organized around meeting the needs of their elderly parents. Seldom was help expected from their older brother. After the death of their father, the daughters continued to provide care for their elderly mother until her death.

The adult daughters' residence on the farm was linked to their relationship to their parents. They lived on the farm as long as they were providing care for their elderly parents. Thus, upon the death of their mother, the daughters had to move off the farm and into another residence. The older son assisted his unmarried sisters in the purchase of a house close to the farm. The primary reason for the change in residence was to enable the older son's eldest son to move onto the farm with his young family.

For Amish, the need to provide assistance to dependent elderly is seen as a way to honor their parents. Their family life and religious values coincide to provide support to elderly family members. The older and younger adult generations are attuned to the probability that a female family member will provide primary assistance with the care of the elderly.

Separation from the World

Following their interpretation of the Bible, the Amish seek to be separate from the world. Their family life is organized around activities within the Amish community, and they have little time for involvement with the world (non-Amish people). Amish elderly have little reason to become involved in the world. Throughout life, work and social activities center around the family and other members within the Amish community. There is no reason for a change in this pattern when an Amish person is older. In fact, the social structure encourages continuity of relationships for older Amish. Moving into the grandfather house involves little physical distance. Many older Amish are still living on or adjacent to the land they have farmed throughout their adult lives. Thus, the move may involve a decrease in responsibilities but little change in the social relationships of the Amish.

Involvement in the world may occur when the health of the elderly Amish person declines and hospitalization is necessary. Generally, an ill Amish person continues to live at home and receive in-home assistance. Occasionally, the ill older person is admitted to the hospital for more specialized care. As noted above, while the older person is in the hospital, Amish family and friends regularly visit and provide support. Every attempt is made to return the older person to his or her home as soon as possible. Consequently, nursing home residence is an unlikely option because the family and the Amish community will provide assistance.

The reluctance to receive any assistance from the government (e.g., Social Security) is an attempt to be separate from the world. There is no financial dependency on the outside world. As Hostetler (1980) notes, "Economic subsistence is maintained without government aid of any kind. . . . The community's sensitivity to sharing and practicing mutual aid and its abiding interest in the well-being of those in need are great assets to older people" (p. 170). Older Amish are able to continue their separation from the world because there is a strong family and community support network.

Differences between Amish and other Ethnic Groups

The Amish differ from other ethnic groups in the United States in several ways. Separateness from, and coexistence with, the dominant culture contribute to their uniqueness as an ethnic group in the United States. Specifically, the lack of assimilation, lack of migration, and irrelevancy of social class suggest differences between the Amish and other ethnic groups.

The Amish do not wish to become assimilated into the dominant culture. Unlike a number of other ethnic groups, such as Polish Americans (Lopata, 1981), Italian Americans (Quadagno, 1981), and Japanese Americans (Kikumura & Kitano, 1981), the Amish society is premised on nonassimilation. They do not seek acceptance into the dominant culture. The Amish have been successful in developing a social structure that encourages their uniqueness and separation for all age groups. Consequently, older Amish do not deal with the problems of assimilation experienced by many other ethnic groups. The older Amish are reservoirs of information about a culture that younger generations are seeking to perpetuate. Because Amish farms are not premised on the use of the latest technology, older Amish men are not outmoded by new technology. Similarly, older women are able to provide useful information to younger Amish women. Thus, older Amish are not viewed as representing an antiquated way of life. Rather, the older Amish are seen as successful in living the life-style that is valued by younger Amish.

Another difference between the Amish and many other ethnic groups is the lack of migration of the Amish. Bengtson (1979) noted that one of the problems with ethnic elderly is that they are born into a culture that defines old age one way; then they migrate to another culture with a differing definition of aging. For the Amish, this conflict in expectations about aging seldom occurs. There is little migration. Older Amish are likely to live in the same community into which they were born. If they do move, they move to another Amish community. Consequently, there are few differences in expectations associated with aging.

Social class is an important factor in analyses of many ethnic groups (e.g., Blacks, Jewish Americans). Indeed, Gelfand and Kutzik (1979) suggested a need for more knowledge about the interrelationships of ethnicity and social class when studying ethnic groups. For the Amish, social class is an irrelevant factor. As Huntington (1981) states, "The Amish are a small, homogeneous group within which social class has no meaning" (p. 308). The Amish are not class-conscious, and the social structure is not organized around class differences. Similarity is the theme. The Amish seek to be a homogeneous group. Thus, unlike other ethnic groups, analyses of older Amish do not need to consider social class as an issue.

The continuity of the lives of older Amish is remarkable. Amish are a part of the Amish community from birth till death, and older Amish continue patterns developed when they were younger. They retire to a smaller house on the same farm where they raised a family. In later life they continue the same activities with less responsibility. If ill, family members assist them in the same house where they lived before they became ill. The social activities of the older Amish continue to revolve around the family and friends with whom they have lived their entire lives. In many ways, elderly Amish illustrate the continuation of a life-style in which few changes can be attributed to aging.

Solidarity of the family and community is another characteristic of the lives of older Amish. The values of family and community are consistent, and they support the elderly. Older Amish know that they will receive assistance from family. They know that government assistance will not be needed. If the family cannot provide the necessary assistance, the Amish community will be there. Religious ideals and values reinforce the strong family unit and support from the community.

Older Amish know that they are a peculiar people. The social structure developed by the Amish place the older Amish in a respected position, and they are not dependent on external agencies. Rather, as a peculiar people, they know they are members of a family and a community. They are able to continue their life-style into their later years with little change. The lives of today's older Amish are similar to the lives of their grandfathers. And their religious traditions suggest that this pattern will continue for many generations in the future.

9

Ethnicity in the Informal Networks of Older Sunbelt Migrants: A Case History of the Finns in Florida

Eleanor Palo Stoller

The importance of family, particularly adult daughters, in providing assistance to community-based elderly raises questions about the informal support networks of older persons who migrate to sunbelt retirement communities. These migrants are largely married couples in their sixties, in relatively good health, with higher than average levels of education and income (Biggar, Longino, & Flynn, 1980; Ferraro, 1981; Rives & Serow, 1981; Wiseman, 1980). Little is known, however, about the experiences of these older migrants and how they cope with life-course transitions. Using an exchange-theory perspective, this chapter integrates research on caregiving, migration, and ethnic identity to explore the impact of shared ethnicity on support networks among elderly migrants. The research is focused on a community of retired Finnish Americans in Florida. The study of this particular ethnic group's experiences with life-course transitions may serve to shed light on the problems faced by sunbelt migrants in general.

Research on Caregiving: Implications for Sunbelt Migrants

Family and Caregiving

Contrary to the myth of family abandonment of the elderly, three decades of social gerontological research have documented the continuing importance of family members in caring for the frail elderly in America (Brody, 1981; Shanas, 1979b). Friends and neighbors may also provide help, although this assistance is supplementary, "helping to strengthen [kinship networks] by relieving some of the burdens from caretaking kin" (Lowenthal & Robinson, 1976; p. 440). Assistance from friends or neighbors is reported more frequently by single elderly, although they are rarely mentioned as a source of help for activities of daily living or personal care in long-term illness (Cantor, 1979; Cicirelli, 1981; Johnson, 1983; Stoller, 1982).

Several explanations have been developed for the salience of family as a late-life support group. Litwak (1985) argues that permanent group membership and long-term emotional commitment make families best suited to providing long-term care. The short-term and equivocal nature of many neighbor and friend relationships often results in the desire by both the older person and the helper to maintain balance in any exchange, thus reducing the utility of these ephemeral relationships as sources of support for frail older persons unable to reciprocate. However, older persons who have experienced little geographic mobility often have developed lifelong friendships that exhibit the long-term affective commitment usually associated with kinship (Atchley, 1985; Ward, 1984).

Another structural feature of families conducive to caregiving is the presence of cross-generational ties. Primary groups based on age peers decrease in importance as older persons experience increasing frailty (Dono et al., 1979) because changes in the mix of needed assistance can undermine the ability of age peers to provide the level of help required. In contrast, the cross-generational contact within kinship groups provides older persons with younger helpers better able to meet their care needs.

Several researchers have argued also that the responsibilities of caring for a frail older person are inconsistent with the normative expectations surrounding less intimate and lasting relationships (Johnson & Catalano, 1983). Similarly, Hooyman and colleagues (Hooyman, Gonyea, & Montgomery, 1985) suggest that performance of personal care or body contact tasks may be perceived as more stressful than impersonal housekeeping tasks because of the incongruity between actual caregiving demands and expectations and norms regarding appropriate behavior. Nevertheless, as Brody's research has clearly documented, despite pressures associated with caregiving, children and grandchildren of today's elderly continue to subscribe to norms of filial responsibility (Brody et al, 1983; Brody et al,1984).

Existing Informal Supports

This importance of kin and long-term friends raises questions about the informal support networks of older persons who migrate to sunbelt retirement communities. These older migrants frequently leave behind potential caregiving resources. Several researchers have suggested that life-course transitions such as widowhood, diminished economic viability, and deteriorating health may motivate these long-distance migrants to return to their original community to bolster the resources available to meet their expanding needs; frail elderly also express greater preference for moving near relatives, particularly adult daughters (Bryant & El-Attar, 1984; Longino, 1979; Longino & Biggar, 1981; Pampel, Levin, Louviere, Meyer, & Rushton, 1984; Wiseman, 1980).

Although no direct tests of this migration-crisis-return model have been made, existing literature shows some support for this model. Wiseman (1980) reports that large streams of older migrants from noncontiguous states to Florida and California were in part counterbalanced by smaller streams from Florida and California to the state of origin. Other research suggests that older counterstream migrants leaving Florida were likely to be older, female, widowed, and poor (Longino, 1979; Longino & Biggar, 1981).

Return migration among sunbelt retirees experiencing difficulties in life-course transitions may also reflect decreased physical, emotional, and financial capacities for coping with the demands of living in the new environment. An environmental perspective suggests that a person's sense of competence is less a reflection of actual abilities than of the fit between capacity and environmental demands (Kahana, 1974, 1975; Lawton, 1977). Existing research indicates that many retirement communities set high expectations of activity and participation by members (Hochschild, 1973; Jacobs, 1974). Increased difficulty in fulfilling these community norms may undermine the morale of older persons, especially those experiencing declines in functional capacity. Rather than activating an informal support network, increasing frailty may socially isolate older persons who are reluctant to burden new friends and neighbors with demands for which they will be unable to reciprocate. Even admitting that they are experiencing health problems may decrease their sense of competence. Several researchers have found that declines in physical or mental capacity undermine social status within some communities of elderly (Gubrium, 1975; Hochschild, 1973; Jacobs, 1974). Thus, return migration not only provides greater access to the primary group best suited to provide long-term support but may also allow the impaired older migrants to escape the experience of incompetence.

New Informal Supports

Whether difficulty experienced in life-course changes induces a second migration decision among sunbelt retirees, either to a place of previous residence or to the current residence of an adult child or other relative, depends in large part on the resources available within the retirement community. Return migration, however, is not the only response to inadequate support. Some older persons may instead seek to activate informal support systems in their new location. This strategy may be elected more often among retirees who have experienced mobility throughout their life and report few local ties to their community of origin (Meyer & Speare, 1985; Wiseman & Roseman, 1979). Retirees who followed relatives or friends to an amenity-rich retirement destination would also be less likely to select return migration because they would have access to informal helpers with whom they share ties of long-term commitment.

Older but healthy persons not part of such chain migrations may attempt to ensure future support from neighbors by building up obligations through small favors, exchanges that are governed by a strict code of reciprocity (Francis, 1981). Even without the emergence of dyadic helping relationships, the norm of generalized reciprocity, which "requires that people help those who now need the type of help they themselves may need from others in the future" (Nye, 1979; p. 8), may also encourage this provision of support if the helper has faith in the continued viability of the larger community.

Several characteristics of residential environments appear to generate such exchanges of assistance. As suggested above, migration patterns are one factor. Chain migration could create clusters of migrants whose relationships exhibited the length of commitment usually associated with kinship. Degree of residential concentration is another. Helping with tasks of everyday life is facilitated by residential proximity, and the availability of a number of potential helpers alleviates the demands on any one caregiver.

Community Identification

A particularly important feature of retirement destinations is the extent to which migrants identify with the community. Several writers have stressed the importance of a sense of community based on homogeneity as a characteristic of retirement communities that encourage mutual assistance (Hochschild, 1973; Keith, 1980; Rosow, 1974; Ross, 1977). Ethnicity is a potentially important dimension of homogeneity, implying a shared history, common place of origin, similar culture, and, frequently, common organizational ties, religious preference, and residence (Cool, 1980; Holzberg, 1982). Although research focusing on ethnic minorities has frequently conceptualized ethnicity as a handicap or barrier (see Dowd & Bengtson, 1978, for a review of this "double jeopardy" perspective), other research stresses the positive potential of ethnic membership on the experience of growing old.

Ethnic membership provides continuity in both self-concept and social participation, buffering the effects of role losses in other areas (Cool, 1980; Yinger, 1985). Ethnic cohesion, like kinship, neighborhood, or common life-style, serves as a potential medium for the solution of both personal and social problems (Myerhoff & Simic, 1978), whereas ethnic membership provides older persons with opportunities to "sustain continuity in their repertoires of already familiar lifestyles and culturally stylized patterns of social involvement" (Holzberg, 1982; p. 253). Along this line of reasoning, Cool (1980) suggests that interest in ethnic identity might be revived in old age when the individual has lost or modified other roles, providing the older person with "a source of identity that is distinct from those conventional identities based on sex, age or occupation" (p. 187).

Second, to the extent that shared ethnicity can generate patterns of mutual assistance, ethnic ties may also be a valuable substitute for kinship among older persons who have moved some distance from their original homes. As is true of kinship groups, ethnicity can involve permanent membership. Belief in the continued viability of the ethnic community can activate the norm of generalized reciprocity because older persons providing help to those facing problems today will feel that they may also rely on assistance from the community in the face of future needs. Friendships that develop in retirement communities may lack the long-term commitment characterizing family relationships or friendships originating early in life, but shared ethnicity may partially compensate for the absence of longevity. Trela and Sokolovsky (1979) argue that ethnic identification may generate strong kinlike ties within a community of age peers. As Chrisman (1981) points out, ethnicity is accompanied by an ideology "promoting beliefs about social characteristics and the likelihood of predictable social relationships" (p. 267). Fellow ethnics, he argues, are in some ways known in advance, and because of this expectation of shared orientation, a greater potential for interaction exists. Gans (1979) suggests that ethnicity may provide mobile people with an excuse to get together. Woehrer (1982) adds that an ethnic community may be especially important for retirees, widows and widowers, and individuals without family members close by.

Informal Supports of Older White Ethnics

Relatively few studies have explored the informal support networks of older White ethnics (Holzberg, 1982; Place, 1981), even though White ethnics are less likely to utilize formal services than older persons in general (Gelfand, 1982; Guttmann, 1979). Several studies have demonstrated a preference for both friendships and professional relationships within the ethnic group (Cohler & Lieberman, 1980; Place, 1981), but this research has focused on respondents who maintained residential continuity.

Several studies shed more direct light on the role of ethnicity in the helping networks of elderly migrants. Myerhoff's (1978) ethnographic research highlights the importance of ethnic attachment among the surviving members of a once active community of retired eastern European Jews in Venice, California. Although she does not stress instrumental assistance, her research highlights the role of ethnic identification in the elderly residents' search for meaning in life. The community provides a forum for celebrating individual biography, for sharing the lessons of survival, and for coping with the daily reminders of the losses that accompany aging. Myerhoff avoids the fallacy of viewing ethnic identification with an immigrant subculture derived from an Old World heritage, which, as Gelfand and Kutzik (1979) warn, negates the importance of ethnicity for later generations. Rather, her view of ethnicity is fluid, incorporating past experiences but also responding to present needs.

Chrisman's (1981) study of a Danish-American community in the San Francisco Bay Area also provides evidence of the integrative potential of ethnicity. Although residentially scattered and culturally invisible, these Danish Americans have maintained a set of ethnic voluntary associations and stable interpersonal relationships for over a century. Chrisman argues that integration of new migrants into the community is facilitated by an ideology of common descent and a national network of ethnic organizations linking Danish-American communities throughout the United States. These voluntary associations not only provide newcomers with an organizational entry into the community but may create indirect ties among new and earlier migrants that provide both hospitality and resource assistance. Whether such communal bonds would generate long-term assistance to recently integrated but impaired migrants and whether ethnic organizations would emerge to meet the instrumental needs of frail older members are questions beyond the scope of Chrisman's research. Nevertheless, his work is important in pointing out the integrating mechanisms and exchange systems provided by organizational networks linking ethnic communities, and it provides a departure point for my case study of Finnish self-help networks in Florida.

The Finns in Florida: A Case Study

Community History

An important focus of my research in progress in a Florida community of retired Finnish Americans is exploring ethnic attachments among sunbelt migrants. Several thousand older Finnish Americans live in the West Palm Beach/Boca Raton Standard Metropolitan Statistical Area (SMSA), and the number is estimated to grow by more than 10,000 during the winter months. The community is not a planned retirement settlement. Members are scattered throughout several towns in the area, linked through a variety of ethnic organizations.

The community began in the late 1940s, when retired Finnish immigrants moved south from New England and the upper Midwest. Residents today include first- and second-generation retirees from both the United States and Canada, primarily Northern Ontario. In addition, there has been a sharp increase in immigration from Finland to Florida since 1960. Interviews with these recent arrivals suggest that most are drawn by the existence of the Finnish community in the area (Copeland, 1981).

Many of the retirees moved from Finnish-American ethnic communities in Massachusetts, Minnesota, Michigan, Ohio, Wisconsin, and northern Ontario. First- and many second-generation Finns, who represent today's elderly population, remained geographically concentrated, exhibited endogamous marriage patterns, and maintained a relatively strong attachment to the ethnic community (Olson, 1979). Chain migration patterns have meant that many new migrants arrive with preexisting ties to current residents. As with the Danes studied by Chrisman, chapters of national ethnic organizations, including the Finlandia Foundation, Knights of the Kalevala, and Ladies of the Kalevala, provide entry points for new residents. There are three ethnic religious congregations in the area, which still sponsor Finnish-language services. Finnish communities traditionally sponsored "Finn Halls," whose activities provided a focus of ethnic participation. The Finnish Tourist Club of Lake Worth (*Turisti-halli*), founded in 1940, was the first ethnic association. A more politically oriented organization, the Finnish Workers Educational Club of Lake Worth (*Kentta-halli*) was formally organized 2 months later. Both organizations still maintain buildings and sponsor active cultural and social programs. Although the political divisions that separated participants in the two halls during the early years have become less salient, identifiable yet overlapping social networks still distinguish them. Several informants stressed the fact that only one of the halls serves alcohol at social events. A recent development with respect to long-term care was the establishment in 1970 of the Finnish-American Rest Home, which now includes a skilled nursing facility. Residents proudly explain that construction of the facility was financed from an endowment based on contributions by the Finnish-American community. In addition to providing care for frail elderly, the rest home is a focal point for the community; programs, coffee parties, and birthday celebrations are frequently scheduled in its dining room.

Community Ties

Informal interviews with several residents suggest that friendships within the ethnic community may compensate for the absence of kin in providing support for retirees who encounter increasing frailty. Several residents reported "doing favors" for fellow residents, who could later be relied on to reciprocate with needed assistance.

Several key questions remain to be answered. Chain migration from ethnic communities "up North" means that many new migrants arrive with preexisting ties to current residents. How important is chain migration in influencing the structure and content of informal helping networks? Do older migrants rely most heavily on long-term friendships originated in their prior residence or can common ethnicity substitute for the lack of long-term commitment characterizing kinship? What is the effect of level of ethnic integration on return migration decisions and long-term care plans? Although most of these questions require data on individual networks, several characteristics of this ethnic group contribute to an understanding of the Florida community's response to growing old.

Community and Ethnicity

In exploring the role of ethnicity in coping with the problems of aging, it is important to note the small size of this ethnic group. Of the total number of immigrants in the United States up to 1920, Finns made up less than 1%. Maintaining an ethnic community requires greater organizational effort with so small a population, although smaller ethnic groups may be more concerned about cultural survival (Glazer, 1980).

A number of factors heightened the importance of the ethnic community in the lives of many first- and second-generation Finnish Americans. The height of Finnish immigration coincided with a growing nativism. Although both northern European and Protestant, Finns were viewed as part of the "new immigration," composed largely of southern and eastern Europeans (Aaltio, 1969). Modernization in Finland occurred later than in other western European countries, and most Finnish immigrants were poor, had little formal education, and lacked industrial experience. Speaking little if any English, they found employment as miners, lumberjacks, mill operatives, domestics, and laborers clearing farms (Jalkanen, 1969; Olson, 1979). Furthermore, because the main wave of immigration coincided with the rise of nationalism in Finland, many immigrants brought with them an intense loyalty to their native culture. Nationalists promoting ethnic consciousness were active in immigrant organizations (Hoglund, 1960).

Another relevant feature of this group is its history of organizational activity (Greeley & MacReady, 1974; Greeley, 1974; Woehrer, 1978). In addition to religious congregations, temperance societies, benefit organizations, socialist locals, and sports and social clubs, Finnish immigrants developed various cooperative enterprises, including stores, creameries, and boardinghouses (Hoglund, 1960). This tradition of cooperative organization along ethnic lines provides a structural foundation for collectively coping with problems associated with aging.

Women's Role in the Community

Another important legacy of the immigrant experience has been the role of women within the community. Since the 1890s, the majority of female immigrants from Finland were young single women who came alone, often settling in major cities where Finnish men were rare (Wargelin-Brown, 1986b). Most had no more than a *kansakoulu* (elementary) education, and many spoke no English. A large number found work as *piikas* (domestics) in the homes of middle- and upper-class American families, learning English and American life-styles. The *piikas* enjoyed high status within the immigrant community because of their relatively high wages, economic independence, facility in speaking English, and familiarity with American culture (Koivukangas, 1986; Penti, 1986). Hoglund (1960) argues that because they tended to acquire an economic status equal to that of immigrant men, Finnish-American marriages were relatively egalitarian.

In addition to economic independence, first-generation Finnish-American women assumed active roles within the immigrant community. They grew up during a period of gains in women's rights in Finland, resulting in enactment of women's suffrage in 1906. In the United States, immigrant women were active participants and leaders in the three major institutions of the immigrant community: the temperance movement, the socialist workers' clubs, and the Finnish synods of the Lutheran Church. This legacy of economic independence, relative equality within marriage, and political activism provides elderly Finnish-American women with a tradition of reliance on networks of female peers in coping with problems encountered in old age (Wargelin-Brown, 1986a).

Finnish-American Distinctiveness

Although Finnish Americans share several characteristics with other White ethnics, they also exhibit distinctive features. Like other immigrants arriving in the late 19th and early 20th centuries, Finns faced strong nativist sentiment. Although they shared northern European origins and Protestant religion with earlier waves of immigrants, language barriers and geographic concentration heightened community cohesion, and small size and Finnish nationalism strengthened commitment to ethnic solidarity. Although both Finnish immigrants and immigrants from southern and eastern Europe came from rural backgrounds, Finns had a history of small, family-owned farms. They did not share the legacy of serfdom with other southern European immigrants, which Schooler (1976) argues encouraged passive responses to problems, dependency in social relations, decreased feelings of autonomy, and lessened capacity for rational planning. Instead, a tradition of cooperative organization along ethnic lines provided a structural foundation for collectively coping with problems associated with aging. Finally, women within the immigrant community possess a history of organizing and problem solving that extends beyond the family unit and emphasizes reliance on networks of other women.

Despite the preliminary nature of this research, there is evidence that the Finns in Florida have continued their earlier patterns of cooperation and ethnic organization in coping with late-life transitions. Several questions need further exploration in determining the generalizability of the Finnish experience to other ethnic groups. What has been the effect of the legacy of independence and reliance on female peers that social historians have described among the first-generation *piikas* (domestics) on strategies for coping with old age? Has this tradition been maintained among second-generation women, many of whom experienced their childbearing years during the 1950s?

Shared Ethnicity and Aging

This chapter has suggested that shared ethnicity may partially compensate for lack of kin in the support networks of first- and second-generation ethnics in sunbelt retirement communities. The importance of this argument hinges on the continued salience of ethnicity. Cross-sectional research suggests that the salience of ethnic identity is positively correlated with age (Hoyt & Babchuck, 1981; Place, 1981). An assimilationist perspective would suggest that this is a cohort effect, reflecting the concentration of first- and second-generation ethnics among the elderly. As these older cohorts are gradually replaced by generations further from the immigrant experience, the salience of ethnic identity among the elderly could be expected to decline.

More recent writing, while recognizing that assimilation and acculturation continue to take place, has argued that a new form of contemporary ethnicity has developed. This perspective views ethnicity as a continuous variable rather than an ascribed attribute and has stressed the importance of identifying the conditions under which ethnicity is particularly salient (Yancey et al., 1976). Variously described as "emergent" (Yancey et al., 1976), "symbolic" (Gans, 1979), "situational" (Paden, 1967), and "latent" (Pavalko, 1981), ethnicity is seen as largely voluntary, a label that an individual may choose to project in particular situations (Padgett, 1980).

Gans (1979) found that symbolic expression of ethnicity may persist among third- and fourth-generation ethnics who have had little involvement in immigrant cultures and organizations, citing as examples the persistence of ethnic identification among Scandinavians, Germans, and Irish. Several explanations have been offered for this persistence of ethnic identity. Ethnicity, at least based on a European ancestry, entails few disadvantages. As argued above, it can satisfy internal identity needs of late adulthood, providing a source of continuity in both self-concept and social participation, buffering the effects of role losses in other areas (Myerhoff & Simic, 1978; Cool, 1980).

This chapter has suggested that shared ethnicity may generate community networks on which retired migrants can depend in coping with increasing frailty. Among many first- and second-generation ethnics in today's elderly population, these exchange relationships may reflect a continuation of lifelong involvement in an ethnic community. Alternatively, renewed emphasis on ethnic identity may be a reaction to loss of other roles and opportunities for social participation (Hoyt & Babchuck, 1981). In the case of chain migration, these friendships may have lasted many years and resemble kinship in longevity. Even among more recent acquaintances, the sense of shared identity and faith in the continued viability of the ethnic community may activate norms of generalized reciprocity even when friendships lack long-term commitment.

Although the form of ethnicity may have changed in generations further removed from the immigrant experience, symbolic ethnicity may still contribute to satisfying needs for continuity and sociability. Shared ethnicity among older sunbelt migrants, particularly when reinforced by similarities in age, life-style, socioeconomic status, and residency, may generate a sense of community in the new environment. However, this new form of symbolic ethnicity is also characterized by its lack of demands on other areas of life. Gans (1979) argues that third- and subsequent-generation ethnics

> look for easy and intermittent ways of expressing their identity, for ways that do not conflict with other areas of life. . . . Ethnicity takes on an expressive rather than instrumental function in people's lives, becoming more of a leisure-time activity. (pp. 12–13)

Symbolic ethnicity may form the basis for new friendships among migrants. Whether this new form of ethnicity will also generate exchange relationships with sufficient strength to cope with increasing frailty remains an empirical question. It is also possible that belief in the continued viability of the new community will activate norms of generalized reciprocity and encourage organizational efforts paralleling the institutional completeness of the older immigrant neighborhoods. This awaits the results of further investigation.

10

Social Support Among Black, Mexican, and Chinese Elderly

James E. Lubben and Rosina M. Becerra

The support system of the elderly can be characterized as an interwoven network of informal services provided by family and friends and formal services provided by public and private agencies. Much research has studied the role of support systems, particularly family members, and their impact on the mental and physical well-being of the elderly (Lee, 1979; Shanas, 1979a). This research, however, has led to many contradictory findings, when examining the familial support system of ethnic minority groups. For example, Cantor (1979) found that there was no difference between Black and White elderly in their levels of interaction and support from their children, whereas Mutran (1985) showed that there was a significant difference in intergenerational helping behavior between the two groups. Usually marital status and age have been demonstrated to strongly influence support networks (Anspoch, 1976; Antonucci & Depner, 1981). However, Taylor (1985) did not find that these variables affected support networks for Black elderly.

What does seem to hold true across studies, controlling for gender and social class, is that Hispanic elderly consistently have higher levels of interaction and support from their children than either Black or White elderly have (Cantor, 1979; Valle & Martinez, 1981). Although little has been written about Chinese family support systems, some recent work suggests that Chinese elderly, compared to Hispanics and Blacks, are the most likely to be married and not live alone but least likely to visit or be visited by friends. Moreover, Chinese elderly are most likely to turn to family for help with housework and meal preparations (Cuellar & Weeks, 1980).

130

Some of the differences reported about social support between ethnic groups in the United States can be attributed both to culture and to immigration patterns. Both Chinese and Mexican elders are the most likely to be foreign-born and to continue to live in ethnic enclaves. For example, Lum et al. (1980) points out that many Chinese elderly elect to remain in "Chinatowns," where their sociocultural needs can be met, whereas their U.S.-born children move to the suburbs.

The purpose of the following analysis is to examine support networks of Black, Mexican-American, and Chinese-American elderly to determine if these data support or refute some previous findings on ethnic/racial differences. This investigation utilizes the social support system theory advocated by Ell (1984). She suggests that "social network" and "social support" are conceptually different. Social networks are an individual's social contacts, from which social support may be given. Supports include the nature and extent of social exchanges between an individual and his or her social network. The following analysis will examine familial and friendship networks and determine what type of social support is given the elderly person in that constellation. Besides ethnic variations in social support, particular attention will also be given to the role of marital status, age, and level of acculturation.

The California Senior Survey

The source of the data was the California Senior Survey (CSS) conducted in 1982 and 1983. CSS respondents were all over 65 years of age and MediCal recipients (California's Medicaid program). CSS respondents were randomly selected from a central MediCal identification file and administered a close-ended questionnaire in a face-to-face interview. They reflected California's ethnically diverse population. The CSS random sample included 1,037 elderly respondents. Nine hundred fifty-two elderly, representing 603 Whites, 170 Blacks, 100 Mexican Americans, and 79 Chinese Americans were used for this study. Those groups omitted were other Latinos, Asians, and members of various other ethnic groups. None of these groups was large enough in number for detailed analysis of their social networks and supports.

Because of the nature of the data, the sample represents California's poor elderly population. An advantage of restricting this analysis to the low-socioeconomic population of elderly is that other research has shown social supports often to be the result of socioeconomic factors (Mutran, 1985). The high correlation between lower socioeconomic status and minority status has often been a confounding factor in studies examining ethnic differences. However, in this instance social class was controlled.

With respect to the sample, about three out of four respondents in all groups were women, with a slightly higher proportion of men represented among the Chinese (Table 10-1). The higher proportion of women to men in the total sample might be accounted for by the differential life expectancy rate between the sexes as further

TABLE 10-1. Major Characteristics by Ethnicity

Characteristics	Total	White	Black	Mexican	Chinese
			% Distributions[a]		
Totals (%)	100	63.3	17.9	10.5	8.3
N	952	603	170	100	79
Gender[b]					
Males	27.8	27.0	28.2	29.0	31.7
Females	72.2	73.0	71.8	71.0	68.4
Age					
65–79 years	64.9	60.6	74.1	71.0	69.6
80+ years	35.1	39.4	25.9	29.0	30.4
Marital status					
Married	22.0	20.1	15.3	30.0	40.5
Widowed	56.3	55.1	60.6	57.0	55.7
Separated/divorced	15.3	17.1	18.2	9.0	1.3
Single	5.6	6.5	5.9	2.0	2.5
Other	1.0	1.3	0.0	2.0	0.0
Education					
None	7.6	3.5	5.9	13.0	35.4
Elementary	40.0	31.5	58.2	61.0	39.2
High school	33.5	40.3	30.0	16.0	11.4
Beyond H.S.	18.9	24.7	5.9	10.0	13.9
Religion					
Protestant	45.3	44.4	79.5	17.9	15.8
Catholic	22.8	22.4	4.5	69.5	5.3
Jewish	11.4	18.5	0.0	0.0	0.0
Other/none	20.4	14.7	16.0	12.7	79.0

[a]Unless otherwise noted, all distributions are significant at the .05 level using a chi square test for independence.
[b]Not significant.

exemplified by the high widowed rate among all ethnic groups (56% for the total sample). The slightly higher representation of Chinese men (32% compared to 28% for the total sample) may be because today's Chinese elders are often those who arrived in the United States during the early part of the century. At that time many young, single Chinese men emigrated to the United States seeking work as laborers. However, Chinese women were not as readily admitted; thus, there tends to be a slightly higher male-to-female ratio in this age cohort of Chinese elders (Jackson, 1980).

Two-thirds of the total sample were 65 to 79 years of age, and the balance were 80 years or older. Approximately 30% of both Mexican and Chinese elderly were 80 years or older. Blacks were the youngest group, with only one of four respondents being 80 years or more. The oldest group were Whites, with nearly 40% 80 years or older. These racial differences probably are indicative of higher mortality rates at younger ages, especially among Blacks, because of a higher rate of severe health problems among minorities.

The White subsample was more highly educated than the other ethnic/racial groups. Approximately one-third of the Chinese elderly indicated no formal education. This lack of schooling among Chinese elderly probably resulted from the fact that a high proportion of them were part of a Chinese immigration pattern at the turn of the century that represented the poorer, uneducated class. Furthermore, a lack of English-speaking skills and a necessity to work precluded formal education. Perhaps also because of language barriers, the Mexican elderly had a high proportion reporting either no schooling (13%) or else only a few years of primary school education (61%). Similar to the Chinese, Mexicans of this age cohort often entered the United States seeking unskilled jobs. Many Mexicans, also lacking English-speaking skills, did not obtain any further formal education. In general, both of these groups came to the United States in earlier immigrant waves to fill positions in low-wage jobs. Though many had plans of returning to China or Mexico, they remained and grew old in the United States.

With regard to religion, Blacks were more likely to be Protestants (80%), and Mexican Americans were more likely to be Catholics (65%). The largest proportion of Whites were Protestant (44%), the remaining being Catholic (22%), Jewish (11%), or claiming no organized religion (20%). Because Chinese often view religion more as a philosophy of life, they were most likely to state they had no formal religion (79%).

Less than one-fifth of Whites and Blacks were married, compared to one-third of Mexican or Chinese elderly. Approximately one-half of the total sample were widowed. Though Mexicans and Chinese were just as apt to be widowed as were Whites or Blacks, the Mexican and Chinese elderly were the least likely to be divorced, separated, or single, reflecting strong cultural values among these two groups of being and staying married.

Social Networks

Social networks were used here according to Ell (1984), as the source of ties, frequency of contact, and closeness of ties. Many ethnic differences were observed in structural and interactional aspects of social networks (Table 10-2). More than 60% of the White and Black elderly, regardless of age, lived alone. However, a majority of the Mexican and Chinese elderly resided with another person. Of those who lived with others, the two most common living arrangements were with a spouse or with an adult child. The young-old (65–79 years) Mexican and Chinese elderly were more likely to be married and thus more likely to live with a spouse. For opposite reasons, the Black elderly were least likely to live with a spouse. However, among the old-old (80 years plus) there were no ethnic differences in living with a spouse. This was undoubtedly because of the large number of widows among all ethnic groups in this older age category.

Age increased the likelihood of all elderly to reside with one of their children. Its most profound effect was among the Black elderly. Whereas young-old elderly Blacks exhibited a pattern similar to Whites, old-old Blacks were much more likely than Whites to live with one of their adult children (24% for Blacks compared with 15% of old-old Whites). Overall, the Mexican and Chinese elderly tended to live with their children more often than either Blacks or Whites. In either age category, Mexicans were three times more likely to live with one of their children than were Whites. Differences between Chinese and Whites were even more profound, almost one-half of the Chinese elderly lived with one of their children. This greater likelihood of certain racial/ethnic groups to live with their children is both cultural and possibly functional. Because ethnic minority groups tend to have fewer economic resources and to suffer more health problems than Whites, it may be more necessary for minority elderly to reside with their children. Additionally, ethnic groups who have maintained strong cultural ties, as have many Mexicans and Chinese of this age group, are more likely to live with their children, particularly after retirement.

TABLE 10-2. Social Network Characteristics by Ethnicity and Age

Characteristics	Age group (years)	% Distributions[a]				
		Total	White	Black	Mexican	Chinese
Lives Alone	65–79	59.1	65.6	61.2	41.8	35.9
	80+	65.9	70.5	64.3	46.4	47.8
Lives with spouse	65–79	28.0	26.7	21.0	36.9	40.7
	80+[b]	12.6	13.9	7.1	10.7	14.3
Lives with child	65–79	15.7	10.9	12.3	35.4	47.8
	80+	21.9	14.9	23.8	41.4	55.6
Siblings						
Has	65–79	73.5	73.1	80.8	80.3	50.9
	80+[b]	58.6	58.3	56.8	67.9	54.2
Sees weekly	65–79	28.5	29.5	40.6	16.4	0.0
	80+	30.2	33.3	44.0	10.5	0.0
Children						
Has	65–79	74.6	72.7	64.5	88.7	94.6
	80+	76.4	76.8	59.1	82.8	95.8
Sees weekly	65–79	73.8	71.6	76.0	87.3	65.3
	80+[b]	81.3	82.0	80.8	83.3	73.9
Grandchildren						
Has	65–79	73.5	71.0	64.3	88.4	90.9
	80+	76.5	77.2	58.1	82.7	95.8
Sees weekly	65–79	51.7	46.3	54.3	72.1	49.0
	80+[b]	46.3	41.9	60.0	62.5	47.8
Close friends						
Has	65–79	73.3	74.5	81.0	73.2	47.3
	80+	67.7	74.3	63.6	55.2	25.0
Sees weekly	65–79	79.8	82.7	86.3	72.6	38.5
	80+[b]	79.1	79.0	82.1	80.0	66.7

[a]Unless otherwise noted, all distributions are significant at the 0.05 level using a chi square test for Independence.
[b]Not significant.

Some differences in parents living with their adult children can be accounted for by the differences in having children. Blacks (62%) were least apt to have children, and Chinese (95%) were most apt to have children. Blacks have higher birth rates than all other groups but higher death rates by various causes than other groups, which might account for the Black elderly in the current study having a lower probability of having living children. Additionally, there was a fairly high percentage of never-married Blacks in this sample (6%).

Moreover, a higher percentage of Mexican (87%) and Chinese (92%) elderly had grandchildren, whereas fewer than three-fourths of Whites or Blacks had grandchildren. More than one-third of the Mexican and Chinese households were multigenerational (i.e., elderly persons, child, and possibly a grandchild all living in one extended family household) but fewer than half that number of Blacks or Whites lived with their children.

The young-old Chinese (51%) were much less likely to have siblings, but among those who did, few reported seeing them weekly. Perhaps a large number of Chinese elderly in the sample immigrated alone because families were often not allowed to immigrate until the late 1960s (Carp & Kataoka, 1976); thus, siblings might still live in China. Although most Mexican elderly reported having siblings, most also reported a very limited interaction with siblings. As with the Chinese, many of the siblings may reside outside the United States. Thus, White elderly saw their siblings more frequently than either Mexican or Chinese elders. Blacks, more than any other group, reported a high degree of interaction with siblings. This may be because low-socioeconomic Blacks tend to live in Black communities with extended kin and have more opportunity to see each other frequently, whereas Whites tend to be more geographically dispersed, thus inhibiting as frequent visiting.

With respect to the frequency of interaction with children and grandchildren, Mexicans and Blacks were more likely than Whites to see them at least weekly. However, among the 80+ cohort there were no ethnic differences in frequency of contact with either children or grandchildren. Increased frailty may be the reason why contact with grandchildren decreased with age, whereas regular contact with children increased.

The Role of Acculturation

Today's Mexican elderly span the acculturation continuum. Although these elderly tend to adhere more to traditional Mexican cultural patterns, there is also wide diversity within the group. One measure of acculturation to American values and norms is English-speaking ability, which generally accounts for approximately 60% of the variance on most acculturative scales (e.g., see Padilla, 1980, or Cuellar, Harris & Jasso, 1980).

In order to examine the role of acculturation with respect to social networks within the Mexican sample, the sample was divided into the Mexican English-speaking (MES) and the Mexican Spanish-speaking (MSS) (i.e., those who speak Spanish only). A little more than half of the Mexican elderly spoke English (57%). The MES, as expected, exhibited a pattern between that of Whites and the MSS. This pattern reflected the bicultural nature of many of the MES elderly.

Mexican elderly in general were less likely than Whites to live alone, but that was even more true of the MSS. The MSS were most likely to live with one of their adult children; thus, contact was facilitated. This difference between ethnic groups and subgroups is both cultural and perhaps necessary because of the lack of English-speaking skills combined with generally lower economic status. However, the strong traditional Mexican value of elder care seems also to be indicated by these data.

Both Mexican subgroups had siblings, but the substantial differences in frequency of contact can probably be explained by geographical proximity. The MSS were probably more likely to have siblings living in Mexico, so weekly interaction was probably not feasible.

There is a great cultural emphasis on family ties and on having children in Mexican families, which may account for the large differences in the reporting of having children and grandchildren. Although there was no significant difference in the frequency of contact with children, the trend was toward the following pattern: the more acculturated the individual, the less extensive the family interaction. Thus, cultural differences with respect to social networks appeared to diminish as an individual became more acculturated to American society.

These findings would probably have been similar among the Chinese as well. A comparable acculturation analysis of the Chinese sample was not conducted because there were too few English-speaking Chinese. Only 13 of the Chinese elderly spoke English, suggesting that this group of elderly were more likely to adhere to traditional Chinese cultural patterns and be less acculturated to American values.

Quality of Social Networks

How close one feels to one's social networks is one measure of perceived quality of that network. With respect to Whites and Mexicans, the feelings of closeness to family increased with age. However, an opposite trend was observed in Black elderly, where a smaller percentage of old-old (50%) felt close to their family than did young-old (58%). Blacks and Whites were more likely to report having close friends than were Mexican elderly. However, Mexicans were much more likely than either Blacks or Whites to report being close to their families. Chinese elderly rarely reported feeling close to their families or having close friends. In fact, these results may only reflect a cultural trait among the Chinese that disclosing a feeling of closeness to a number of family members or friends might be construed as "bragging" or unnecessary elevation of the self.

Overall, it appears that with respect to social networks, White and Black elderly related more to siblings and friends, whereas Mexican elderly were more likely to direct their attention to children and grandchildren. Whites and Blacks tended to report frequent contact with brothers and sisters. The Mexican subsample was as apt to have siblings as were Whites and Blacks but reported considerably less contact with them. Perhaps the Mexicans' siblings still resided outside the United States, or it may be that limited sibling interaction was a trade-off for increased contact with children. Mexican elderly reported the highest frequency of weekly contact with children and grandchildren of any ethnic group.

The Chinese patterns were less obvious. Though Chinese elderly were more apt than any other ethnic group to live with one of their children (49%) and almost all (95%) had children, Chinese elderly reported the lowest frequency of regular contact with children (65% compared to 74% for the total sample). This difference has been noted by Chen (1979) as a decrease in filial piety among Chinese children. It may be that as Chinese children become more acculturated they tend to move away from their parents and not visit them regularly. Chen notes, "Several Chinese-American elderly complained bitterly about their children's unfilial attitudes. The common remark was that 'my son is just like an American' " (p. 93). Fewer of the Chinese reported having siblings, which might account for some of the social interaction differences with brothers and sisters (e.g., the greater propensity for small families among the Chinese might explain this) and, as with the Mexicans, Chinese siblings may also reside outside the United States. However, interaction differences were quite extreme because *none* of the Chinese reported weekly contact with a sibling.

Social Supports

According to Ell (1984), social support encompasses material aid and services that are obtained from one's social networks. The analysis examined support for activities of daily living (ADL);

however, among the young-old (65–79 years), only one-fifth of the sample reported help with ADL. Though this percentage rose to 40 for the old-old (80+ years), very few ethnic differences were noted. The most important difference in ADL was that Whites and Chinese were slightly more apt to receive help from a spouse than were Mexican or Black elderly. Mexicans tended to get that help from an adult child, whereas Blacks most commonly got ADL help from formal support (e.g., home health aide, homemaker, visiting nurse, etc.).

The largest ethnic differences observed were in housework and laundry chores. Blacks and Whites were much more likely to use formal support than were Mexicans or Chinese, who got their help from informal sources. Mexican and Chinese spouses and children were both common sources of domestic support. Spousal support differences disappeared with age, perhaps because of the higher numbers of widows and/or possibly because of the frailty of the spouse. However, increased adult child help seemed to compensate for the loss of spousal support for the old-old Mexican and Chinese elderly, whereas no such increase was observed among Whites or Blacks. These differences may be partially accounted for by the greater likelihood of Mexicans and Chinese to live with their children, thereby enabling them to help with housework and laundry.

Mexican and Chinese children were more common sources of help with shopping and transportation than Black and White children. This difference was not affected by increased age. Mexican and Chinese young-old seldom participated in formal meal preparation programs. Whether this was due to increased opportunities for informal support or a dislike for formal meal programs is unclear. (These two groups often shun formal programs because such programs often do not provide the ethnic foods they prefer.) Mexican young-old were especially unlikely to get formal meal support (less than 5%).

The effects of acculturation on social support were explored among MES and MSS subsamples. Generally, the MSS subsample was more likely to get informal support than were the MES or White elderly. This was almost entirely due to the extensive support given by children of MSS. These trends were similar to comparisons made between MES and White subsamples. MES elderly were a little more likely to get help from a child than were White elderly. MES elderly tended to get more help with housework and laundry than were either MSS or White elderly. This was probably because of the greater likelihood for MES to live with a spouse.

Ethnic Differences in Social Support

Because some ethnic differences in social supports were due to variations in marital status and age, the following analysis controls for both of these factors. A logistic regression model was used to test the likelihood of an elderly person getting support for a given function as well as the likelihood of help coming from a particular source. Again few ethnic differences were observed in ADL. Therefore, Table 10-3 reports only results for housework, laundry, meals, shopping, and transportation. Methodological details on the logistic regression model are described in a note appended to this chapter.

After controlling for both age and marital status, it was observed that many ethnic differences in social supports disappeared. For example, differences in spousal support were no longer significant,

TABLE 10-3. Logistic Regression Analysis of Social Support

			Partial correlation coefficients[a]			
ADL	N	Age	Married	Black	Mexican	Chinese
Housework & laundry						
Gets support	951	.19	.10	NS	NS	NS
Formal support	627	.04[b]	−.16	NS	−.11	−.10
Informal support	627	NS	.19	NS	.09	.07
A child helps	474	.06	−.16	NS	.16	.11
Meals						
Gets support	951	.16	.25	.11	.03[b]	.08
Formal support	356	NS	−.25	NS	−.07	−.04[b]
Informal support	356	NS	.24	NS	NS	NS
A child helps	281	NS	−.29	NS	.08	NS
Shopping						
Gets support	951	.20	.07	.08	NS	.04
Formal support	580	NS	−.14	NS	NS	NS
Informal support	580	NS	.17	NS	NS	NS
A child helps	455	.09	−.18	NS	.07	NS
Transportation						
Gets support	951	.20	NS	NS	NS	NS
Formal support	507	NS	−.08	.05[b]	NS	−.10
Informal support	507	NS	.07	NS	NS	.06
A child helps	395	NS	−.09	NS	NS	.07

[a]All partial correlation coefficients from the logistic regression models are significant at least at the .05 level unless otherwise noted.
[b]$p < .10$.
ADL, activities of daily living; NS, not significant.

suggesting that if one was married a spouse was equally likely to help. Being married reduced the likelihood of both formal support and informal support delivered by a child. Regardless of ethnicity, having a spouse was strongly related to the overall likelihood of getting help with a function and also getting that help from informal sources.

These data also augment the previous findings, which indicated Mexican children were more likely to help with laundry, housework, meals, and shopping than were White children. Chinese children were also more apt to help with housework, laundry, and transportation than were White children. There did not appear to be any difference in the helping roles of Black children and White children.

Finally, another logistic regression model examined the determinants of whether or not one lived alone. This model, which also controlled for age and gender, indicated that Blacks and Whites tended to live alone, whereas Mexican and Chinese elderly are apt to live with others, particularly children. These data suggest that if an elderly person is living with another person, the likelihood of having critical social supports would be greatly enhanced regardless of ethnicity.

Ethnic Traditions, Change, and Social Support

The data revealed some clear ethnic differences. It continues to support the view that Chinese and Mexican elderly are more likely than either Black or White elderly to share housing and receive help from an adult child. This phenomenon is believed to be the result of two major factors: cultural values and economic need. When acculturation level was examined, it indicated that the closer one's ties to traditional culture, the greater the parent-child supportive behavior. However, this relationship may also be confounded by economic need. Inability to speak English tends not only to maintain stronger cultural ties but also to inhibit use of other types of formal services. Limited English-speaking skills may also aggravate an elderly individual's low socioeconomic circumstances, requiring greater assistance from the elders' children, including provision of living arrangements.

Both the Mexican and Chinese cultures have strong traditions reinforcing adult child responsibility for parents. That is not to say that other cultural groups do not also hold this value but rather that the degree to which it is reinforced in a culture may differ. For historical reasons, Blacks differ to some extent on this issue. The dispersement of families early in their history made it difficult to maintain the same ties. However, when one examines within Black families rather than between ethnic/racial groups, as in this comparative analysis, one still notes the supportive strength of Black extended families as they respond to the elders' needs (Taylor, 1985). Similarly, Brody (1985) found that White families offered extensive support to their elderly parents. The present study merely suggests that Chinese and Mexican children do more.

Perhaps Mexican and Chinese elderly are much less likely to seek formal help because of a strong informal support system. However, Mexicans and Chinese encounter some extra barriers to alternative forms of support. Limited English-speaking ability might especially impede use of formal services in these two groups, whereas that would be less true for Blacks and Whites.

A key to the existence of helping supportive systems seems to be whether one lives alone or not. However, even in living arrangements there appears to be possible cultural reasons for observed differences. American society values independence and nuclear family autonomy more highly than supportive interdependence and multigenerational living arrangements. This was indicated in the examination of the differences in acculturation levels of the Mexican elderly. Those who were more acculturated (closer to American norms) were more likely to live alone.

The findings from these data pose some questions with respect to further research on ethnicity and aging. A possible confounding issue in this analysis, of course, was the age-old problem of sorting out what can be attributed to ethnic status and what can be attributed to economic need. Even though economic status was largely controlled in this study, gradations in socioeconomic status, even within this low-income sample, could have caused sufficient differences to explain variations between ethnic groups. For example, children of the elderly welfare recipients included in this study might come from very different economic strata. Thus, the "opportunity costs" of extensive caretaking of an elderly parent might be much higher for some children than for others. This difference is likely to be ethnically biased given income disparities among ethnic groups in American society.

Clearly, age was the most important factor in the present analysis of social support. Age may impede the development of other social contacts that could be called on to nurture a support system. Marital status itself may not be as important a factor in receiving social support as whether an individual lives alone or not.

The findings of this study and the issues discussed are relevant and applicable to all aged who are members of ethnic subgroups who maintain strong cultural ties or who are not completely assimilated into the mainstream of American life. Our data again suggest that there is an ethnic factor in social support, but what needs further clarification is the degree to which it operates.

Socioeconomic status, living arrangements, age, and marital status can all be confounding factors when ethnic data is analyzed. The multivariate approach used here attempted to sort out some of these factors. However, the sample size of some of the subgroups, particularly the very old, precluded additional partitioning. Furthermore, the high correlation between marital status and living arrangements required the elimination of one or the other from a multivariate model. We chose to control for marital status, but larger samples could control for both and thus examine the relative influence of each on social supports.

The findings of this study also suggest that future research might first develop criteria for defining the norms for those who might be defined as "Americanized" and to use this as a standard against which to measure ethnic differences. Second, these comparisons need to control especially for age, acculturation, social class, and living arrangement differences among ethnic groups. Finally, such analysis should use sufficiently large samples to control for fine gradations of economic circumstances. This would better respond to the issues concerning the role of economic need versus the role of traditional cultural values as we examine the many facets of life that affect elders of various ethnic groups.

Methodological Note

The logistic regression models reported in Table 10-3 regress various types of social support onto age, marital status, and ethnicity. Age was entered into the model as a continuous variable. Marital status was a dichotomous variable, with 1 representing currently married. Similarly, Black, Mexican, and Chinese were dichotomous variables, with 1 indicating membership in that ethnic group.

Thus, the major reference group in the model was that of White elderly not currently married. A significant ethnic variable suggests that that group differed from White unmarried elderly in terms of the support variable examined. The total sample was included in models on whether one got help, but only those who got help were included in models on whether that help came from formal or informal social supports. This accounts for the smaller sample sizes in the formal and informal support models compared to the models regarding receiving help. Conceivably, those who got help were of comparable frailty, differing primarily in source of support.

Similarly, the models testing the likelihood of help from a child were further restricted to only those who had a child. Thus, these models control for the propensity of certain ethnic groups to have children, thereby focusing on the likelihood of a child to help an elderly parent. If this restriction had not been employed, Chinese and Mexican children variables would have generally been even more significant because those two groups were much more apt to have children than were Black or White elderly.

11

Organizational Activities, Cultural Factors, and Well-Being of Aged Japanese Canadians*

K. Victor Ujimoto

The degree to which ethnic identification factors are retained by aged ethnic minorities can be observed in their family or kinship interaction patterns and participation in voluntary organizations and various other social activities. From family and kinship interaction patterns, the retention of traditional roles and values by the aged ethnic minority can be observed if the aged still occupy positions of authority and prestige and if they play a role in daily family decision making. Despite the growing body of literature on activity patterns and general well-being of the aged, very little attention has been given to differences in the patterns of daily activities by ethnic minorities.

The relatively few studies that recognized the ethnic variable made the assumption that the ethnic group was more or less homogeneous. As a result, intergenerational differences were not accounted for. In addition, the socialization processes experienced by each generation varied, although they may share a common ethnic or cultural heritage. Regardless of the generational dif-

* The study on which this paper is based was made possible through a research grant from the Social Sciences and Humanities Research Council of Canada (Grant No. 492-81-0006). Their support is gratefully acknowledged.

ferences, however, the extent to which an ethnic minority is able to maintain traditional culture and values may be associated with the degree to which the members are able to participate in their own ethnic institutions and social networks. For the aged ethnic minority, their well-being may, in turn, be related to the various ethnic identification factors noted by Driedger (1978), namely, identification with an ethnic culture, identification with ethnic institutions, identification with historic symbols, identification with an ideology, identification with an ecological territory, and identification with charismatic leadership. With reference to aged Japanese Canadians, this chapter examines generational differences in the participation in organizational activities, differences in the retention of ethnic cultural factors, and their subjectively perceived well-being.

Earlier studies that examined well-being and daily activities did not go beyond conventional methodologies and reported only the frequency of participation in selected activities. Our study employs both time-budget and life-satisfaction instruments that enable us to determine (a) the social context in which various activities occurred, (b) the duration and frequency of single and multiple activities, and (c) the general well-being or satisfaction of our aged respondents. By not having preselected activity categories and by asking respondents to record their sequence of daily events, we have the advantage of relative objectivity while at the same time preserving much of the content of daily life experiences (Moss & Lawton, 1982). In aging research, the duration of participation for some activities appears to be more important than the frequency of activity. For example, visits of several hours in duration by a relative may be more meaningful to the aged than ritualistic and much shorter regular visits. The time-budget methodology employed in our study permits us to secure the appropriate data on the frequency, duration, and sequence of various daily activities.

Time-Budget Methodology

Time-budget methodology involves the collection of data on various activities over a specified period of time, such as the 24 hours of the day, the weekend, or over the whole week. The data are essentially observations of what people do in time and space, and thus they can be easily recorded at specified intervals by trained observers or by the survey respondents themselves. Although this may appear to be quite simple and straightforward, the usage of time-budget method-

ology for the study of age-related behaviour is a relatively unex-
plored area in social gerontology.

There are several reasons why a time-budget methodology has not
been utilized in gerontological research. The first reason stemmed
from the fact that the methodology required respondents to record
their daily activities for the previous day based on recall, and for
aged respondents this created problems in both validity and reliability of the data because of their limited recall ability. This problem
has been reduced considerably in recent studies (Ujimoto, 1985a) by
having respondents record their activities regularly at their con-
venience, throughout the day as they take place.

The second reason for the reluctance in employing time-budget
methodology in studies on aging was based on difficulties in analyzing a plethora of data. Time-budget studies yield a very rich source
of data about our research subjects. In addition to the information
on the temporal distribution of daily or weekly human activities, a
time-budget methodology permits the researcher to obtain additional information on each of the activities, such as duration, frequency,
and location of activities; the social networks involved, for example,
kinship or friendship; and the sequence of events. Therefore, prior to
recent developments in information technology and computer programs capable of analyzing vast quantities of data, researchers were
understandably reluctant to collect time-budget data.

Another reason why time-budget methodology has not received
wider recognition in research on aging stems from the very nature
of previous social gerontological research itself. Until very recently,
specific hypothesis testing did not encourage the use of multiple
measures of a given phenomenon. A good illustration of this can be
found in those studies on life satisfaction or well-being of the elderly
in which various activities in daily living were noted only as a
single objective measure in terms of what people did. Other objective measures such as duration, frequency, and sequence of activities, as well as the social environment in which various activities
took place, were not considered. Furthermore, the qualitative
aspects of each of the activities were seldom addressed.

Finally, time-budget methodology can be a costly and time-con-
suming technique for data acquisition if the research objectives are
not very clearly specified at the outset. The research objectives
should be grounded in gerontological theory and time budgets utilized as a methodology to secure additional information on the phenomenon to be analyzed. In what follows we will provide a very brief
overview of earlier studies on activity patterns and well-being of the
aged and indicate some of the limitations in these studies. We will

then introduce several studies that utilize the time-budget methodology to show some of its advantages, particularly with reference to
the multidimensionality of activity data. Finally, we will describe
our study of aged Japanese Canadians, which uses the time-budget
methodology to secure data on their participation in various activities, cultural factors, and their well-being in late life.

Activity Patterns and Well-Being

One of the important studies on activity patterns and well-being of
the elderly was the study by Teaff, Lawton, Nahemow, and Carlson
(1978). In their study, six indexes of well-being were developed
based on activity participation, family contact, morale, housing
satisfaction, and friendship behavior. Activity participation was
derived from "the number of on-site activities named by the subject
as engaged in during the past year." Although activity participation
is only one aspect of the well-being index for this study, the limitations of the data are fairly obvious. Activity data secured on the
basis of recall will certainly not be as accurate as time-budget data
recorded daily.

The other indexes of well-being in the Teaff et al. (1978) study,
namely, family contact and friendship, also suffer the limitations
imposed by the single-question approach to obtain activity data.
Family contact data are based on how often respondents see their
relatives. Similarly, friendship data are based on the number of
friends, number of friends visited, and/or visits by friends during
the past week. Both family contact and friendship data are therefore
limited to numbers or frequencies only and lack information on
duration and quality of seeing relatives, visiting friends, or visits by
friends. Duration and the qualitative aspects of daily activities are
of particular importance for the elderly, and it is worth noting that
recent developments in time-budget studies (Cullen & Phelps, 1978;
Michelson, 1984; Ujimoto, 1985b) attempt to integrate the objective
and subjective dimensions of daily life.

Another method that is commonly used to obtain activity data is
to ask participants to keep an active diary. Hooker and Ventis
(1984) employed the active diary method to examine the relationship between daily activities and retirement satisfaction. They
obtained not only the number of activities but also data on perceived
usefulness and pleasantness of those activities. This is an important
aspect to consider because the same activity may have different
meanings for different people. Indeed, Hooker and Ventis also note

that the same activity may have different meanings for the same person at different times of the day. A good example of this is watching television as an educational activity as contrasted to a passive activity merely to kill time.

There are several recent studies on activity patterns that employed the time-budget methodology. In the study by Moss and Lawton (1982) participants were asked to recount for the interviewer each sequential activity of the previous day from the time the participant woke up. For each activity, participants were asked to state the location of the activity, the social context in which the activity took place (i.e., with whom), and the qualitative aspects of the activity (like, dislike, etc.). The time-budget methodology enabled Moss and Lawton to compare the daily life patterns of the four subgroups in their sample in terms of the proportion of time (mean minutes) spent on obligatory and discretionary activities and in different social and environmental contexts.

Another study that utilized time-budget data is the study by Altergott (1985), which investigated how marital status in late life influenced social participation in various daily activities. Her study was based on a secondary analysis of a national time-use survey conducted by Juster et al. (Juster, Courant, Duncan, Robinson, & Stafford, 1977). In this survey, participants provided reports on their activities for a single day on two weekdays and on weekends. The time budgets provided a record of the duration of activities, social context, and details on other peripheral activities that took place at the same time as the primary activity. Of particular significance to our discussion of time-budget studies are the data-analysis strategies presented by Altergott in order to examine her time-budget data. First, at the aggregate level, Altergott was able to present data on the average time spent in a particular role relationship as well as in other more general social involvement. Second, multiple regression analysis enabled Altergott to provide some indication of the effect of marital status and gender while controlling for health and propensity to interact, on individual social involvement.

Perhaps one more example of research on activity patterns that employed a time-budget methodology will suffice to illustrate its diverse utility. The study of Ujimoto (1985a) used time budgets to investigate the degree of social integration of aged ethnic minorities by determining their time-use patterns for daily activities and to see if there were any differences when compared to the activity patterns of the majority members of the community. The community selected for this study was La Villeneuve, France, because it was a planned community developed to accommodate a wide range of socioeconomic, age, and diverse ethnic groups. Based on the assumption that planned social and physical environments facilitate the degree of integration of the aged ethnic minorities by providing opportunities for social involvement, it was hypothesized that the time-use patterns for participation in various activities by the majority French and minority non-French elderly would be similar if the non-French elderly were integrated into the planned community. This hypothesis was examined using the combined techniques of participant observations, time-budget records of sequential daily activities, and a questionnaire for sociodemographic information. The data obtained provided the following information: (a) the frequency and duration of activities, (b) the social context in which various activities took place, and (c) information on whether or not a given activity was initiated by self or by someone else, for example, by a visitor or a social facilitator in charge of organized activities.

Time-budget methodologies can differ from study to study depending on the research resources available and the specific research objectives. In the Moss and Lawton (1982) study, interviewers were hired to record the sequential activities of the previous day as recounted by the respondents. This may pose a recall problem, especially when respondents are older people. This issue was minimized in the Ujimoto (1985a) study by spreading the data acquisition phase over 2 consecutive days. During the first day, the interviewer established the rapport in order to administer the survey questionnaire and to provide instructions on how to complete the time-budget activities form for the following day, commencing with the time the respondent woke up. The time-budget form employed in the study was a slightly modified version of the form developed by Robinson (1977) in that the time-recording technique used by Leroy and Deliege (1982) was incorporated. This enabled the aged respondents to easily record the start and end of each activity. They were encouraged to fill in their time-budget forms as often as possible throughout the day. This procedure minimized the loss of information due to recall loss.

The studies briefly described above illustrate the various ways in which time-budget methodology is currently employed and confirms the observations made by Little (1984) that there is a growing usage of time-budget methodology applied to the study of age-related behaviour. The once broad collection of time-budget activities data is now being supplemented with subjective evaluations of how each of the various activities is perceived. This multidimensional aspect of activities data provides a more meaningful assessment of the general well-being of the elderly.

Time-Budget Methodology for Research on Aging

Although the main advantages of time-budget methodology for research on aging may be self-evident from the brief overview of the various studies provided above, there are other significant aspects of the time-budget methodology that should be noted, particularly with reference to research on aging. The daily time expenditure for all primary activities must add up to 24 hr or 1,440 min. (Juster & Stafford, 1985; Little, 1984; Szalai, 1972). Therefore, within the constraints of the 24-hr day, it is obvious that the time expended for a particular primary activity can be increased only if the time spent on other primary activities is decreased. This is an important factor to note in longitudinal studies in which changes in frequency and duration of a given primary activity must be determined. For example, a person who is in relatively good health may sleep quite soundly during the night without any interruptions for 8 hr. At a later date this same individual may experience a health problem that necessitates frequent visits to the toilet. In this case, the time expended on washroom activities during the night may only be at the expense of sleep. This specific example may appear to be quite trivial; however, changes in activity patterns over a period of time can provide meaningful information in terms of the well-being of the elderly. The precise measurement in the allocation of time to a given activity at two different points in time can provide an accurate assessment of change, which may enable social policy planners to base their decisions on crucial information and not on speculation.

Activity patterns for older people may differ considerably compared to those of younger people, and time-budget data are helpful in establishing the specific nature of these differences. For example, retired older people do not have the constraint of reporting for work at a predetermined time, and consequently, the allocation of time to various activities tends to shift throughout the day and eventually throughout the week. Similarly, as one ages, the nighttime activities of the aged also tend to vary. Golant (1984) has shown that nighttime activities of old people do indeed vary depending on individual attributes and environmental variables.

An aspect of time-budget data that is of interest to the study of well-being of the elderly is the possibility of analyzing the allocation of time for those primary activities perceived to be satisfying to the elderly in terms of location and social context. Szalai (1984) notes that the distinction between the main or primary and concomitant activities are at the discretion of the individual; however, if the frequency, duration, location of the activity, and the social context or with whom the activity takes place are examined in conjunction with a subjective evaluation of the primary activity, this will provide the researcher with additional information in differentiating between satisfying and unsatisfying activities. It is quite conceivable that we may find a given primary activity in a certain environment to be less satisfying than that same activity in another context. Listening to music for several hours in solitude may be the primary activity, but this may not be as satisfying as listening to music with someone with whom one may share and discuss certain aspects of the music. This example illustrates the significance of the social context of an activity when the subjective dimension is introduced in our analysis.

Aged Japanese Canadians

As argued by Kalish and Moriwaki (1979), the significance of the life-span developmental perspective becomes apparent when studying the relationship between ethnicity and aging:

> The older Asian Americans cannot effectively be theorized about, understood, or provided for without a grasp of four factors: a) their cultural origins and effects of earlier socialization; b) their life history in the United States and Canada; c) those age related changes that occur regardless of early learning or ethnicity; and d) their experiences concerning what it means to be old. (p. 266)

Indeed, unlike many other ethnic minorities, aged Japanese Canadians have an extremely unique history. Like aged Japanese Americans who were uprooted and incarcerated by U.S. Executive Order 9066 on February 19, 1942, Japanese Canadians were similarly uprooted and incarcerated on February 24, 1942, when Canadian Order in Council P.C. 1486 empowered the Canadian government to remove Japanese Canadians from the designated "Protected Area" of the Pacific Coast. The forced removal stripped Japanese Canadians of their property, and to this day full compensation for the losses incurred has not been made and is only in the discussion stage with the Canadian government. Daniels (1977) argues that the Canadian dispersal measures were much harsher and more enduring than the American policy. He notes that Japanese-American citizens were free to live where they wished 7 months before V-J Day. In stark contrast, the last of the Canadian government restrictions on the mobility of Japanese Canadians ended on April 1, 1949, almost 3½ years after the end of World War II.

Another very important difference to note was that Japanese Americans were provided with the opportunity to demonstrate their loyalty by enlisting in the U.S. military service. Such was not the case in Canada. The nisei, or second-generation Japanese Canadians, were banned from the Canadian military forces, and volunteers for special service were assigned to the British forces.

In order to survive the uprooting and incarceration during World War II, traditional Japanese values facilitated in coping with the daily stresses of life. Traditional values such as loyalty, diligence, *gaman* (forbearance), and *enryo* (restraint) facilitated the maintenance of family cohesion by emphasizing the interdependence of family members. For the *issei,* or first generation of Japanese immigrants, this general pattern of devotion to the family or to the family occupation was a very common one, in which social interaction with others in the community was minimal because of various circumstances. First, it was extremely difficult to converse in English. Unlike today, there were no English-as-second-language facilities. Second, external discrimination and prejudice forced the Japanese to form their own social networks within their own communities as a means of survival. Third, the geographic dispersal of the Japanese further meant that the sense of community and social interaction were extremely limited to special occasions only.

Today these *issei* are now retired, and therefore, an interesting question arises as to whether or not there are any discernible differences in what they do in time and in space as compared to the aged nisei, given the vastly different sociodemographic characteristics of the Canadian-born and -educated. This is an important question to consider, as there are relatively few studies that recognize the intergenerational differences in ethnic minority groups. To obtain the data for our study, we utilized a time-budget methodology that provided a record of activities by aged Japanese-Canadian respondents. Because of space limitations, we will report only on their participation in organizational activities.

Social Demographic Characteristics of Our Sample

Our sample of respondents ($N = 374$) was selected from a list of aged Japanese Canadians living in four major Canadian urban centers (Vancouver, Winnipeg, Toronto, and Montreal) and four relatively rural communities in the Okanagan Valley of British Columbia

(Kelowna, Vernon, Salmon Arm, and Kamloops). The rationale for selecting these various cities across Canada stems from the fact that there are sociodemographic differences in the Japanese-Canadian communities depending on the region. For example, many of the aged Japanese Canadians currently residing in Winnipeg were interned or evacuated as families to farm projects on the Canadian prairie. In contrast, those who went farther east were mainly individuals who possessed entrepreneurial skills. Our data also revealed that there were rural/urban differences in the retention of traditional cultural values. For example, 71.6% of the Okanagan Valley respondents stressed discipline and perseverance as important factors that contributed to their successful aging and well-being. In contrast, discipline and perseverance was noted by only 13.3% of the Montreal respondents, 21.5% of the Winnipeg respondents, and 23.8% of the Vancouver respondents.

A crucial variable to consider when examining postretirement activities is the level of education. As noted by Hendricks and Hendricks (1979), the central thesis of the activity theory is that the greater the number of optional role resources with which one enters old age, the better one will be able to adjust to the changes brought about by the aging process. For the aged Japanese Canadians, it is not clear just what is meant by optional role resources because in most cases their level of education and skills possessed may be lower than for other aged Canadians in the same age category. Our data ($N = 369$) reveals that the level of education possessed by both *issei* and nisei respondents is relatively high. For example, 77.9% of the *issei* and 80.9% of the nisei had high school education. In contrast, only 48.1% of the *kika* nisei respondents had a high school education, and 37% indicated no formal education. The *kika* nisei are those who were repatriated to Japan either during World War II or immediately after the war and then returned to Canada at some later time.

Participation in Organizations

As can be expected, the organizations listed by our respondents were mainly those organizations or associations specifically for Japanese Canadians. For example, the Japanese Canadian Citizens' Association, Japanese Canadian Cultural Centre or its equivalent in various cities and communities, and various churches were the main ones noted by our respondents. An examination of our data on participation by level of education reveals that there is consistent participation in at least one to four organizations regardless of the level of education.

Our data also indicate that, regardless of age, there is an even distribution of participants in one to four organizations. There are two possible explanations to account for this general trend. First, it is necessary to examine the nature of participation in the various organizations. It is generally expected by the *issei* and older nisei that all Japanese Canadians be active members of the National Japanese Canadian Citizens' Association. This expectation is most strongly held by those who still retain a very strong sense of moral and social obligations to the association for past assistance. Active participation usually means keeping up with the payment of one's membership dues only, although members may be called upon to contribute some time for volunteer activities. Second, participation in Japanese cultural associations is not based on any prerequisite such as level of education, which is the case for joining professional associations. The fact that age is not a barrier to participation in Japanese culture and community-oriented associations is clearly shown in our data. The feeling of *kansha,* or gratitude and respect, accorded to aged Japanese Canadians is still quite strong.

Our data also reveal that the level of income does not have a significant bearing in terms of participation in one to three different organizations. Participation data in the one- and three-organization categories reveal that those with lower income levels are more numerous than those with very high income, and thus it does not appear that income levels influence participation. However, there are more participants in the four-organization category in the higher income bracket. What this suggests is that we must be more precise in terms of the type of organization in which aged Japanese Canadians actually participate.

Another interesting aspect of participation in organizations by aged Japanese Canadians is the data on differences in participation by marital status and sex. Our data on participation by marital status indicate that the highest proportion of single respondents belong to at least one organization. The widowed group constitutes the second-highest category in terms of participation in two or three organizations. There is only a very slight difference in participation in one, three, or four organizations by marital status. Similarly, there is very little difference in participation by sex. However, the number of female respondents who were nonparticipants is almost double the number of male nonparticipants.

With reference to participation in organization by the *issei,* nisei, and *kika* nisei, the largest proportion of nonparticipants are the *kika* nisei, followed very closely by the nisei. In the one- and two-organization participation category, the nisei participation is the lowest and the *issei* the highest. This may reflect the fact that many *issei* are members of Japanese culture and community-oriented organizations because they feel morally obligated to belong to them as these were the organizations that fought on their behalf during periods of adversity during World War II. In contrast, our data indicated that the nisei and *kika* nisei were both greater participants than the *issei* in the four- and five-organization category. This stems from the fact that many of the nisei are also members of non-Japanese community associations and professional organizations in which the language of business is English.

Although our questionnaire provided data on organizational participation, it is necessary to examine our time-budget data to determine the extent to which our respondents participated in organizational activities. Table 11-1 illustrates the variations in the allocation of time to organizational participation by generation: *issei,* nisei, and *kika* nisei. There is a remarkably similar allocation of time by *issei* and nisei. For the *kika* nisei, a much smaller proportion of respondents indicated having spent from 30 min to 2 hr on organizational participation; however, a proportionately greater percentage of *kika* nisei respondents spend from 3 to 4 hr on organizational participation in contrast to the much smaller proportion of *issei* and nisei who indicated having spent 3 to 4 hr in organizational activities. Note, however, that this trend is slightly reversed when it comes to organizational participation between 4 and 5 hr. This is a manifestation of time allocation to leadership and other management activities, which of course is limited to a very small number of *issei* and nisei.

Traditional Japanese Values and Life Satisfaction

In our questionnaire we asked our aged Japanese-Canadian respondents to indicate those aspects of their cultural heritage that may have assisted them to grow old successfully. This was an open-ended question designed to solicit the respondent's own views on traditional Japanese values and culture. An interesting variation in responses by generation was obtained. As might be expected, 21.1% of the *issei* respondents indicated that perseverance was the key to successful aging, as compared to 13.8 and 17.4% by the nisei and *kika* nisei, respectively. However, 25% of the nisei and 34.8% of the *kika* nisei stressed discipline, compared to only 14.1% of the *issei*.

TABLE 11-1. Allocation of Time to Organizational Activities by Generation

Allocation of time (hr)	Generation[a]		
	Issei (%)	Nisei (%)	Kika nisei (%)
.00	8.5	10.0	11.1
.50	.0	.0	.0
.75	.4	.9	.0
1.00	8.1	8.2	3.7
1.25	5.5	2.7	3.7
1.50	16.1	14.5	14.8
1.75	11.9	10.9	3.7
2.00	11.9	14.5	7.4
2.25	13.2	10.0	3.7
2.50	8.1	10.0	7.4
2.75	3.0	2.0	—
3.00	2.5	5.5	11.1
3.25	.8	—	7.4
3.50	.8	2.7	11.1
3.75	.8	1.8	11.1
4.00	2.1	.9	3.8
4.50	1.7	1.8	—
4.75	—	.9	—
5.00	3.8	2.7	—
5.50	.8	—	—

[a]$N = 373$.

Surprisingly, the nisei placed more emphasis on the filial aspects to respect elders (13.8%) than did the *issei* (5.4%). There were no significant differences by generation for the other traditional cultural values such as group loyalty, sense of duty, moral obligations, thriftiness, and pride in Japanese culture.

Our respondents were also asked to indicate those aspects of their cultural heritage that may have hindered them from growing old successfully. Although more than half of the respondents in each generational category indicated nil cultural factors that hindered them, 14% of the *issei,* 18.6% of the nisei, and 5% of the *kika* nisei indicated that *enryo* (reserve or restraint) hindered them. The lack of general aggressiveness and false modesty was also mentioned by 10 and 5% of the nisei and *kika* nisei, respectively.

Life satisfaction in terms of one's finances, family relations, and health was also examined in relation to traditional values and culture. Generally, those respondents who stressed discipline, perseverance, and self-reliance were satisfied or very satisfied with respect to their financial situation. Of those respondents who emphasized discipline as an important factor that contributed to their successful aging, 81.5% were either satisfied or very satisfied. Of those who indicated perseverance as an important factor, 89.9% were satisfied or very satisfied. In contrast, 5.7 and 25.7% of those respondents who had indicated that *enryo* was a hindering factor indicated dissatisfaction or mixed feelings, respectively, with reference to financial satisfaction.

In terms of family life satisfaction, a generally high satisfaction pattern was indicated by our respondents. Of those who stressed perseverance as an important factor, 93.2% were satisfied or very satisfied. Similarly, 85.2 and 87.5% of the respondents who stressed respect for the elderly and pride in Japanese culture, respectively, were satisfied or very satisfied. Again, a very small proportion of our respondents who were dissatisfied or had mixed feelings about their family relations centered on those who had indicated *enryo* and lack of aggressiveness as hindering factors to successful aging.

Although our data revealed a generally satisfied or very satisfied group of respondents in terms of their financial and family relations, such was not the case for their health status. Our data indicated that the lack of fluency in expressing oneself, the lack of aggressiveness in stating one's true feelings, and false modesty are important factors that influence one's well-being in terms of health status. Of those respondents who had indicated that *enryo* and lack of aggressiveness were hindering factors, 42.9 and 33.3%, respectively, were either dissatisfied or of mixed feeling. This finding underscores the importance of understanding the traditional cultural values of ethnic minorities when providing effective health care services.

Summary and Conclusions

We have shown in this chapter the importance of recognizing the generational and cultural variations within a given ethnic minority group, the aged Japanese Canadians, when assessing the degree of their perceived well-being. The approach utilized in our study was that of a time-budget methodology to secure our data. The time-budget approach to data acquisition has several important implications, especially in comparative ethnicity and aging research. First, regardless of the ethnic group under study, the amount of time that can be allocated to various activities in a given day must add up to 24 hr. This means that within the common frame of reference of the 24-hr day, variations in the allocation of time to various activities can be obtained for each of the ethnic groups for a single day or for a whole week, depending on one's research resources. Second, the time-budget methodology enables us to capture the duration and frequency of single and multiple activities as well as the social context in which the activities take place. Such information can tell us the differences in priority or importance that individuals place on the allocation of time to various activities. In particular, information on the sequencing of certain activities may provide vital clues with respect to future social and leisure activities planning and programming. Third, the relationship between what people do in time and space, the allocation of time to each activity, and the social context in which various activities occur can be assessed in terms of the sociocultural and ethnic-identity-retention factors of individuals. For example, the degree to which the cultural aspects of ethnicity are retained can be observed in family or kinship interaction patterns, ethnic community participation, and other forms of traditional ethnic social activities and rituals. The retention of traditional roles and values by the aged can be observed if the aged still retain positions of authority and prestige and influence family decision making.

The significance of the above three factors are clearly manifested in our research. Our data indicated that organizational membership by the aged Japanese Canadians was mainly in those organizations or associations specifically for Japanese Canadians. However, our time-budget data revealed that the actual participation in these organizations is rather limited and that membership appears to be based on moral or social obligations and *kansha,* or gratitude, for past associational assistance in securing their basic rights of citizenship and franchise privileges. This appears to be supported by the observation that the *issei* have the highest organizational membership and the *kika* nisei the least.

Although we were able to illustrate our time-use data for organizational activities only, we have argued that, unlike traditional studies of activity patterns, the additional information on duration of activity, sequence, and social context in which the activity takes place makes it possible to render a more meaningful comparison of ethnic groups. For example, it is possible to show particular sequences of activities in a given social context that may lead to greater life satisfaction for a particular ethnic group. This is especially significant for ethnicity and aging research because the sequence of activities for the aged, particularly aged ethnic minorities, may be quite different from that of the younger and more dominant members of society. Furthermore, by delineating those activities most predictive of well-being for members of different ethnic groups, we are in essence witnessing ethnic variations in coping behavior, that is, the ways in which stress situations can be reduced and general well-being maximized. The implications for future social policy are obvious, and it remains for a further analysis of our data to determine the most appropriate combination of activities for successful aging.

Part III

Practice, Policy, and the Ethnic Dimensions of Aging

At various points in their lives, individuals may utilize ethnic background as an important element in their identity. This contention is supported by Luborsky and Rubinstein's chapter in Part I. Disman (Chapter 5) views ethnic identity as a element providing continuity in the lives of older people. In Part II Stoller finds older Finns transplanted to Florida able to reestablish an ethnically based community that provides important assistance to its members.

Whatever the importance of ethnicity for older individuals, it is dangerous to overestimate the assistance the ethnic community or family is going to be able to provide individuals who are in their seventies or eighties. Clearly, these older adults will require services from formal as well as informal sources. We need to ascertain the types of services needed and develop the policies that support effective and efficient services.

Ascertaining what these services are requires extensive research in homogeneous ethnic communities as well as among older individuals living in heterogeneous communities. As the authors of many of these chapters can attest, practice among ethnic groups can be a difficult endeavor. This difficulty can extend to the practice of research. Limited education, a lack of understanding of the research process, limited fluency in English, and suspicion can all combine to make the lot of the researcher difficult. This difficulty may prevail even if the research instruments are translated into the native tongue and the researcher is from the same ethnic background.

To list the difficulties does not mean that they are insurmountable. In Chapter 12 Cox describes some of the difficulties and approaches that can be viable in overcoming them. Her article is based on research in California with three diverse groups: Portuguese, Hispanics, and Vietnamese. Although each of these groups has distinct cultural traditions, the approaches she outlines should be helpful to researchers, practitioners, and policymakers concerned about the delivery of services to older ethnic people.

Successful completion of a research project may highlight the diversity within an ethnic group as well as among ethnic groups. Kozaitis' probing analysis of the older Greek community in Chicago uncovers important differences among the older Greeks she studied. Based on her finding of a "continuum of acculturation from values of the mother country to those of the host nation among the older Greeks," Kozaitis elaborates on how services should be oriented toward this diverse group. Her recommendations may surprise some readers because they do not accept all of the traits of the older Greek Americans as a basis for services. Instead, her call for a service delivery orientation that is based on *bifunctionalism* requires changes among Greek Americans as well as among service providers.

Even having the best of intentions, service providers may be dismayed to find that the older individual does not welcome their help. To some extent this lack of service utilization may stem from a desire not to utilize assistance outside of the ethnic family or community. On the other hand, a lack of service utilization may stem from a combination of factors. Harel, McKinney, and Williams attempt to bring these factors into a framework that can assist practitioners involved in providing or planning new services. The effort to link the characteristics of the older person, the informal service-delivery system, and the formal service-delivery system is a necessary step toward adequate assistance for the older ethnic person.

At this point it would be hard to classify the service-delivery system for older people in the United States or Canada as adequate. MacLean and Bonar contend that a reliance on the family for assistance by older individuals often stems from the fact that "services are available in principle but not in practice." They view the precarious situation of many older people as resulting from "socially constructed hardships." Examining the problems in service provision, they call for more cooperation among individuals dedicated to serving ethnic elderly people. This cooperation must include both the informal providers in the community and professionals. This contention would seem to be indisputable, given the multidimensional social and health needs of older individuals and the interdisciplinary focus of the field of aging. Unfortunately, the administrative structure of services often makes the clear need for cooperative practice impossible to implement. MacLean and Bonar's call for cooperation must remain in the forefront of our thinking.

Adequate services and cooperative practice must stem from policies that target the needs of the ethnic elderly. Gibson's provocative chapter indicates that the meaning of retirement may not be the same for Black elderly as it is for Whites. A major factor in the different meaning of retirement for Blacks is their difficulty in obtaining a stable work role. Her data, taken from a major study of Black elderly, indicates that individuals who do not have continuous work histories, who are disabled, or who do not collect a major portion of their income from retirement benefits may not regard themselves as "retired." Instead, she terms this group the "unretired-retired." Neglect of this group brings into question the validity of current retirement research.

Gibson raises a number of important policy issues relating to older Blacks who do not fit the standard parameters by which retirement is defined. She also provides some disturbing results if we view ethnicity and aging in a future-oriented, rather than only a present-oriented, time frame. As she notes, current high unemployment rates among Blacks may mean that future cohorts of older Blacks, particularly Black men, will have fewer resources than current cohorts of older Blacks. This possibility is in stark contrast to the hope that each successive cohort of older individuals will have greater economic resources in their later years.

Gibson's concerns are also reflected in Torres-Gil's writing. In the final chapter Torres-Gil highlights the trends that have had and will continue to have an impact on policies for the minority elderly. These trends include continued growth among certain minority groups as well as an increased consciousness of the importance of policies that affect older persons.

This consciousness is only one aspect of an extremely complex configuration of forces that determine policies. These forces include the attitudes of taxpayers of younger ages, general economic conditions, and divisions as to appropriate directions among older individuals themselves. Although he does not provide any easy answers, Torres-Gil raises the necessary questions for us. Importantly, he views North American society as becoming more multicultural rather than less multicultural.

The dilemma for many practitioners and policymakers will be how to respond effectively to this continued multiculturality. In a period when funds are limited it will be difficult to provide discrete services for all of the diverse ethnic elderly groups in North America. Separate senior centers for Greeks, Poles, Italian, Blacks, Chinese, and Japanese, as well as the groups lumped together under the label of "Hispanic," may not be possible. Many providers may have to develop innovative programs that allow ethnic group members to maintain a desired sense of uniqueness within a setting that serves a number of groups. At the same time the setting should also allow individuals to interact with other ethnic groups if they so desire. Developing cooperation and tolerance, or even avoiding continued historic hostilities among ethnic groups, is a major task for providers concerned about serving diverse ethnic elderly populations and yet minimizing their costs. An understanding of the relationship of ethnicity and aging will be a requirement for successful completion of this task.

12

Overcoming Access Problems in Ethnic Communities

Carole Cox

Research, an essential base for the provision of effective services to the ethnic elderly, cannot begin until access into the communities is achieved. In many instances obtaining this access can be very difficult, actually impeding efforts for program development. Accessing ethnic communities, particularly those that are insulated and where cultural traditions and ties remain very strong, can be a formidable task for the researcher, even when members of the ethnic community are themselves used as interviewers. An inherent distrust of persons asking questions and seeking information can present insurmountable barriers that prevent researchers from obtaining adequate samples and essential data. The residents of ethnic communities may resent "outsiders" and bureaucrats coming into their turf, attempting to change the established order (Greeley, 1976). These barriers against intrusion can be strongest in those persons who are the least assimilated to American culture and who feel they have the most to protect. Concurrently, these are also the persons who may be most in need of formal services.

In most ethnic groups, the least assimilated, those with the strongest sense of ethnic identity, will be the elderly, who are most likely to be the first-generation immigrants. As the first or second generations in the United States they tend to maintain the closest ties with traditional ethnic attitudes and culture. These ties provide older persons with an identity based on cultural norms, which may shelter them from many of the problems encountered by other older persons. Within the ethnic group age alone may vest them with prestige and respect and the right for assistance from their families.

165

Conversely, as ethnic traditions begin to break down in the younger generations, older persons may find themselves isolated and discontent as children no longer adhere to traditional filial values (Cox & Gelfand, 1987). However, formal social programs to meet the needs of these persons are not always available. Moreover, existing services may not be used because of the elderly's lack of familiarity with them or cultural reluctance to seek formal help.

Two particular obstacles to the use of formal programs by the elderly are language barriers and programs that are insensitive to cultural traditions and beliefs (Harbert & Ginsberg, 1979). The elderly are the least likely in the ethnic groups to speak English. If they have managed to remain within ethnic neighborhoods and to have children who were responsible for interacting with the dominant society, their need for English was often minimal. However, as this group grows older and children move away, they often find themselves reliant on services that they are unable to understand and that do not understand them. Furthermore, they may need to be educated regarding the use of programs and their rights to service (Guttmann, 1979). Without such education and an overall assumption among service providers that the families provide most of the care for these older people, these older ethnics are at risk of being neglected and isolated by service providers.

Ethnicity, which can shield persons for many years from the difficulties of role loss and status change often associated with assimilation, can in old age become a barrier to the development of needed policies and services. By remaining insulated, often within ethnic enclaves, the needs of the older persons may remain unknown to policymakers and agencies. In order for policies and services to be developed for these populations, the groups must be reached. Access becomes one of the critical underlying factors in meeting the ongoing needs of these ethnic elders.

The problems involved in access include suspiciousness and distrust of programs of the dominant culture. In fact, the failure of many social programs to meet the needs and solve the problems of ethnic persons can be caused by the ethnic culture itself as it sees these outside actions as threats to its very existence (Wright, Saleebey, Watts, & Lecca, 1983). The research process, fundamental to the development of policy and programs, is sometimes seen as being irrelevant and its results inaccurate. The persons sought as providers of information may feel resentful as they do not see its purpose (Sue, Ito, & Bradshaw, 1982).

Although access is crucial to the development of research and policy, there is a dearth of data on issues involved in accessing older ethnic persons. Available information concentrates on means of interacting and the importance of cultural traits in the interaction process. For example, initial contacts with ethnic elderly must demonstrate respect so that an atmosphere of trust and cooperation can develop. Specific ways of interacting, including the use of first and surnames, eye contact, seating, and touch, can all have important effects on the ensuing relationship (Kadushin, 1972; Zuniga-Martinez, 1983). The openness and the sharing of feelings that indicate maturity in relationships in the dominant culture may be negatively perceived in comparison to the ability to control expression (Watanabe, 1973). These fundamental differences can prohibit effective interaction. However, these studies, useful in defining and prescribing relationships, do not deal with the fundamental issue of reaching these older people, whether for providing services, for assessing needs, or for research.

The purpose of this chapter is to describe the problems and methods involved in accessing older ethnic populations. A framework for access has been developed that is based on a model derived from social work and community organization. The framework was utilized in a research project that studied the health care of elderly Portuguese, Hispanic, and Vietnamese living in Northern California (Cox, 1986). The issues involved in reaching these diverse populations should be applicable to researchers and service providers attempting to reach other populations of ethnic elderly. The following description of the three populations in the original study illustrates some of the issues involved in understanding and accessing ethnic elderly.

Elderly Ethnics in California

Vietnamese

The Vietnamese were the least assimilated of the three groups, with almost all having arrived in the United States in the late 1970s. All of the 100 persons are first-generation immigrants. The median education of the group is 4.6 years and income approximately $4,170 per year. Almost all persons live in households with their children, often remaining alone and isolated during the day. With younger family members leaving the home for school or work, the older people are responsible for caring for the young children. Lacking language skills—only 2% percent spoke English—the group is at risk of depression and other emotional problems (Kamikawa, 1982). The difficulties associated with assimilation and a mourning for relatives and a country they won't see again often serves to increase a sense of despondency.

Portuguese

The Portuguese population is mainly from the Azores, the first immigrants having settled in California in the 1880s. The older persons have tended to remain in two communities in the county in which they have Portuguese churches, stores, and senior centers. Both the education (2.3 years) and income levels ($5,250) of this group are low. Younger people, as they have become assimilated to the American culture, have gradually moved away, leaving the elderly to live alone. English is a problem for a majority of these persons; they remain dependent on local ethnics to assist them with the use of services. A sense of ethnic identity is reinforced through the popular media by Portuguese newspapers and radio stations serving the community.

Hispanics

The Hispanic population in the study was primarily from Mexico, although approximately half of the respondents were born in California. The majority had no difficulty speaking English although they tended to use Spanish in the home. Of the three samples, the Hispanics had the highest median education (7.8 years) and income ($8,210). The Hispanic population is located in specific areas of the county in which there are many ethnic stores and churches. As the geographic areas are large, they have tended to remain heterogeneous in terms of age and social class. Younger people have not moved out of the community and thus may be more available to the older persons. At the same time, all of the formal social service and health care agencies have bilingual staffs.

Each of the three groups of elderly has maintained a strong sense of ethnic identity through their use of the mother tongue and maintenance of cultural traditions. These are supported in the community by ethnic media, churches, services, and in some instances bilingual providers.

Accessing the Ethnic Elderly

As a means of accessing these three groups for the research project, the following framework was developed. A description of the major stages of the access process that was evolved can make it utilizable as a guideline for application to other ethnic populations. These stages of access are

1. Selection of groups.
2. Understanding of cultural attitudes of the ethnic groups particularly as they may affect access.
3. Specification of geographic areas.
4. Involvment of community leaders.
5. Publicity and support.
6. Selection and training of interviewers.
7. Development of the instruments.
8. Selection of the samples.

Selection of Groups

Obviously, the first step in attempting to access specific ethnic groups is to identify the persons to be reached. This involves deciding how ethnicity for the purposes of the project will be defined and whether it will include only first-generation immigrants or also include second and third generations. Will all members of the community be included regardless of race or religion (Chinese Vietnamese, Puerto Rican Hispanics, Buddhists, and Catholics)? Is the interest primarily in older persons who have continued to adhere to cultural traditions and behaviors, such as those of language, dress, foods, and beliefs, or is it in persons who have assimilated into the dominant culture?

Decisions on the groups to be included must be made before the plan for access is developed because varying segments within the broad population can have different attitudes and behaviors. These variations need to be taken into account in the initial design of the study.

Understanding Cultural Attitudes

In developing the plan for access there must be a basic understanding of the attitudes that may affect the access process. As stated above, certain groups may feel threatened by persons asking questions, even if they are of the same ethnic background. This distrust needs to be clarified before access can be achieved. For example, many of the older Vietnamese have had terrifying experiences in Vietnam, being questioned many times in their houses by the North Vietnamese or Viet Cong. In some instances they had been promised that they would not be harmed only to have everything taken away from them later. Thus, many persons in this population remained suspicious of Vietnamese interviewers whom they did not know. In order to deal effectively with this problem, it was necessary that the respondents knew the interviewer either personally or through his or her reputation. With this sense of security the response rate greatly increased.

Suspicions toward interviewers may also develop when persons have information they are trying to conceal. If many members of an ethnic population entered the United States illegally, even if years ago, they are likely to be nonresponsive regardless of the purpose of the study. This commonly occurs within the Mexican population, where many older persons may be undocumented residents (Valle, 1983). The lack of formal documents makes these persons unwilling to respond and also impedes their use of services. Access to these elderly can be obtained only when they trust and feel secure with the interviewer.

However, if ethnic groups are seeking to obtain more services and attention from the greater community, they may be very eager to participate in studies. Although this receptivity may provide access to the community associations or leaders, it does not guarantee access to the individual respondents who may still be reluctant to provide information and continue to be suspicious of "outsiders."

For example, the leaders of the Portuguese community felt ignored by the dominant society because of a lack of ethnically sensitive services or bilingual personnel serving their elderly. They were anxious to have research done on the needs of this segment of the group. However, the isolation of the community meant that the older people themselves were often reluctant to participate. It was difficult for them to understand the relevance of the interviews to the issues and problems that concerned them.

As a means of developing a basis for understanding the culture, attitudes and needs of the Vietnamese, Hispanic, and Portuguese groups, a training workshop on these ethnic elderly was held prior to the initiation of the study. This program was aimed toward increasing the sensitivity of service providers toward the three cultures. The presenters were social workers, physicians, nurses, and professors from the Vietnamese, Hispanic, and Portuguese communities.

In addition to providing insight into the culture and needs of these populations, the training session helped to establish credibility for the project within the ethnic communities. Community leaders were made aware that the directors of the project were interested in learning about the needs of their elderly and in having this information shared with service providers. This public forum served to legitimize the intent of the research, a necessary condition for future access.

Specifying Geographic Areas

A primary issue in attempting to access ethnic communities is specifying their geographic location. Unfortunately, census data is of little assistance in this regard except in the broad classifications of ethnicity—Black, Hispanic, Asian—that may be defined by census tracts. Locating specific ethnic populations, such as the Portuguese, requires a familiarity with the community, which may be obtained through contacts with local planners and ethnic leaders. Limited funding and time frames can make the definition of the areas crucial to the design and success of the project.

In the present study community persons from each of the three groups served as resources in identifying the geographic boundaries of the populations. Spending time with these persons in the communities also familiarized the researchers with the types of housing, services, and programs. Furthermore, through these persons, informal contacts with others in the ethnic communities were made.

Involving Community Leaders

The involvement of community leaders in the study is critical to its subsequent success. These leaders are the persons who are identified within the ethnic communities as having authority and influence. In the community organization literature, they are known as the community notables (Rein & Morris, 1962). The involvement of these persons in the project further legitimizes it and can facilitate access to participants. Thus, it is an essential primary task for the researcher to identify and obtain support from these persons.

In working with ethnic populations, it is important to recognize that those persons identified as community leaders will not be the same for all ethnic groups. Cultural values affect the selection of these persons as varying traits affect the determination of status. It is imperative to learn what persons or traits are respected within the community, particularly by the elderly. For example, within the Vietnamese population the leaders were primarily men who had been heroes or respected officers in the South Vietnamese army. These were men whose history of power and importance continued in the new country, where they maintained an inherent status and respect in the community. This respect was manifested in voluntary positions they held such as president of the Vietnamese Assistance Association, president of the Parent Teachers Association, and editorial contributors to the Vietnamese newspapers. In attempting to obtain access to the Vietnamese population, it was important to involve these persons in the project and to have their active support.

Within the Portuguese community, the Catholic clergy play prominant influential roles, particularly in the lives of the older persons. Two large churches dominate the Portuguese communities and are the focus of much of the social life. The active role of the church is demonstrated in its sponsorship of a senior center staffed by Portuguese nuns. In working with the Portuguese population, a basis for extended interaction with the elderly was through the initial involvement of the clergy.

The important role played by the Catholic church in Hispanic communities has been documented many times (Clark & Anderson, 1967; Padilla, Ruiz, & Alvarez, 1975). Although its influence may decline with younger persons, the older Hispanics continue to view the church as an integral source of support, with the clergy maintaining positions of respect and authority. As with the Portuguese community, the initial involvement of the clergy provided a base for the development of the study.

Another influential group within the elderly Hispanic population are retired professionals. These persons, assimilated to the dominant culture but maintaining links with the ethnic community, are often active in civic and political affairs. The involvement of these retirees in the project served dual functions in that they had a particular status in the community and they could relate to the older persons as peers, sensitive to their needs.

Within all three of the populations, identified community leaders were incorporated into the study from its earliest planning stages. They assisted in the design of the study, the development of the instruments, and the plans for obtaining the data. This early involvement assists in making the project a community effort rather than one imposed by outside researchers (Rossi, 1969). Gelfand and Tow (1978) have described the usefulness of this type of cohesive effort in applied research in mental health settings. It creates the feeling of a team rather than that of an elitist group of outsiders. This team approach was underscored in the present project in that the directors of the study included a Portuguese professor from the local community, a Hispanic professor, and an Asian professor.

As a further means of increasing support within the communities and in order to familiarize the groups with the aims of the project, a large reception was held at the university. This was attended by university faculty members and deans of the schools involved in the project. In San Jose the university plays an important role in the community, being geographically located in the midst of these three ethnic populations. Many of the younger members of the ethnic groups are students at the university, further integrating it into the community. Being invited to a reception and meeting with the professors was viewed as an honor by the ethnic leaders. At the same time, the reception gave the staff an opportunity to stress to these persons the important roles they played in the project and the need for their assistance.

Publicity and Support

During this phase an immediate need was for publicity for obtaining ethnic interviewers and for informing the older persons about the impending interviews. Knowing beforehand that they may be contacted for an interview and that it had the sanction of respected persons in their ethnic groups could help to encourage participation. The ethnic media played a very important role in this context in all three populations. Overall, the media is an important source of information for older people, who spend a large proportion of their time listening to the radio, watching television and reading (Bosse & Eckerdt, 1981; Moss & Lawton, 1982). Within ethnic communities the media is an important link for older persons with the traditional culture and language as well as being an important source of information (Gelfand, 1986). In the present project the ethnic media played a vital role in publicizing the study through both radio announcements and newspaper articles.

The role of the church in ethnic communities has been discussed by many researchers (Moriwaki & Kobata, 1983; Kitano, 1969; Padilla et al., 1975). The church may therefore play an important role in publicizing and gaining support for projects. At the conclusion of both Portuguese and Hispanic masses, the priests discussed the research study and its aims, indicating their endorsement of it. As well as preparing persons for the possibility that they would be interviewed, these announcements also assisted in providing ethnic interviewers for the project.

Interviewers

One of the most difficult tasks encountered in the process of ethnic research is that of locating and recruiting ethnic interviewers. The interviewers are the direct link into the community. If they are not accepted by the potential respondents, access cannot be achieved.

Having interviewers of the same ethnic group as the respondents can reduce potential barriers to participation, as the respondents can more easily identify with and relate to these "insiders." These persons often have special insights, sensitivity, and credibility in relation to their particular populations. These factors may be of increased importance with older ethnic persons who maintain stronger cultural traditions than the younger population and who may also be less willing to accept outsiders.

This specific project required three groups of interviewers, Vietnamese, Portuguese, and Hispanic. However, within these ethnic groups are particular cultural distinctions that could also impede access. Chinese Vietnamese, Portuguese-speaking persons from Brazil or Portugal, rather than from the Azores, and Hispanics from countries other than Mexico could be unacceptable to the majority of the elderly. The dialects and traditions of these persons are not necessarily congruent with those of the respondents. In this interviewer-selection phase, it is imperative that their fluency in the mother tongue and their dialect be evaluated by a member of the ethnic group to determine its compatibility with the population in the study.

The interviewers were interviewed in both English and their mother tongue. As might be anticipated, the greatest problem was in obtaining qualified Vietnamese interviewers. Most of these persons were still in the process of learning English themselves, so there was uncertainty with their level of comprehension of the training and instructions. All of the training was done in English.

Traditions and customs of the ethnic groups can affect the interviewing and research process. The Vietnamese have an attitude of traditional Asian deference to others. This affected their subsequent interviewing behavior in that they would often say that they understood instructions when they did not. As an example, one Vietnamese interviewer completed 20 interviews in 2 days. Wanting to satisfy the researchers, he had hired two relatives to assist with the interviewing, not understanding that only those persons who had been selected and trained were qualified as interviewers.

Within all three ethnic groups it was difficult to get persons to adhere to schedules. Interviews expected by certain dates were routinely late. Schedules and time frames do not have the same importance to other groups that they have to researchers. This lack of congruence can result in much frustration in the latter group, which is attempting to adhere to a specific schedule. An understanding of ethnic differences and cultural attitudes in respect to these factors can allow accommodations to be made to prevent subsequent problems.

Throughout the interview and data collection process it is essential that the interviewers be closely monitored. Ties need to be maintained with the staff so that questions can be immediately answered. The amount of needed supervision will depend on the sophistication and experience of the interviewers. In the present study, the relative lack of experience meant a great deal of supervision was required.

In working with interviewers it is a prerequisite to understand their attitudes toward the elderly. In the three populations of this study all of the groups had a traditional sense of respect and filial piety toward older people. Therefore, in training the interviewers, it was not necessary to discuss with them how to approach the elders. In fact, after initial pretesting of the instruments, it became necessary to train persons in terminating or shortening interviews. Once having established rapport, the tendency of many of the older persons was to attempt to keep the interviewer as long as possible. Cultural deference to the aged made it difficult for these interviewers to interrupt the responses, often making the interviews several hours long.

Developing the Instruments

In developing the instruments, attention must be given to the relevancy, structure, and complexity of the questions. The items must be culturally relevant to the populations so that inaccurate responses and interpretations of questions do not result. In a study (Dohrenwend & Dohrenwend, 1969) of psychopathology among Puerto Rican, Jewish, Irish, and Black respondents in New York City, the Puerto Ricans consecutively scored higher in disturbance. Dohrenwend and Dohrenwend's conclusion was that this reflected their cultural tendency to express distress rather than their actual higher rate of illness.

Other problems in cross-cultural research can result if the questions do not mean the same in English as in the mother tongue. The usual technique in preparing questionnaires in another language is to have the questions written first in English, translated into the mother tongue and then translated by another person into English (Sinnott, Harris, Block, Collesano, & Jacobson, 1983). This gives some assurance that the meaning of the questions is congruent across groups. Throughout this process the interview questions must be sensitive to the values and mores of the respondents. If they are considered offensive, rapport can be difficult to maintain and further access into the community impeded. Thus, obtaining accurate data from elderly persons on sexuality or intimate relationships may be difficult. Researchers need to balance the importance of gathering data on sensitive issues with the threat of offending respondents and thwarting future access.

The design of the questions is also an important factor in the interview process. Most ethnic elderly are not familiar with multiple-choice questions or scaling. Reducing the number of possible categories for answers can ease the interview task. The use of closed categories in conjunction with probing for further descriptions can provide meaningful data while being more easily answered by the respondents. Including several open-ended questions, although more difficult to code, provides ethnic elderly with the opportunity to give responses and information that may have been overlooked. These responses can also increase the rapport with the interviewer.

Selection of the Sample

As in all research, the type of sample used needs to reflect the purposes of the study. However, researchers attempting to study elderly ethnic populations often encounter obstacles in their sampling design. The optimal design for most studies is that of a random sample because it best reflects the issues and problems of the whole population. But in working with ethnic groups, recruiting a completely random sample can be a formidable if not impossible task. Both financial and time limitations may prohibit door-to-door canvassing, and cultural attitudes and traditions can influence the participation of respondents. Those who do agree to participate may differ significantly from nonparticipants particularly in their degree of assimilation to the dominant culture. Moreover, letters of support provided by the interviewer or mailed prior to the interview are of no assistance if the potential respondent is illiterate or has vision problems that make reading difficult or impossible.

The most efficient type of sampling may be purposive. In this sense ethnic elderly are selected in a random manner from the available membership lists of ethnic associations, churches, and agencies. The basic assumption must be made that the persons known to these programs do not differ significantly from other ethnic elderly. Within insulated ethnic communities, this assumption may be more valid than in those where there has been much assimilation. As an example, the Vietnamese elderly, selected from the lists of the resettlement agency and the Vietnamese Association of the Elderly were assumed by the resettlement and refugee personnel to be representative of most elderly Vietnamese in the area. To determine generalizability of findings, comparisons can also be made between demographic characteristics such as income, education, marital status, health status of the selected group with data on other samples of the same ethnic population.

Summary and Conclusions

Research into ethnic communities, particularly that relevant to the needs of the older ethnic members, is often impeded by barriers that prevent access to this group. Cultural traditions, attitudes, mistrust, and a suspiciousness of outsiders are some of the factors contributing to these barriers. However, as described in this chapter, through careful planning and the involvement of the ethnic community, access can be achieved.

It may not be necessary in all instances to follow each of the stages outlined in this chapter. However, adherence to certain fundamental factors would appear to be necessary for the successful development of the project.

Fundamental to the access process is the establishment by the researcher of a working relationship with the ethnic community leaders. This relationship should involve these persons in the project from its earliest phases, as this involvement provides credibility to the study and a basis for future access. It is important that the community accept the purposes of the research and its proposed outcomes and believe in the integrity of the researchers. In this project this was achieved through a training workshop prior to the study aimed at sensitizing service providers to the needs of the ethnic populations. However, meetings with local leaders and older persons regarding the purposes of the intended project may also be an effective means of obtaining community support and involvement.

Researchers must be continually sensitive to the values and norms of the ethnic group. This sensitivity is critical in all phases of the project, including the development of the instruments, the selection and training of the interviewers in their patterns of work, and the recruitment of the sample. A lack of awareness or sensitivity to these values can in itself be a barrier to access. It must also be recognized that older persons may adhere more closely to traditional values than do the younger members of the ethnic community, so obtaining the approval of the younger generation does not in itself guarantee the participation of the elders. Using interviewers whom these persons trust can assist in dispelling their resistance and improving the chances for access. Again, the selection of these acceptable interviewers requires both knowledge and sensitivity to the values of the community, which can be acquired through close relationships with the ethnic group.

In conducting studies of ethnic elderly, a willingness to accept less than a perfect random sample of the population is important. As described in this chapter, many factors impede the development of such a design. However, the lack of such purity should not inhibit the research process. Researchers must be willing to use purposive samples and to make comparisons and generalizations from them. Creative efforts and risks are essential if data on the issues and problems confronting these ethnic populations are to be obtained.

Access into older ethnic populations can be a challenging and slow process, requiring careful planning and the coordination of many groups. But as the needs of the ethnic elderly remain unclear and often unmet, efforts to access these populations must continue. The stages of access described in this chapter are presented as a guideline for such efforts, emphasizing many of the factors that must be considered in the process. Using this guideline, new and innovative strategies for reaching these populations of elderly can be developed.

13

Being Old and Greek in America

Kathryn A. Kozaitis

Greeks in the United States

The Greek-American community is the largest population of Greeks outside the mother country itself (Saloutos, 1980), and Chicago is reputed to host a population of Greeks second only to that of Salonica, the second largest city of Greece. Immigration to the United States came chiefly in two waves. The first, fueled by an increasing population in Greece and increasing scarcity of resources toward the end of the 19th century and afterward, continued from 1900 into the 1920s. The majority of these immigrants were unskilled men who expected to return to their families in Greece with money earned in the United States, but only half actually returned. This wave also included poor women who sought husbands in a country where dowries were not required. The second wave came after World War II, particularly after the 1965 Immigration Act ended the quota system. This group included more educated, professionally or technically trained individuals from Athens and central Greece. Predominantly, however, this group included women and children, families that came with intentions of settling in the United States in order to take advantage of economic and educational opportunities (Saloutos, 1980).

Individuals in both waves of immigration share many traits that serve as markers of Chicago Hellenism. Coming from bleak rural backgrounds, many new Chicagoans sought economic independence in the establishment of small businesses. The Chicago Greek often started out shining shoes, waiting on tables, or peddling fruit or flowers; later he would use his hard-earned savings to buy a small business, such as a confectionery, a produce business, a floral shop, a dry cleaning shop, or some sort of food-service establishment (Moskos, 1980).

In general, the Greek-American community in Chicago has excelled at maintaining its separate cultural identity while achieving great success in the business sectors of American society (Kopan, 1982). Yet many Greeks, especially recent immigrants, continue to find themselves in a problematic sociocultural continuum that often impinges their otherwise functional existence. As the present study reveals, for a significant sample of elderly Greeks in Chicago, "worst of two worlds" more accurately describes their plight, taking into account their inability and unwillingness to participate in a fruitful retirement as defined by American culture and the lack of culturally appropriate contexts and resources in which to practice in-group values and aging patterns as defined by the participants themselves. It is the mission of this study to examine the influence that common heritage, collective identity, shared history, traditional rituals and customs, common language, and similar life-styles has on how elderly Greeks perceive and experience aging, what expectations they have from their community, and what strategies they employ to resolve problems intrinsic to aging.

Chicago's "Greek Town"

The Greek population of Chicago has been estimated at about 250,000. One neighborhood, however, stands out as being predominantly Greek in character, that of the Ravenswood area of Chicago's northside. This community became the home of many of Chicago's immigrants when the "Greek Town" of more than half a century at Halsted was displaced in the 1960s by the construction of the University of Illinois at Chicago (Kopan, 1981). Centered at the intersection of Lawrence and Western Avenues, two major thoroughfares, this community's own "downtown" is defined by Greek bakeries, Greek grocery stores, Greek coffeehouses, Greek gift shops, and a Greek bridal shop. Numerous other Greek-owned enterprises, including beauty salons, a nightclub, a flower shop, doctors' offices, and dry cleaning shops, also characterize this Greek-American community. Many of the non-Greek businesses hire Greek employees, and all places of business, from drugstores to banks, are filled with the distinctive conversation of their Greek patrons. The unifying focus of any Greek-American community is the Orthodox church, and St. Demetrios serves the needs of this growing community of Greek immigrants.

Elderly in Greek Town

The primary objectives of the present study were to assess the needs of Greek elderly relative to senior citizen status, and to investigate their respective adjustment patterns and coping strategies. The settings where these seniors assemble regularly became the central sites for observation and data collection. These include the Office of Hellenic Family and Community Services (HFCS), a local, nonprofit agency devoted to meeting the needs of Greek Americans; the Joseph and Sarah Levy Center, a senior recreational facility located at the center of the community; and the Hollywood House, a Greek-owned and -operated retirement residence on the northside of Chicago. Though outside the boundaries of the study community, Hollywood House is populated largely by Greek elderly (32%) and houses the administrative office of HFCS. Other observation sites include the "Young-At-Heart" biweekly socials held at St. Demetrios, the weekly "Rap Session" organized by HFCS conducted at the Levy Center, and the local coffeehouses, where elderly men leisurely shared their impressions and experiences about old age in America.

This study is based on 10 months of field research conducted from September 1983 through May 1984 and during July and August 1985. The ethnographic techniques employed include participant observation in organized activities, careful monitoring of focal samples and ad lib contacts, and both structured and unstructured interviews with primary informants. Issue-focused discussions in informants' homes, informal yet issue-oriented conversations with elderly individuals in public places and accidental data gathering at bus stops, park benches, restaurants, and waiting lines in banks—where subjects were often unaware of a Greek-speaking listener—also contributed to the data collection process.

The degree of acquaintance with the subjects varied. Formal, 2-to-3-hr interview sessions were conducted with most respondents. With others only a couple of 1-hr arranged meetings occurred, during which only topic-oriented questions were addressed. Spontaneous revelations by respondents at impromptu meetings also contributed valuable and relevant information.

The focal samples of the 164 respondents include the 59 Young-At-Heart participants, 12 Rap Session participants, 63 Hollywood

House residents, and 19 individuals who identified themselves as clients of HFCS. In addition, there were approximately 20 ad lib contacts at St. Demetrios' Sunday coffee hours, community socials, their children's homes, public businesses, and cultural events. One hundred eight participants were women and 46 were men. Their ages ranged from 61 to 94 years, but most of the respondents' ages fell between 65 and 78 years.

Of the 164 participants, 23 fall in the category of Americanized Greeks, i.e., either they were born in the United States or immigrated here at the turn of the century as youths or adolescents. Eleven of these respondents report minimal primary school education. Only nine men attest to formal education or professional training, and three women report having completed high school. The second category consists of 93 Greek Americans, primarily widows who immigrated to the United States before World War II in their twenties as brides of early immigrants. With the exception of one woman who had completed 3 years of secondary schooling in Greece, the rest of the respondents report 2 to 5 years of elementary schooling. The third group consists of recent immigrants, i.e., individuals who immigrated to the United States with young families in the late 1950s and 1960s and those who arrived during the 1970s in order to join their children in the United States. The respondents in this category report 2 to 5 years of primary schooling. All respondents identified themselves as permanent residents of the United States. It should be noted that though this is not a random sample, it is a cohesive group of Greek elderly, uniquely appropriate for the microfocus and issue-oriented approach of this research project.

Intracultural Diversity and the Greek Elderly

During the early stages of the field research, it became apparent that the sample of Greeks under investigation did not constitute "*the* Greek elderly." The community is clearly not homogeneous. The members of this elderly community share only two characteristics: a common heritage and a chronological life stage. Correspondingly, their attitudes and their needs vary according to the degree of their acculturation to American mainstream values. Another characteristic that varies significantly is the degree of proficiency in the English and/or Greek languages, a crucial indicator of ability to function socially outside Greek boundaries. The dominant dialect used by the group may be characterized as "Greeklish," a form of Greek liberally interspersed with Hellenized English words. Consequently, all of the interviews and discussions with informants were conducted in this dialect. Whenever this author addressed a group in the role of guest speaker, group facilitator, or researcher, standard modern Greek was used, much to the satisfaction and admiration of the listeners.

Americanized Greeks

The first category of elderly is composed of 23 Americanized Greeks. These respondents identify themselves as relatively healthy, expressing feelings of economic security, satisfaction with life in general, and a comfortable orientation to American mainstream values concerning retirement. Independence, self-reliance, and self-determinism were concepts that *they* used to describe their present life course. They identified family propinquity, financial security, and good health as the determining factors in good retirement. The members of this group express an appreciation for an active life, and a keen awareness of services available to seniors, and they indicate frequent participation in community events and membership in Hellenic professional organizations as well as self-initiated social gatherings.

Many of the conversations focused on their place in the spectrum of Greek ethnicity and preference in leisuretime activity. These individuals express a preference for Greek-affiliated social outlets, claim membership in almost exclusively Greek-American professional societies and organizations, and remark that they are more likely to participate in community affairs organized by and for Greeks rather than non-Greek events. Although they relate a definite preference for a Greek-affiliated social life, they insist that such is not a mandatory qualification. They are perfectly comfortable, adjusted, and capable of functioning in non-Greek settings, but, as one man explained, "When you are with your own it's different, better, more meaningful," a sentiment very much representative of other respondents' points of view. This group of people conceives of Greekness primarily in terms of heritage, of Greece as their country of birth, and their ethnic status is only incidental to the way they design and conduct their lives. They do not identify with contemporary Greeks. Rather, they have romantic images of Greece and often relate idyllic and nostalgic reminiscences of their experience as tourists in Greece. All of the respondents explained that at some point earlier in their lives they had contemplated returning to Greece to retire, but they now unanimously agree that "Greece is not equipped to accommodate old people."

Perhaps the most important finding reflecting the world view of this group is their exhibition of balance in the dichotomy of ideal and real behavior. They demonstrate a thorough sense of self and an awareness of their privileges and limitations as elderly people in the United States. They understand the appropriate coping mechanisms, are informed of available resources, whether endogenous or exogenous, and possess the skills and inclination to use them. Irrespective of their ethnic identity as Greeks, culturally they exhibit a strong mainstream American orientation in values and attitudes, and maintain a life-style consistent with this code.

This orientation was most prominently demonstrated by a group of eight men in their eighties who claim to be healthy, spirited, and active. As Greeks, they thrive on long, leisurely conversations with other Greeks, the chance to speak the Greek language, and the accompaniment of good food. At the same time, their American socialization has equipped them with the initiative to schedule weekly lunch dates downtown, the inclination to assemble in a non-Greek restaurant, and the ability to discuss current events in Greek, of which they become informed by American media. Their attitude toward mobility allows them to maintain their friendship despite the fact that they live in different communities and offers opportunities to take advantage of non-Greek "goods and services."

The acculturated women also report a flexible participation in both Greek and American activities. Although many admit to limiting their leisuretime activities to church-affiliated organizations such as the Ladies' Philoptochos Society (Friends of the Poor), others report providing volunteer services to local hospitals, nursing homes, and social service agencies, roles that require English-language skills, independent transportation arrangements, and value orientations that reinforce an independent, active, and productive retirement. Furthermore, the men and women in the first focal sample report a far greater interest and participation in cultural and social events and in domestic and international travel than do their unacculturated counterparts. Their accounts reflect a conflict-free, fulfilling retirement and a life-style that combines Greek and American aspects that allow them to function fruitfully in both cultures.

Greek Americans

The second group of elderly consists primarily of widows who often refer to themselves as Greek Americans. Most of them are members of the St. Demetrios Young-At-Heart senior citizen club and the weekly Rap Session and are residents of the Hollywood House. As a group they exhibit the greatest degree of marginality. Often they describe themselves as being in a dilemma or state of mental conflict by reason of inevitable confrontation with two different, often contradictory cultural milieus. The domestic work orientation, sheltered existence, marital dependency, and self-sacrifice that characterized all of their adult lives has not prepared them for a life stage free of child-rearing responsibilities, domestic burdens, and "husband-tending." Quite suddenly most of these women find themselves regretfully wondering, "How does time pass now?" In one group interview, nine women disclosed two of the most powerful obstacles to an enjoyable retirement, namely, guilt and shame. Not only are they aware of the American ideal retirement occupations such as extradomestic work, volunteering commitments, travel, arts and crafts classes, and participation in the numerous social, cultural, and recreational activities available through local community centers, but they consider them quite attractive and admirable. Although they view the beneficiaries of such goods and services as "privileged," when they are questioned about their hesitancy to follow their example they describe the same activities as frivolous, selfish, ostentatious, and "inappropriate." In the pathetic lament, "Those things are not for us," one easily perceives a helpless note of envy, regret, and hopelessness.

This group clearly exhibits both unawareness of and correspondingly limited adaptation to mainstream American patterns of aging. Ideally, they *aspire* to such values as independence, future orientation, high activity level, and self-cultivation but clearly lack the language skills, awareness of available resources, and confidence and inclination to pursue these desired ends. For example, when questioned about how they prefer to spend their leisure time, three of five women in one group responded with very vague answers such as "going out, seeing people, doing things," indicating a desire to be socially active but a timid resistance and an unwillingness to participate in community senior citizen services and make use of available resources. When questioned about their actual use of leisure time, the same women admitted that most of their time is spent at home involved in household chores, sewing, knitting, watching television, and listening to the "Greek Hour" on the radio. Actual outside activities consist of church attendance on Sundays, and 3-to-4-hr Young-At-Heart gatherings, which consist solely of bingo playing for the women and card playing for the men. It is no wonder that most of the women describe these meetings as "something to do but often boring." The church is obviously the primary social center of this group. It should be emphasized that the high participation in church-affiliated events is not to be attributed exclusively to the spiritual function of the church but rather on the ethnicity factor. What attracts them to church as a social center is the familiarity and cultural identification with the setting—a place where "we find our own."

A high interest in social activities, senior organizations, and cultural events was consistently expressed, provided that these programs were organized by Greeks and exclusively with Greeks in mind. Members of this group complained that "the community" (referring to Chicago's population of Greeks) and the Greek agency are not providing enough or adequate services for the elderly. Participation in non-Greek social programs and utilization of non-Greek formal supports is practically nonexistent. For example, the Levy Center, a very comprehensive social and recreational facility for elderly located in the heart of the Greek community, is minimally used. Although the center is geographically accessible to the Greeks, the only times that they visit the facility are when the HFCS holds the biannual dinner dances at the center's social hall and to attend the weekly Rap Sessions. The reasons given by a number of informants for not using the center more frequently included feelings of alienation, unwillingness to take part in non-Greek activities, and most important, being *unable* to participate in the type of recreation available. For example, participation in the Book Club requires command of the English language, a skill that this group of Greek elderly lack. Furthermore, dance classes, fitness and nutrition programs, and trips to art institutes are activities whose value is not recognized or appreciated by this group of elderly.

The difficulty in relating to activities with a mainstream orientation was exemplified by the great discrepancy between the prescribed mission of the Monday afternoon Rap Sessions, as defined by the agency, and what was actually accomplished by the members during the meetings. Participation in the group is open to anyone interested, so the number of individuals varies weekly but usually includes about ten women and a couple of men only sporadically. The prescribed purpose of the group is to encourage the participants to express "feelings" on a particular issue or problem suggested by a member of the group. Participants are expected to take turns and share with the group their feelings on an agreed-on subject without interruptions. The intent of the session is not to engage the participants in a discussion. Rather, focus is on individual disclosures, often of a personal nature. Each meeting is organized by an American-born volunteer who, under sponsorship of the HFCS, had been trained to "facilitate" such "encounter groups." Her duties include restating the mission and method of the Rap Session at the beginning of *each* meeting. Despite this, the participants persistently transform the process into an unstructured melange of opinions, reminiscences, and gossip, often in the form of a discussion. Occasionally a number of people all speak at once, ignoring one another's comments. The facilitator consistently interrupts and attempts to redirect the group to its intended purpose, usually without success.

The men and the women often comment on how glad they are to have a place to meet on Monday afternoon but complain about the rules of the meetings. They do not wish to be restricted by having to come up with a topic or necessarily concentrate on one suggested by another participant. Expressing feelings about personal matters is not encouraged in the Greek culture, particularly by women, and especially to strangers, a designation given to anyone outside the nuclear and extended families. The public image orientation so characteristic of Greek culture does not permit honest, intimate revelations of emotions, especially dissatisfactions and needs. The individuals who attend the Monday afternoon session having their own ideas of what they want and need from the meeting. They seek company, a social outlet where they can see other Greeks, "something to do." The group unanimously appreciates having the space arranged by HFCS but is unable to conform to the objectives of the meeting. Consequently, the Rap Sessions are not used for their intended purpose but for a culturally meaningful one as defined by the participants.

All of the respondents describe themselves as either financially secure or "secure enough to live well." Although financial matters do not appear to be an overriding concern, at least for the present, many participants express anxiety and puzzlement about coping with future problems such as extended care. The younger respondents in this group deny the importance of planning for later life and often react with such remarks as "We have time" or "It is too early to think of old age now" or "I hope not to live long enough to suffer and to need extended care."

When questioned about options relative to functioning during the more frail aging stages, most were at a loss for words. They were clearly unprepared for what may await them in their later years. To many this issue brought tears to their eyes. A few widowers said that they hoped to spend old age with their children, mostly because of their inability to be self-reliant. However, most of the respondents explained that living with their children would be undesirable either because the move would necessitate a separation from their community of friends and their church congregation of 30 or so years or because they feared being a burden on their children. Some even expressed a desire to live alone, admitting that the hectic life-style of the young family would be a burden on their own life.

Of crucial importance are the reasons many of the women give for their "position of disadvantage." They emphasize repeatedly that their failure earlier in life to take the necessary acculturation measures such as learning the English language and obtaining a driver's license are responsible for their current problematic existence. As one 65-year-old woman regretfully remarked, "We paralyzed ourselves out of ignorance and backwardness so that we could accommodate the wishes of our husbands and to protect our name." Others repeated the prevailing attitude of this generation toward change: "Those things are not for us." They resigned themselves to a *separate* existence that may have served feasibly during young adulthood and middle age but is clearly obstacle-ridden now. Their current life stage demands skills for a socially *integrated* life-style, one that minimizes limitations to social functioning and that would optimize life satisfaction.

Recent Immigrants

The third group of elderly comprises the category of the recent immigrants, i.e., those who arrived in the United States during the period between the late 1950s and the present. A predominant majority of the elderly in this group immigrated to Chicago in their thirties and forties from a rural environment. They came from a nonindustrialized, nonmechanized, agrarian economy that had a conservative code of moral conduct and a social climate with a tightly defined prescription of sex role behavior. Short of religious services on Sundays, a typical day centers around the home, the family, listening to the "Greek Hour" on the radio, and neighborhood visits. The single most serious problem reported by this group was the language barrier. As one man said, "Without language you are a nobody," a sentiment expressed by many. Lack of control and self-government, feelings of helplessness, and a correspondingly fatalistic orientation characterize the world view of these elderly immigrants. Their disposition is passive and their temperament predictable. Decision processes are strongly linked to the ways of the "fatherland," and efforts to adapt to the new, often threatening ways of the new land are minimal. Opinions, judgments, and points of view are placed in the framework of how things are done in

Greece, or at least how they remember things to have been in the village when they left it.

The need for a community network is vital to this group. The village life that provided them with personal safety, security, support networks, familiar townsmen and environment, homogeneity of value orientations and codes of conduct, and control in housing matters is a far cry from the isolated and restricted existence they maintain in this country. The message clearly communicated by this group of elders is that their adaptation patterns are not only of a cultural nature but of an environmental one as well. The transition from a Greek way of life to an American one is only complicated by adjustments demanded by an urban setting, one in direct contradiction to the way of life in rural Greece.

Value conflict between some of these elderly and their children is an additional burden. The second generation, with its American-born offspring, has acculturated to a significant degree, which often places them in a conflicting situation with their aging parents. Those individuals who came from Greece in the 1970s to live with their children because of economic and functional difficulties express much helplessness and distress. They perceive their status as that of a "permanent guest," a burden that no proud Greek can carry easily. Unlike the respondents in the first and second categories who live alone, a number of the very recent immigrants are forced to live with their children, who have already moved to the suburbs. Their dependent status and lack of freedom and autonomy are in contrast to the living arrangements of the elderly as they knew it in Greece, where one of the children lives in the parental home, not the other way around. The accommodations that some of these elderly are confronted with in this country deprive them of self-respect, integrity, and their much cherished liberty.

Dependence on their children, however, is not only of an economic nature. One male key respondent, who often complained about having been placed in "a jail with open doors," referring to his son's suburban home, explained that he and many of his widowed buddies must live with their children so that their daughters or daughters-in-law may accommodate their daily needs. Respondents from this group, whether living with their children or alone, express a great deal of loneliness, more so than respondents in the other two groups. As one woman remarked during an afternoon tea at a neighbor's home, "Loneliness in a foreign country is unbearable. In Greece, even when you are alone, the sun and the clean air keep you company; you are never lonely."

This group of elderly is least likely to use available services or to participate in social events. Although they admit to experiencing economic, functional, and psychological problems, these elderly do not reach out to formal support systems, either because they are not aware of available services or because expressing a need for professional help is considered "shameful" within the Greek value system. Three women admitted that they are forbidden by their children to request outside support. Most of these elderly remarked that they do not understand the concept of social work, nor do they know what their rights and benefits as elderly are or how to initiate contact with support systems. They are not vocal about their needs; they attribute their plight to fate and continue to lead a stressful and passive existence.

In contrast to the other two groups, participants in the third category perceive their destiny to be strongly in the hands of their children. Their fears of the future have as much to do with financial concerns as with dying alone in a strange (non-Greek) place. The problems experienced by these individuals are much more complex, more serious, less easily resolved, and fewer culturally meaningful remedies are available. The difficulties they are confronted with daily result from their relatively recent immigration status, which isolates them from potential resources. Their cultural orientation, which does not permit self-determination, independence, and self-reliance, exacerbates problems associated with their aging process significantly and leaves them with few if any alternatives and appropriate remedies.

The findings reveal that an immigrant's experience with aging is significantly influenced by country of origin, point of entry to the United States, and processes of acculturation and integration to the mainstream American social system. Each of the three groups of elderly identified is at different points along the continuum of acculturation from Greek to American values and behavioral patterns. Correspondingly, each group exhibits different needs, problems, and patterns of aging. The segmented acculturative continuum strongly correlates with how aging is perceived and how relative problems are confronted. The American-oriented individuals exhibit a high degree of integration, flexibility, and positive adjustment, whereas the intermediate transitionals disclose a visibly disoriented and insecure disposition. The more recent immigrants admit to feelings of helplessness, fear, and bewilderment about growing old, and they demonstrate minimal effort toward altering their destiny.

Among the elderly Greeks in Chicago the level of acculturation is also related to the use of social services. Those Greeks born in the

United States or who immigrated here at a young age utilize such formal supports as government agencies, senior clubs, and social organizations, especially when these are affiliated with the Greek community. The middle group of immigrants relies heavily on church-affiliated activities, and expresses a definite need for more Greek-based support systems. The recent immigrants, confronted with serious problems of alienation and adjustment, report consistent underutilization of services relative to their needs. This latter group relies primarily on the family for support, which often is inadequately skilled or unavailable. They attribute underutilization of professional services to culturally insensitive programs, values and attitudes relative to help seeking, lack of familiarity with the process and procedures of professional services, the language barrier, and unawareness of available resources. It is clear that the culturally integrated, functional orientation of the first group, the marginal status of the middle group, and the socially peripheral position of the third group significantly affects how ethnic aging is experienced and how these elderly Greeks confront the problems associated with this life stage. It is concluded that ethnic aging must be conceptualized not only by the membership of elderly persons in a given ethnic group but also by the significant intracultural variation present within any given ethnic population of elders.

Intervention Strategies with Greek Elderly

The continuum of acculturation from values of the mother country to those of the host nation among the older Greeks interviewed forces reconsideration of the overall strategy for meeting the needs of socioculturally diverse aging groups. The need for increased and improved services to the aged in this Greek community is obvious, but the implementation of relevant and culturally appropriate services is partly contingent on the attitudinal orientations of the Greek community at large. Fundamentally, the establishment of necessary services is prohibited by virtue of the scarcity of Greek bilingual/bicultural helping professionals, particularly social workers. Given this reality, should such scarce resources be directed toward attempts at meeting the particular needs of each group previously outlined, or could efforts be better spent on strategies designed to close the marginality gap by teaching basic skills conducive to *bi-functionalism* within American society and institutions?

One approach might be to recommend intervention strategies for "situational acculturation" on the rationale that it is an impossibility to provide culturally tailored services to an infinitely diverse client population. However, this rationale may not be appropriate for older persons. Acculturation strategies may be the preferred approach with younger individuals for whom the investment is rewarded by a lifetime of necessary and useful transactions with American social institutions. However, for an elderly population, the rewards do not appear great enough to encourage and promote participation in acculturation strategies on the part of potential clients with a limited life expectancy. Correspondingly, intervention approaches must be of a somewhat palliative or ameliorative nature, with programs designed to increase the comfort of the remainder of their lives to as great an extent as indigenous resources will allow. Since a comprehensive Greek nursing facility remains an excessively ambitious project, more culturally meaningful programs must be implemented with the needs and aspirations of today's aged in mind. The following recommendations for short-term interventions are suggested in response to the immediacy of currently expressed needs of the study community:

1. Institute an "umbrella agency" to administer and coordinate services ranging from information and referral to socialization programs, counseling services, and short- and long-term medical care in the center of this Greek enclave.
2. Mobilize a large volunteer unit to provide home visitors, interpreters, and shopping and transportation assistants.
3. Provide a social recreational drop-in center conveniently close to community residents.
4. Establish a day-care facility for Greek children of working parents where elderly may function as caretakers, transmitters of Greek culture, and teachers of arts and crafts to successive generations of Greek-American youth.
5. Staff all programs with professionally trained bilingual–bicultural service agents, administrators, and policymakers.
6. Include input by representatives of the aged community in the policy and planning stages of service provision.

Appropriately implemented, these recommendations point the way to an increase and an improvement of culturally relevant services for the present community of Greek elders. The preference for this approach is dictated by both the urgency of the problems and its ameliorative emphasis. Ideally, a "cure" might be thought of as independent and successful functioning within American society, although *not* necessarily at the expense of surrendering in-group values, customs, and traditions. The objective is to minimize a socially marginal status and the stresses of cultural boundary crossing, and to maximize *bi-functionalism,* the eclectic participation in both cultures as social situations demand.

Intervention and Prevention

Because this remains an ideal state for a largely struggling elderly community today, long-term *preventive measures* for future generations of Greek elderly must not be overlooked. Given the fact that it takes time to implement acculturation strategies, and even more time to yield desirable results, it behooves the policy and program planners to confront the needs of increasing elderly populations by intervening with the ethnic *aging* long before they become the *aged.* As many of the elderly respondents in this study admitted, "If only we knew better; if someone had warned us, we would have learned to mobilize ourselves, to drive, to learn the language, to become involved!" These laments suggest a call for strategies to warn younger generations of marginal individuals of the necessity for acculturation so that *they* "will know better." For every 70-year-old widow interviewed in this study who does not speak English, cannot manage private or public transportation, is confined to a life of "disengagement," and is unable to make use of available resources, there are five or more Greek housewives, aged 40, who also are not proficient in English or cannot function outside the boundaries of their church community. As was revealed by their older counterparts, many middle-age persons do not feel the pressure to acquire functioning skills, failing to consider what their needs will be in 30 to 40 years. The forecast revealed in this case study calls for recommendations aimed at cultivating in those individuals of Greek descent who currently maintain a nonintegrative existence initiative and responsibility for future planning relative to old age. Such preventive measures are intended to minimize unnecessary difficulties during the late, more frail stages of life and to assure a culturally richer, more active, and conflict-free retirement for successive generations of Greek immigrants.

Conclusion: Ethnicity, Aging, and Bi-functionalism

The implications about ethnicity and aging inferred from this case study suggest new avenues for addressing the problems of ethnic aging in general. The most important general principle to be learned from this study is that "American ethnicity" as a social label is not merely a singular concept of separateness or boundary maintenance. Rather, it defines a continuum of adaptive capabilities and levels of acculturation on the part of people ranging from individuals socially and functionally isolated from American society to those who relate with ease to the cultures and institutions of both host and mother nations. Thus, in order to understand a given segment of the population, as an end in itself or for the planning of services, it is not enough to know merely that it is "ethnic" or more specifically, Greek or Italian, because these terms describe such a wide range of individuals. This study suggests that a meaningful understanding of a given population includes knowledge of the immigration wave in which the individuals took part, their rural or urban background in the country of origin, degree of their isolation within a geographic enclave, settlement patterns, participation in the labor force, command of the English language, level of education, economic security, and success or satisfaction in cross-cultural boundary crossing. One might further surmise that any other ethnic population that matches the Greek community in such factors as agrarian background in the country of origin, lack of English-language skills, and lack of education would be expected to exhibit similar needs and to benefit from social programs similar to those designed for the Greeks. This hypothesis should be tested by further ethnographic research in other communities that have relevant demographic profiles.

It is expected that programs designed to acculturate and socialize elderly persons of non-American origin would meet resistance, and this study has documented that non-Greek ideas and services were vigorously rejected by the group interviewed as being "not for us." This study also reveals that the provision of services tailored to each of the different needs of the multifaceted Greek elderly population is beyond the resources of this particular ethnic community. Therefore, the more "curative" approach would be the long-term one of providing acculturation services to the middle-age ethnic populations who are at risk of becoming problematic elderly. In this respect, this community study acts as a lesson for populations of any ethnic affiliation, particularly populations where indigenous resources are at a premium, making more short-term culturally sensitive and ameliorative efforts very costly, albeit necessary.

It should be recognized that these recommendations are not meant to promote the "assimilation" of immigrants into American society. It makes no more sense to encourage the exchange of Greek values and attitudes for American ones than it does to socially

handicap ethnic aging individuals with culturally separate interventions grounded on such ethnocentric principles as insisting on
Greek-based transportation and meals-on-wheels services because,
as one man audaciously remarked, "Strangers [non-Greeks] cannot
be trusted." Such culturally sensitive interventions, provided they
are accessible, do little to promote the ability of clients to function
comfortably and independently within the context of American society while still maintaining their ethnic identity and their respective
cultural orientation.

A more realistic yet effective approach is one in which *bifunctionalism* is promoted, a state where an individual possesses at least
English language and driving skills and enough knowledge of the
relative customs to function in two worlds, the ethnic community
and the larger host society, when these are at variance. Old age is
inevitably burdened with physiological and psychological difficulties, natural complications that must not be exacerbated by social
functioning limitations when these can be avoided. The promotion
of an acculturated, more integrative participation in American society will not only enable ethnic elderly to celebrate their unique and
precious heritage more fully but will empower them to take advantage of a culture increasingly sensitive and accommodating to
the needs of the aged, irrespective of national origins and ethnic
affiliations.

14

Aging, Ethnicity, and Services: Empirical and Theoretical Perspectives

Zev Harel, Ed McKinney, and Michael Williams

In recent years there has been an increased concern for the well-being and/or vulnerability of elderly members of ethnic communities. The significant increase in the numbers of persons aged 65 and older and the higher percentage of older persons in the higher age groups have resulted in an increased demand and need for health and human services (Harel et al., 1985). The need to explore the importance of racial background and ethnicity for the well-being, vulnerability, and service needs of the aged becomes, therefore, more obvious. As Marjorie Cantor (1976) states in her research:

> Meaningful social planning requires precise knowledge of both the extent to which the aging process is similar for all older people and the degree to which racial, ethnic, and socioeconomic differences require varying types of community facilities and services to sustain older people independently in the community for as long as possible. (p. 242)

Only after the function of ethnicity in the lives of the elderly has been understood better, can health and human service professionals plan and organize more effective services for these elderly.

The concept of ethnicity has been defined and measured in a variety of ways. It has included concerns for membership, traditions, culture, beliefs, identification, experiences, behaviors, and practices (Gelfand & Kutzik, 1979; Hays, Kalish, & Guttmann,

1986; Mindel & Habenstein, 1981; Rosenthal, 1986). For the purposes of this chapter, ethnicity is defined as consisting of structural aspects (ethnic affiliation), cultural aspects (ethnic identity), and behavioral aspects (ethnic practices), and it is recognized that these dimensions may be useful in the assessment and discussion of ethnic individuals, groups, and communities. In this chapter, our concern is for elderly members of both ethnic and racial groups sharing an identity as related to or influenced by historical, traditional, social, cultural, religious, and language characteristics.

Operationally, ethnicity includes (a) affiliation(s) with groups and associations of ethnic or racial communities, (b) elements of ethnic identity, and (c) practices that are related to background or membership in an ethnic or racial community. This operational definition incorporates structural aspects, cultural and symbolic elements, and behavioral patterns, as suggested by Rosenthal (1986). There are many ways in which ethnicity is presumed to affect the well-being/vulnerability of the aged (Guttmann, 1979; Harel, 1986; Rosenthal, 1986). Our discussion of the effects of ethnicity will focus on the exploration and use of benefits and services by the ethnic aged.

Elderly persons who enjoy a strong association with a particular ethnic or racial group may have more sources of informal support than those having a weaker or no association (Guttmann, 1979). A strong ethnic association, therefore, would benefit the elderly ethnic. At the same time, members of ethnic and racial groups may have limited economic resources, may not know about or not intend to use benefits, even though they may be entitled to them. Furthermore, some ethnic aged may not utilize services available from organizations if they lack procedural knowledge about resources and/or if their attitudinal predisposition precludes relying on need-determined benefits from formal organizations for meeting their needs. These persons may overburden informal sources of support or often go without the assistance they need and that is available for their use.

It is therefore important to differentiate clearly between the defining elements of ethnicity, factors that determine ethnicity, and the effects and consequences of ethnicity. There is a clear need to explore the following three major questions:

1. What is the relative importance of sociodemographic and socioeconomic status, along with other factors that contribute to ethnic affiliation, ethnic identity, and ethnic practices?

2. What is the relative importance of ethnicity, along with sociodemographic and socioeconomic status and other factors, in determining the well-being, vulnerability, service need, and service use among adult and aged members of ethnic communities?

3. What is the relative importance of personal variables, along with the configuration of resource variables, in determining service initiation, service use, and service outcomes?

Well-being in this conceptual context is defined to include good health and functional status, adequate economic resources, adequate social resources, adequate coping skills, positive life perspective, adequate knowledge, and access to benefits and services. Vulnerability is defined to consist of (a) health and functional status impairment; (b) limitations on personal security (income), personal resources (coping and morale), and social integration; and (c) limitations in knowledge and access to benefits and services. Service need is defined to consist of the need for attention and assistance with personal health, personal care, personal management, and household management. In the following pages of this chapter findings from research on ethnicity and racial background related to service needs and usage of services among the aged will be reviewed, and a conceptual approach to services for the ethnic aged will be presented.

Determinants of Service Use

Research indicates that in addition to sociodemographic background, health, and functional status, knowledge about and access to benefits and services play important roles in the prediction of service utilization (Krout, 1983). Many older people are unlikely to have information about social resources and services that might directly enhance the quality of their lives (Branch, 1978). Lack of knowledge about resources and services is likely to reduce both the search for benefits and the search for information about services. Even when people have a general knowledge about available services, they may not be able to relate them to their own needs or to the needs of others around them (Harel, Noelker, & Blake, 1985). Recent research on the Older Americans Act–connected service users found considerable variation in knowledge about and access to services (Harel, 1985). In a review of research on service use by the aged, Krout (1983) concludes that the elderly's perception of services, their access to services, and their intent to use services are far from uniform and/or consistent. In examination of senior center utilization by Black elderly, Ralston (1984) found that sociodemographic variables (sex, age, and marital status), health, and transportation did not have a significant effect. Factors found important were a commitment to become involved in senior centers, perception of senior centers, and contact with family and friends.

Informal support and the interface between formal and informal support are also important determinants of service use among the elderly (Harel et al., 1985; Jackson & Harel, 1983; Krout, 1983). The informal system is more likely to provide emotional support and assistance with personal care and household management. In contrast, the formal system of public and voluntary agencies provides entitlements to housing, education, safety, and transportation, as well as health and social services (Comptroller General of the U.S., 1977).

Most older Americans have a viable and functioning informal support system. Older persons and their informal caregivers turn to formal organizations for assistance when the nature of their problems becomes too difficult for them to handle alone (Cantor, 1976; Comptroller General of the U.S., 1977). One major survey of impaired elderly found that it was a spouse or adult child caregiver who helped with personal care tasks (Noelker & Poulshock, 1982). For the older population in general, 50% of all in-home services are provided by the family, and for those who are severely impaired, the rate climbs to 80% (Comptroller General of the U.S., 1977). Anderson and her colleagues (Anderson, Patten, & Greenburg, 1980) reported that 78% of home-care service users received help from family and friends and that the informal system rendered significantly more care than did the formal organizations.

There is extensive evidence about the significance of informal support for the well-being of the aged. There is only limited evidence, however, about the ways in which membership in a racial or ethnic group determines mutual help, informal support, knowledge about and access to services, as well as attitudinal predisposition toward service utilization. In the absence of adequate empirical evidence, informational bases about the service needs of adult and aged members of racial and ethnic communities is based on assumptions and, to a very limited extent, on professional observations and research evidence.

Research has indicated that the ethnic population does not tend to take advantage of health and social services (Biegel & Sherman, 1979; Guttmann, 1979). Guttmann found that ethnic group members preferred to receive assistance from their own families. If family assistance was not possible, their next source of preferred assistance was an ethnic or church-related organization. The reason for this preference is often a lack of knowledge about the availability of resources and an unwillingness to leave the ethnic community to make use of resources available in unfamiliar surroundings. If elderly members of racial and ethnic communities do reach out for assistance and their requests are not responded to, they often may find themselves isolated both physically and mentally. This isolation may be most severe among those elderly left behind by their culturally and geographically mobile children and those who have not acculturated to the mainstream of American life.

There is a clear indication in these findings that ethnic and racial communities need to play a mediating role in accessing services for their elderly members. There is little systematic evidence, however, about the interest, resources, and ability of ethnic communities to serve the needs of their elderly members. Merely locating health and social services in the racial or ethnic community may not necessarily solve the problem; interviews with non-White and ethnic aged reveal an unwillingness to deal with people perceived as outsiders, often attributable to mistrust and inability to communicate effectively (Guttmann, 1979). Garcia (1979) states that Chicanos cannot be assumed able to care for their elderly without appropriate support systems and that the degree to which services are available versus the degree to which they are perceived to be accessible is a major question to be addressed. The limitations in economic and social resources will result in situations where elderly members of ethnic and racial groups are likely to be homebound without needed services or become candidates for institutionalization.

Family members of ethnic aged are often reluctant to place their aging family members in institutions (Eribes & Bradley-Rawls, 1978). Fandetti and Gelfand (1976) found, however, that whereas most of the Italian and Polish respondents in their study preferred to care for their elderly in their own homes, there was a surprising willingness to consider placement in an institution connected with their respective ethnic communities. Markson (1979) has noted that the Black and ethnic elderly are much more likely to be placed in mental institutions. Often this is done because of the perceived difficulty by professionals to deal with the Black and ethnic aged and the erroneous perception that mental institutions provide cheaper care than alternative forms of health and human services. An investigation of census data on institutionalization for 1950,

1960, and 1970 revealed substantial and consistent differences in the distributions of elderly Blacks and Whites by type of institution; in state mental hospitals Blacks were overrepresented, and in non-profit and proprietary homes for the aged Whites dominated (Kart & Beckham, 1976). These data indicate that knowledge, access, and the availability of informal support also play important roles in the utilization of long-term care services.

Knowledge about the importance of ethnic and racial background is, therefore, not only interesting theoretically but also of considerable importance for the planning and organization of health and social services. Applied gerontological researchers need to understand the possible outcomes associated with assumptional bases regarding the nature and needs of ethnic aged. Viewing ethnic and minority families on the bases of assumptions may lead to the perception that the family as a "natural support system" is adequate and sufficient to care for the service needs of the ethnic aged. The reliance on empirical evidence provides a more objective informational base that highlights both advantages and adverse consequences of ethnicity.

There is also a need for more data regarding alternative approaches in service delivery for ethnic elderly. Biegel and Sherman (1979) propose that more use be made in the delivery of services of the neighborhood and the racial and ethnic community. They assert that the existing mental health services fail to fully utilize the positive neighborhood identification of the urban elderly as a means of overcoming personal and institutional obstacles. Further, they advocate the use of an Empowerment Model. The basic premise of the Empowerment Model is that community leaders and members can work as full partners with professionals in all phases of planning and delivery of services. In their view, with sensitivity and respect for the formal and informal support networks already existing in ethnic communities, professionals can increase the power of these communities to structure and control their own programs while making use of expertise not often available in the community. Thus, after the initial phases of planning and implementation, professionals should find that community input increases while professional direction decreases. Ideally, in this view, through empowerment the formal support system becomes augmented and linked with the informal sources of support in such a way that services are sanctioned; knowledge of available services is highly increased and therefore service use becomes far more acceptable to community members.

Zambrana and her colleagues (Zambrana, Merino, & Santana,

1979) propose the use of two new models for handling the health care needs of the Puerto Rican elderly. The first model is referred to as a modified traditional approach. Basically, this model consists of a team of professionals visiting and evaluating the aged person in his or her own home. The second model, referred to as the intracommunity approach, is based on two premises: that already existing resources in a community can and should be used to provide care for the elderly and that the elderly are an integral resource of the community. Elderly members of the ethnic group are trained as health paraprofessionals and sent into the homes of the ill.

To understand better the service needs and service utilization of elderly members of ethnic groups, applied researchers and health and human service professionals need to be cognizant of two important factors: (a) the ways that ethnicity interacts with other environmental and personal factors and (b) the role that informal support systems and the ethnic communities have in efforts to assure the security and well-being of their elderly members. A better understanding of the ethnic aged and their informal support systems, along with the consideration of service resources in the general and ethnic community, will enable service providers to identify and organize effectively the delivery of services for ethnic elderly.

Respect and understanding of the needs and preferences of service consumers, coupled with effective communications with the elderly and members of their informal support system, are essential in work with ethnic aged. To facilitate a better understanding of the effects of ethnicity on well-being, vulnerability, service need, and service use, we present a conceptual approach aimed at facilitating both research and service efforts on behalf of ethnic aged.

Needs, Resources, and Services

Several points need to be restated in considering the needs of ethnic aged within the boundaries of a comprehensive conceptual approach. First, elderly members of racial and ethnic groups constitute a heterogeneous population. Recognition and consideration of this diversity is essential for any serious attempt to plan interventions on behalf of the aged.

Second, the informal support system is of central importance in the lives of all elderly, including in the lives of ethnic aged. This support system includes children, family members, friends, and neighbors. In addition to family members and friends, churches, civic groups, and organizations play significant roles in the lives of elderly members of racial and ethnic groups. Racial and ethnic institutions provide opportunities for involvement and affiliation and sources of support for the aged. Although informal caregivers play an important role, they cannot alone shoulder all of the responsibility and meet all of the service needs of their elderly family members. Service planners and providers need to be cognizant of the potential and actual involvement of the informal support system in the care of the ethnic aged.

Third, although potentially they may play an important role, most racial and ethnic communities simply do not have the expertise, resources, or services that are needed by elderly members of their respective communities. It is also important to underscore the fluctuations in the public commitment and the fragmented nature of the health and social service system in the United States. The availability of the need-based benefits and services in the United States varies across and within different states and changes from year to year. The extent to which benefits and services may be available for ethnic aged may therefore vary considerably in different locations.

Finally, it is important to underscore that there has been limited research to date that has examined the effects of ethnicity in a conceptual formulation differentiating between different defining elements of ethnicity and also including relevant sociodemographic and socioeconomic status and other personal variables. Moreover, studies of ethnicity have not focused simultaneously on well-being and service needs of ethnic aged.

In the development of a comprehensive conceptual framework that may have greater utility in planning and delivery of services for the aged, the following groups of variables need to be considered: (a) variables characterizing the elderly, (b) resource variables, and (c) service variables (Figure 14-1).

Krout (1983) notes that service utilization research has generally not been based on sound theoretical foundations. However, recent efforts in health and aging services research have operationalized the need for service and service utilization to be a function of the following three variable categories (Andersen, Kravits, & Anderson, 1975; Wan & Arling, 1983). These categories are predisposing variables (demographic and socioeconomic), need variables (physical health, mental health, functional status), and enabling variables (economic resources, living environment, social resources, and personal resources such as life perspective and coping skills).

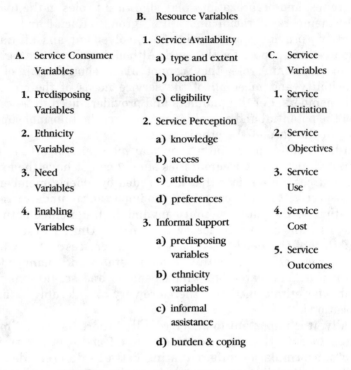

FIGURE 14-1. Aging, ethnicity, and services: an integrated conceptual framework.

In a review of service use and assessment research, Harel, Noelker, and Blake (1985) note that these variable categories in different configurations have been employed in recent years in a significant number of empirical investigations of the service needs of the aged. They note that advancements could be made in health services research and in gerontological research by considering the objectives of human service professionals in the field of aging and incorporating them into the conceptual frameworks of service utilization and multidimensional assessment research. The inclusion of these objectives would result in the generation of data that more directly address the extent to which service objectives are attained and assess whether the services have their intended impact on elderly users.

A review of the health and social services literature reveals that planning and practice efforts of health and human service professionals in the field of aging are guided by the following objectives: (a) providing older individuals and families with effective services that are efficiently delivered; (b) allowing older service consumers as much discretion as possible over the services they use and enhancing their participation in the planning and provision of services; (c) encouraging and supporting family members, friends, neighbors, and volunteers in caring for older persons; and (d) enhancing the coping resources of older service consumers and their informal caregivers (Dunlop, 1980; Harel et al., 1985).

Implicit in these professional objectives is a conceptual approach that includes the need for information about the aged's state of well-being or vulnerability, their knowledge about and preferences for services, and their discretion and choice about the use of services. These objectives imply the need for information regarding the involvement, stresses, and coping resources of the aged's informal caregivers. In addition, these objectives imply the need for information about service variables from the perspective of service consumers as well as from the perspective of service planners and service providers. The use of a more comprehensive conceptual framework in service use research is likely to provide a more systematic data base for the assessment of service need, for the planning of services, and for the evaluation of services.

Four variable categories are included in the conceptual framework suggested for use in research with ethnic elderly. These include (a) the predisposing variables of sociodemographic and socioeconomic status; (b) ethnicity variables; (c) the need variables of health and functional status; and (d) the enabling variables of economic resources, social, and personal (psychological well-being and coping) resources. Three of these four variable categories are consistently used in service utilization research (Andersen et al., 1975).

Several investigations have found that demographic variables (e.g., sex, race, marital status, and living arrangements) and socioeconomic variables (e.g., education, income, and occupational background) only minimally differentiate between members and nonmembers at senior centers and account for only a small fraction of variance in the use of services by community aged (Krout, 1983; Wan & Arling, 1983). Other studies, however, consistently indicate that women, minorities, those who are older, those who live alone, those with lower incomes and less education, and those with limited informal social resources are found to experience greater service needs (Harel et al., 1983; Krout, 1983). Sociodemographic and socioeconomic status are likely to affect not only ethnicity (Harel, 1986) but also physical and mental health, functional status, family and household structure, social interaction, and social relationship (Larson, 1978). Ascertaining the relationship between sociodemographic and socioeconomic status and defining elements of ethnicity appears to be important because few such systematic studies have been conducted. At present, we can only hypothesize about these relationships.

Research to date has tended to focus on racial differences in economic resources, health and functional status, social integration, psychological well-being, and predictors of well-being. Markides (1982) observed that few studies utilized data analysis techniques yielding effects that may be clearly attributable to racial differences beyond those that would be accounted for by sociodemographic and socioeconomic status variables. Until better data are available, we can only hypothesize about how different elements of ethnicity interact with other variables, to affect well-being at different points in time and over time.

The second group of variables, the resource variable categories, are often omitted or underrepresented in service use and assessment research (see the second column in Figure 14-1). The first variable category includes service availability variables, both in the general community and in the racial and ethnic communities. These include availability of resources and services, eligibility criteria, and location of the services. Recent research suggests that these variables are critical because there are great variations in the structure of community-based health and social services in different locations within a state and on a state-by-state basis.

Service use research indicates that the search for and utilization of services is based, to a considerable extent, on knowledge about and access to services. Utilization of services is also affected by organizational characteristics. Stereotypical conceptions depicting non-White and ethnic aged as either not needing services or not wanting services may limit the use of services on their part. Older ethnic aged and members of their informal support system may have difficulty in penetrating the boundaries of bureaucratic health and social service organizations. They may also have difficulty with the fragmented service system that requires consistent and active pursuit of services.

The next variable category includes the service perception variables. These variables include the older persons' knowledge about and access to benefits and community services, their attitudes toward the use of services, and their preference for the type, amount, and source of assistance. At present it is clear that these variables play an important role in the search for and utilization of services. It is less clear that the relationship is between the ethnicity variables, alongside other variables, on knowledge about, access to, and attitudinal predisposition toward the use of services. In addition to ethnicity and other personal factors, an elderly person's knowledge about and access to services may be affected by service availability, by the degree to which service availability is publicized in the media, by the elderly's social resources, and by the preferences of their informal support system. Family, friends, and neighbors may often supply an individual with information about available sources of assistance, serve as "gatekeepers," and frequently serve as referral sources on behalf of impaired elderly persons (Harel et al., 1985).

Lesser acculturation to contemporary U.S. life and culture and lower socioeconomic status may be associated with attitudinal predispositions that preclude the reliance on services. It may also be suggested that ethnic aged of lower socioeconomic status, who lack an informal support system and whose knowledge about and access to services is limited, may be the most vulnerable and are likely to have the highest level of unmet service need. There is clearly a need for more empirical studies, which may specify the configuration of ethnicity and socioeconomic status variables associated with higher levels of unmet service need.

The inclusion of an elderly person's attitudes and preferences toward services in this framework is essential for both researchers and service planners and practitioners. On an individual level, it recognizes that the older person has a right to determine and participate in the choices of services. On an aggregate level, this information is useful to planners in the development of a "demand responsive" community service system.

The third variable category in this column concerns the older person's informal support system. In the conceptual framework proposed here, this variable category is distinct from the social resources included under the enabling variable category. Although the nature and extent of social resources is likely to have an effect on the elderly person's well-being, it is hypothesized that variables included in the informal support system category will have a greater impact on the elderly person's service use. Included in the informal support system variable category are (a) sociodemographic and socioeconomic status, and (b) ethnicity characteristics of the informal caregivers. The configuration of predisposing and ethnicity variables characterizing the informal caregiver, along with patterns of informal support, may affect the extent to which the elderly person will use benefits and services.

The final set of variable categories in the conceptual framework include the service variables (see third column in Figure 14-1).

These are service initiation, service objectives, service use, cost of service, and service outcomes. Ascertaining information about service initiation, service use, and service outcomes will enable service providers and service planners to better plan and evaluate services for various racial and ethnic communities. These variables will also make possible the comparison of service use and non-use and the evaluation of other service use–related outcomes.

A few examples will illustrate the utility of the conceptual framework. Consider the hypothetical case of Mrs. N., an older woman from a major European ethnic group. Mrs. N. lives in an ethnic neighborhood in a large North American city. Her husband died in 1975. Now 82 years old, Mrs. N. lives alone. Her major source of income is Social Security; her husband's pension benefits ended at his death. She is enrolled in both Parts A and B of Medicare but until recently has not had to make extensive use of their benefits because of good health. She now suffers from severe arthritis and hypertension, which limit her ability to take care of her home and do such tasks as shopping.

Mrs. N. arrived in the United States after World War II and never became fluent in English. She relies for information on an ethnic newspaper and a local radio program oriented to her ethnic group. Her children, now in their forties, completed college and are now well embarked on careers as successful professionals. They live outside the city in suburban communities with their families. Mrs. N. does not belong to any organizations and sees very few people during the week. She does talk to her daughters regularly and calls them if she has any problems.

This hypothetical older woman clearly has service needs. The predisposing variables of health and income would indicate a need for assistance. On the other hand, her ethnic culture may dispose her to call on her children for assistance. Formal services may be seen as charity. The services she needs to continue independent living may be difficult to get to or afford.

As the conceptual framework indicates, there is a need to understand the factors that orient Mrs. N.'s disposition and need for services (Figure 14-1, column 1) as well as the factors that orient her to use or not to use services (column 2). The basic issue for Mrs. N. may be her service perceptions or the informal support available from her children. On the other hand, her knowledge about what services are actually available may be very limited. Increasing information about available services through ethnically based information sources such as the radio program and newspaper may bring individuals such as Mrs. N. into existing programs and services.

With these considerations in mind we can review existing and planned services (Figure 14-1, column 3) and ask: Are they oriented toward reaching older individuals from specific ethnic backgrounds? Do their objectives relate to the needs of individuals from these ethnic backgrounds? Do they take the service consumer variables discussed in this chapter into account? Are their rates of utilization indicating effectiveness in reaching the older ethnic person? Are their costs in line with the resources among the older ethnic individuals who are targeted for services? Are their outcomes consonant with the aims of the planners and of the older people who are the intended consumers?

Answers to these questions will require that service providers have an understanding of the diversity of needs and attitudes of older ethnic people and clear lines of communication with them. Planning and providing services without taking the specifics of the ethnic aged into account may result in low utilization rates, frustration on the part of both provider and the ethnic aged, and eventual abandonment of programs that have the potential to have an important impact on the lives of the older ethnic person.

Conclusion

What is clearly indicated in the proposed conceptual framework is a blending and expansion of conceptual approaches employed in service use and ethnicity research. The resulting framework provides sufficient attention to the characteristics of the aged themselves, as well as to variables related to service availability, service knowledge, access to services, and preference for services. It also incorporates the characteristics and involvement of informal caregivers. Furthermore, it focuses on the initiation of service, service objectives, the ongoing use of services, and service outcomes.

Conceptually comprehensive frameworks will permit the development of meaningful conceptual models for the exploration of issues related to the well-being, vulnerability, and service needs of elderly members of ethnic groups. This conceptual approach has a degree of complexity beyond those found in conceptual approaches employed by ethnicity and service research to date. It entails information about the aged themselves as well as about related others, including representation from the informal support system and from planning and service agencies. As such it entails the ascertaining of information from several data sources: the aged themselves, their informal caregivers, representatives of ethnic groups and associations, and representatives of service organizations. Obviously, the exploration of the determinants of ethnicity and the effects of ethnicity on the well-being/vulnerability of the aged will be less complicated than the exploration of the factors that determine service utilization among ethnic aged.

15

Cooperative Practice to Overcome Socially Constructed Hardship for Ethnic Elderly People

Michael J. MacLean and Rita Bonar

The population of ethnic elderly people in multicultural societies such as Canada, the United States, and England is increasing at a significant rate. This increase has recently led to considerable theoretical and applied social science interest that has primarily taken the form of social and health care practice and research into ways of improving care for this population. The message that this interest seems to be conveying is that the society in which the ethnic elderly people are living is concerned about their social and psychological well-being, and it is trying to find ways to contribute to improvements in their quality of life.

This message is expressed by many groups who work with ethnic elderly people. For example, politicians frequently promote the benefits to be derived from living in a multicultural society, and they often speak of the need to maintain the welfare of ethnic elderly people. Researchers refer to the challenge of maintaining this welfare and promote research as a way of developing innovative care leading to improved quality of life for this population. Practitioners such as social workers, nurses, doctors, and community workers acknowledge that they are meeting more ethnic elderly people in their practices, and they often fear that their skills are inadequate to help this population with practical issues of being old in a "second homeland" (Norman, 1985). Finally, ethnic communities also have a strong interest in the quality of life of their elderly members, and they often take direct action to improve the social and health care services for them.

Thus, it appears that there is no lack of interest in the social situation of ethnic elderly people. As such, it could be expected that the quality of life for the majority of this population would be high. However, recent research (Blakemore, 1985; MacLean & Bonar, 1986; Norman, 1985) has indicated that this is not the case—in fact, it appears that the socioeconomic and health care situation of many ethnic elderly people is very poor and that the majority of these people live under conditions of tremendous hardship. The fact that social services have not significantly alleviated this hardship has led Norman (1985) to suggest that there appears to be a double message directed toward the ethnic elderly population. This double message implies that although social and health care services are offered to ethnic elderly people in principle, they are denied to them in practice because of issues related to reduction in services, language difficulties, cultural misperceptions, and discrimination. Thus, it appears that the hardship experienced by many ethnic elderly people in their second homeland may be a result of social conditions in that country. Because this population, according to Norman's double-message argument, does not have equal access to social services, their poor situation becomes worse. This analysis would lead to the conclusion that ethnic elderly people suffer from hardship in old age as the result of social forces rather than of individual characteristics. If this is the case, society at large must accept some responsibility for the difficult situation in which many ethnic elderly people live.

The purpose of this chapter is to focus on an analysis of the social construction of hardship for ethnic elderly people in an attempt to show why these elderly people are in a disadvantaged position despite the considerable efforts of many professionals and volunteers to improve their quality of life. This chapter will focus on the situation of ethnic elderly people in Montreal as a case illustration to show how they are in a disadvantaged position in this city. The chapter will conclude by suggesting how policymakers, researchers, practitioners, and others working with the ethnic elderly population can use a cooperative approach to overcome some of the hardship under which the majority of ethnic elderly people live. A brief case study of an elderly Italian woman in Montreal will be presented to highlight aspects of this cooperative approach.

Social Construction of Hardship for Ethnic Elderly People

The analysis of the social construction of hardship in old age for the ethnic elderly population develops from critical writing about the social situation of elderly people in general that has evolved in the United States, England, and Canada during the past 10 years. This social criticism was initiated by Butler (1975) who, in his book *Why Survive? Being Old in America,* argued that the difficult situation of old people in the United States is a socially constructed tragedy. He suggested that the poverty, poor housing, inadequate and costly medical care, and discrimination that old people in America face is a result of public policy decisions rather than individual approaches to old age.

Butler's (1975) social criticism was followed by other social scientists and health care researchers, who also drew attention to the fact that the majority of elderly people in the United States were in a disadvantaged situation with respect to health, housing, income, and social services. Among others, Levin and Levin (1980) argued that prejudice and discrimination is the plight that most old people in America have to face because of a general tendency to emphasize physical, psychological, and social decline in old age. This argument has also been stated by Crystal (1982), who suggests there are two worlds of aging in the United States: the real world, concerned with social issues such as poverty and inaccessible health care, and the other world, which is concerned with individual issues such as adjustment to retirement and leisure activities in old age. The former seems to be the situation of the majority of older Americans.

This overall pessimistic outlook on old people's lives in the United States has also been developed in England and Canada. Phillipson (1982) has demonstrated that historically the quality of life for elderly people in England has always been poor, and that it appears to be getting worse in the present day. Walker (1982) has clearly documented that elderly people in England are becoming progressively more dependent as a result of social policies that inhibit attempts at independence. The growing awareness of the dismal situation of elderly people in England has recently led to a call for an old age manifesto (Bornat, Phillipson, & Ward, 1985), which argues that significant social change must take place if a decent quality of life for the majority of old people is to become a reality. In Canada, L. Cohen (1984) has focused attention on the abysmal situation of older women, showing that they are often subjected to poverty, overmedication, and unnecessary institutionalization. Shragge and MacLean (1983) have shown that the public pension of elderly Canadians is unrelated to present economic conditions and that there has been little real attempt to help the majority of elderly people have an adequate income. D. Cohen (1984) has supported this analysis by suggesting that the Canadian Old Age Security program has a long history of legislating poverty for older Canadians.

These researchers in the United States, England, and Canada are writing from a critical perspective about the situation of a large percentage of old people in these countries. Elderly people themselves are also becoming actively critical of their situation in these countries (MacLean, 1987; Kuhn, 1980). Their essential message is that the majority of old people live in relatively inferior circumstances, and the social policies of these countries do not seem to be developing ways that will alleviate these hardships.

The adverse circumstances that have been described as characteristic of the majority of elderly people in multicultural societies also apply to ethnic elderly people within these societies. Most ethnic elderly people share the social characteristics that Butler (1975) suggested have contributed to the negative situation for many elderly people. That is, they have had limited formal education and therefore tend to have had a lifetime of difficult, low-paying jobs in their adopted countries. They have often worked for very little money and as a result often end up in old age in relatively poor circumstances with respect to health, housing, and income. As a result of their difficult circumstances, they often seek social services for the first time in their lives. What they frequently find may contribute to a sense of confusion and despair because of the circular nature of social services available to ethnic elderly clientele.

The first place that most ethnic elderly people look to for help with social or health care difficulties is their family. It is well known that, in general, the families of most elderly people provide a considerable amount of informal care; this also applies to the families of the ethnic elderly population. Thus, the family will give any help that it can to improve the quality of life for its elderly members. However, there are many social and health services that the family cannot provide for the ethnic elderly person and help must be sought elsewhere.

The second place that most ethnic elderly people investigate in their search for social or health care services is their local community center. Here they tend to receive a warm reception and are offered the basic services that are available. These services usually include help with government forms, an interpretation of the relevant mainstream social services, assistance in understanding what they can or cannot claim, and referral to other social and recreational services within their community. If this center has access to a doctor or nurse from the ethnic community, elderly people may also be able to receive elementary health care such as blood pressure readings, prescriptions, or health advice.

If ethnic elderly people need more extensive social or health care assistance, they must look beyond the local community center. This means going to the mainstream social services, and it is here that they often have difficulties in getting care that is expected. This is usually because of the attitude of the social service agency toward providing services to ethnic populations. Although all social service agencies would maintain that they provide services to all people who request them, Young (1982) has found that the response of mainstream social service agencies to ethnic populations could be classified into four categories:

Pioneers: those who are highly innovative in meeting the demands of the ethnic communities by creating committees, new positions, and new policies to reflect the change in the services requested by their clientele.

Learners: those who have accepted the view that major changes in policy have to be made to reflect the change in services requested by their clientele.

Waverers: those who are aware of a change in the services requested by their clientele but who feel that the problems raised by these requests are beyond their control.

Resisters: those who deny that the presence of a large ethnic population within their clientele has any implications for the services they provide.

Although Young's study refers to social service agencies in England, the categorization of social services to ethnic populations certainly has implications for such agencies in North America. For example, it would appear that, in the present climate of cutbacks in social and health care resources, ethnic elderly people may have problems in getting the services they need from provincial or state agencies. This would suggest that, in Young's (1982) terms, the majority of mainstream agencies may fall into the category of *waverers* or *resisters* with respect to offering social services to the ethnic elderly population in North America.

At the present time, it appears that ethnic elderly people can potentially experience three basic and interrelated problems in seeking help from the mainstream social service system. The first problem is that most social services are undergoing cutbacks, so many previously available services are no longer in force. This means that there are fewer services to choose from and that there will likely be a strong resistance to developing new specialized services. Thus, ethnic elderly people seeking such services quickly discover that they are not very welcome in the mainstream social service system.

The second problem that ethnic elderly people face is extensive bureaucratic procedures. In times of cutbacks there is a tendency to be careful about the social services that are provided because of the fear that money or services may be misused. Thus, practitioners are hesitant to take undue risk in giving services for which they may be criticized by their superiors. This leads to a system in which paperwork is used to deter service provision, and a client is often passed on to various people in the system before a decision is made about the request. This is confusing for anyone, but it is even more so for ethnic elderly people because of their unfamiliarity with such a complex system, especially one offered in a foreign language.

This relates to a third problem that ethnic elderly people have in approaching mainstream social service systems: they are expected to deal with a complex bureaucracy that uses a language that may still be relatively foreign to them. Often ethnic elderly people do not have access to a social worker who speaks their native language, and as a result, they may become confused in requesting a social service. A frequent response by the social service agency to this realistic confusion is to contact the community center of the ethnic community to help with translation of what the individual wants.

Because ethnic elderly people are often confused and overwhelmed with the problems they encounter in the mainstream social service agencies, they often have to return to the community center from which they initially started. However, the reason they went to the mainstream social services was that they could not get what they needed in their own community, so they are often still in need of the service. This leads to the final stop on the search for social services for the majority of ethnic elderly people—their family. It appears that in many instances the family of the ethnic elderly person has the responsibility to provide the final care for its elderly members. This puts considerable pressure on the family and the ethnic elderly person and contributes to an image of an uncaring society.

In conclusion, the fact that ethnic elderly people often start and finish their search for social and health services within their family reinforces the double message that these services are available in principle but not in practice to this population. Because society does not provide enough social and health care professionals to serve ethnic elderly people in their own language, it is clear that much of the hardship that this population has in old age is socially constructed. With the neoconservative approach to the provision and development of social and health care services that characterizes the 1980s, it appears that the social construction of hardship for ethnic elderly people in Canada, the United States, and England will continue in the immediate future.

Examples of Socially Constructed Hardship for Ethnic Elderly People

In order to consider aspects of the social construction of hardship for ethnic elderly people, some recent experiences of this population in Montreal will be given. Montreal is a metropolitan area of approximately 2.5 million people, of whom approximately 10% are over the age of 65 years, as in the rest of Canada. This total population is primarily made up of people from French-Canadian and English-Canadian backgrounds; but there are more than 75 ethnic communities, although many of these have very small populations.

It was only in 1971 that a policy of multiculturalism was officially introduced in Canada to try to create a society that would be based on the idea of equality for all cultural groups. This honorable ideal has failed to materialize for the majority of cultural groups in Canadian society (Christensen, 1984). This failure can be evidenced in many aspects of Montreal society, but one of the most striking examples of it is in the way ethnic elderly people are limited with respect to their access to services that contribute to a sense of social and psychological well-being. It is clear that this limited access to services because of cultural differences, language difficulties, and social service cutbacks can create considerable hardship in old age for these people.

Hardship for the ethnic elderly population of Montreal relates to their position with respect to social, health, housing, and financial needs. Larson (1978), in a comprehensive review of psychological well-being, suggests that the dependent variables that most often contribute to this state are the individual's housing, health, financial situation, and the extent of community involvement. There are no ethnic distinctions given in this review, but it would be expected that these variables, along with family relations, would contribute significantly to the psychological well-being of all elderly, including the ethnic elderly population. It can be seen that these variables, apart from family relations, are much more influenced by social considerations, such as previous employment conditions, health care benefits, income and pension benefits, than they are by individual differences. That is, many ethnic elderly people end up in old age with poor housing, health, and income conditions because of previous social hardships they have experienced during their lives.

The housing situation for ethnic elderly people in Montreal covers a wide range of accommodation. Many ethnic elderly people live in areas of the city that are predominantly made up of their own ethnic group. They may live in their own homes, their children's homes, rented apartments, or single rooms. However, there is often a problem in housing for the ethnic elderly population who live with their families or in rented accommodation. The individual nature of this problem arises when the family want to move from the ethnic area and the elderly person wants to remain because of access to cultural amenities. This problem creates stress for the individual and for the family, but it can usually be resolved within the family. However, there is often a social nature of this issue that contributes to hardship for ethnic elderly people.

This situation has recently become a social issue for the elderly Chinese population of Montreal who, for the most part, live in the city's Chinatown area. This is the only area that has any social or cultural life in Chinese, so naturally elderly Chinese people want to live there in order to be involved as much as possible in their culture. In fact, many elderly Chinese people who have families in Montreal have opted to live in Chinatown rather than move with their families to better accommodation in other areas of the city. The social problem arises as a result of a proposed redevelopment program for Chinatown that will change the character of this area. One of the main changes that will affect approximately 200 elderly Chinese people is that there will be little low-cost housing for them, and they would not be able to afford the cost of the new accommodation. Thus, many will be forced to move out of the only area of the city that has any cultural significance for them. This is an example of how hardship in housing and community involvement for elderly Chinese people is being socially constructed in Montreal.

The social and health care services for the elderly population of Montreal are, in general, very good because of the provincial and federal programs offered. However, in particular, the social and health services put ethnic elderly people at a disadvantage because the vast majority of services are offered only in French or English. As a result of this linguistic bias, many ethnic elderly people who do not have access to a social worker or medical practitioner in their own language are limited in their use of these services. Some ethnic communities try to overcome this limitation by having a community volunteer accompany elderly individuals to these services to translate their needs. This is often humiliating to ethnic elderly people as they cannot have private discussions with a social worker or a medical practitioner in their own language. This lack of privacy may inhibit ethnic elderly people from seeking services they feel they need.

The Italian community has tried to overcome this problem by having a nurse and a doctor come to a senior citizen center on a weekly and monthly basis, respectively, but according to the director of this center, this does not begin to meet the needs of the elderly Italian population. According to a Japanese community spokesperson in Montreal, elderly people from this community hesitate to use the mainstream social services because there is not a social worker who can communicate with them in their own language. These are examples of how hardship in health and social services is socially constructed for the ethnic elderly population of Montreal.

Loneliness or solitude is a significant problem for many ethnic elderly people that could be addressed by a greater sense of community involvement. In spite of the fact that there are community centers for senior citizens of different ethnic backgrounds in Montreal, there is often a resistance to using them. This can be explained by the fact that many ethnic elderly people are widows who have traditionally stayed at home. Many ethnic communities try to get their elderly people involved in social activities, but this often takes considerable time and resources. An example of such a program was developed by the Portuguese community for its elderly members. This community had an annual grant for 3 years to employ three recreational therapists on a part-time basis to lessen isolation among elderly Portuguese people. Participation in the program increased from 0 to 50 people during the 3 years; but when the grant was finished, the elderly Portuguese people stopped attending the community center because they did not have the security of knowing there would be someone there to lead the activities. The elimination of this program is another illustration of a socially constructed hardship for an isolated group of ethnic elderly people in Montreal.

Income is an important variable that contributes to a sense of well-being in old age. It has recently been estimated that approximately 50% of the elderly population in Canada is living below the official poverty line (Hepworth, 1985). No statistics about ethnicity were addressed in this estimation, but it can be assumed that ethnic elderly people would be in a financial situation similar to the general elderly population. Because many of these people have worked in low-paying employment during their lives, it is not surprising that they would not have much money to supplement their Old Age Security and Guaranteed Income Supplement payments. Thus, the poverty that many ethnic elderly people have in old age is often related to social forces beyond their control.

In conclusion, it seems clear that many of the difficulties that the ethnic elderly population face in old age are related to the social situation rather than to their individual circumstances. Therefore, it is the responsibility of the society to improve the difficult situation in which many ethnic elderly people presently live. It is clear that the Canadian society has not made much effort to help ethnic communities in general (Christensen, 1984), so it is unlikely that it will behave differently toward ethnic elderly people without considerable prompting by various groups interested in this population.

Cooperative Practice Toward Social Change with Ethnic Elderly People

The combination of financial cutbacks in social service programs and the growing population of ethnic elderly people in Canada and the United States has contributed to a situation in which these people are experiencing difficulty in obtaining the social and health care services they need in order to have a reasonable quality of life in old age. This sequence of events tends to put pressure on social and health care practitioners, the ethnic community, and ethnic elderly people themselves, who have to balance the dilemma of a reduction in social services and an increasing population who need them.

This dilemma can potentially be resolved by a cooperative approach among the three groups who are interested in the care of ethnic elderly people. By combining the strengths of social and health care practitioners and researchers, the ethnic community, and the ethnic elderly population themselves, the social care to the elderly population can be improved. The strengths of the social and health care practitioner in this exchange include the following: a knowledge of the social service system; a commitment for social change through the provision of social and health care services;

skills of community organization; a familiarity with the theoretical literature about issues related to service provision to the ethnic elderly population such as the categorization of social service agencies according to their willingness to work with this population; and an expertise in research skills that could be useful to the ethnic community.

The strengths of the ethnic community include their knowledge of ways of helping their older people because of their familiarity with cultural mores, their desire to help each other, and their experience of adjusting to the North American society. The strengths of ethnic elderly people themselves include their experience of adapting to considerable social change during their lives and their knowledge of what it is like to grow old in a second homeland. The combination of these strengths can work toward satisfying the basic social psychological needs of the ethnic elderly population.

A Case Illustration

A case illustration provides an example of how cooperative practice can be used as a way of combining the strengths of ethnic elderly people, the ethnic community, and the social and health care services to help an ethnic elderly person.

Mrs. X. is a 76-year-old Italian widow living alone in her small house in a French-Canadian neighborhood of Montreal. She is crippled with arthritis, and her sight is partially impaired, so her mobility is severely limited. She has two daughters who live outside the province and a son who lives in Montreal, 45 min away from her by car. She does not want to live with her son because she wants to stay in the home that she and her late husband had. Mrs. X's son and his family visit every weekend to do her shopping, cooking, and cleaning, but during the week she is alone and lonely. She has few friends but some acquaintances from her regular attendance at church.

Recently, Mrs. X's health began to decline rapidly, and she stopped going to church. Her son tried to get some home help and social services from the mainstream social service agency but, unfortunately, it could provide these services only in French, and Mrs. X. could speak only Italian and English. Thus, she could not have these services and she could not get out of her home. This worried her son, but there was little he could do apart from his weekend visits to her.

Mrs. X's old Italian acquaintances at church noticed her absence. Some of these women visited her to find out if anything was wrong, and they decided to organize a system whereby Mrs. X would have visitors during the week. These women also got their grandchildren to do some errands for Mrs. X, so she had young visitors to help her on a regular basis. One of the Italian women got her daughter, who is a social worker, involved in an attempt to arrange intermediate social services for Mrs. X. The case of Mrs. X. was also brought to the attention of the authors of this chapter because of their interest in cases like this in Montreal. They have documented this case, and a copy of this chapter has been sent to the social service agency in question to highlight the difficulty that people such as Mrs. X. have in this neighborhood. The agency can use this information to pressure the social services ministry of the province to provide more resources so clients such as Mrs. X. can receive the services they need. The result of these interventions by ethnic elderly people, the Italian community, the social work practitioner, and researchers is that Mrs. X. is much more involved in her community and her quality of life is considerably improved.

This case study illustrates how the strengths of ethnic elderly people, an ethnic community, and social work practitioners and researchers were combined in a cooperative effort to improve the quality of life for an elderly Italian widow. The elderly Italian women who visited Mrs. X. showed their concern for their acquaintance, and they used direct action to help her. They also used family resources to have their grandchildren do some things for Mrs. X. This action involved the Italian community in helping Mrs. X, and through this action an Italian social worker became involved. This led to the case being presented to the authors, who could use their skills to convey to the social service agency issues of social work practice that discriminate against people such as Mrs. X. This cooperative action by these three interest groups have helped alleviate hardship for one person in this case. However, these skills, and others that each of these interest groups have, can be used to improve the quality of life of other ethnic elderly people in general.

The strengths of these three interest groups can also be used in an overall cooperative way to improve the care for the ethnic elderly population. Since much of the hardship the ethnic elderly population experiences is socially constructed, social change will only take place if interest groups pressure governments to make changes in the provision of care for these people. Therefore, social and health care practitioners and researchers, the ethnic elderly community, and the ethnic elderly population have to work cooperatively in educating policymakers about the difficult conditions under which many ethnic elderly people live. Thus, the cooperative work that these interest groups initiate must be directed to the eventual change of policy to ensure that social and health care services that contribute to a reasonable quality of life are available to people who are living out their lives in a second homeland.

Conclusion

It is clear that the increase in the number of ethnic elderly people in Canada and the United States will raise many issues for social and health care provision to this population in the immediate future. Because many of the problems that ethnic elderly people experience have a social rather than an individual origin, they require a social solution rather than an individual one. This means that social service providers will have to develop new approaches in order to contribute to a reasonable quality of life for this population. Unfortunately, this mandate comes at a time when there is a general reduction in human and financial resources in social service fields. This leads to a tendency, in Young's (1982) terms, for many social service agencies to ignore the special nature of requests for social services from ethnic elderly people, or to treat them as outside their control and redirect the responsibility to the family or the ethnic community. Such action conveys a double message (Norman, 1985) to ethnic communities in general and to ethnic elderly people in particular. This double message of having social services available but not readily accessible to ethnic elderly people contributes considerable stress to them at a time when their other resources are limited. This does not contribute to an adequate level of care for this population, and it is not a social solution to the problems that ethnic elderly people have.

A social solution to the problems that ethnic elderly people experience is for those interested in the care of this varied population to use a cooperative approach to change practice and policy in order to alleviate hardship that this population is presently experiencing. That is, social and health care practitioners and researchers, the ethnic communities, and ethnic elderly people themselves can work together and learn from the strengths of each other in the interests of providing adequate care for ethnic elderly people. In this way, we would be, again in Young's (1982) terms, "pioneers" or "learners" in developing new practice and policies to address the needs of this growing population. Such a cooperative approach would also contribute to an old age in a second homeland that has the dignity that ethnic elderly people would expect from this stage of life.

16

Defining Retirement for Black Americans

Rose C. Gibson

This chapter discusses retirement research that is based on the first probability sample of the adult Black population, the *National Survey of Black Americans* (NSBA) (1979).[1] These findings indicate that the unique lifetime work experiences of Black Americans complicate their self-definitions of retirement, and these definitions in turn exclude a large number of them from the major retirement research today.

There are several important reasons for studying the retirement definitions of Black Americans. The first reason is that three fairly new social trends—the declining labor force participation of middle-age and older Blacks, increases in their physical disability, and the increasing availability of disability pay—may be creating a new type of Black retiree, "the unretired retired"; that is, individuals aged 55 years and over who are not working in full-time jobs but do not call themselves retired (Gibson, 1986d). This group appears to be the most overall deprived of the Black elderly (Jackson & Gibson, 1985). But because they may not meet the traditional retirement criteria (age 65, a clear line between work and nonwork, income primarily from retirement sources, and viewing themselves as retired), this very needy group could ironically be screened out of major national retirement research, which uses these traditional operational definitions of retirement. They would therefore be excluded from the planning and policy that stem from that research. Reconceptualizing retirement to include this group could challenge

[1] I would like to thank Dr. James S. Jackson for the use of the *National Survey of Black Americans* data, and Dr. Ralph M. Gibson for his helpful comments on the first draft of the chapter.

some of the past major findings and guiding paradigms of retirement research and make it necessary to alter retirement research designs, planning, and policy.

The chapter first reviews the work, retirement, and role theory literature that is relevant to understanding the meaning of retirement for Blacks. Next, it discusses current procedural definitions of retirement and ways in which the unique retirement definitions of Blacks might exclude them from the major retirement research. Finally, findings are summarized from this author's research on the retirement definitions of Blacks. This research takes into account the particular lifetime work experiences of Blacks, lends further insight into the retirement roles of the Black elderly, and provides a sense of the factors that are most important in creating this new type of Black retiree, the unretired retired. The chapter closes with recommendations for new approaches to retirement research and policy in behalf of older Black Americans that are also applicable to other groups of disadvantaged minorities.

Relationship Between the Lifetime Work and Retirement Experiences of the Black Elderly

A review of more than 20 years of the work and retirement literature indicates that Black Americans have disadvantaged work experiences across the life course—they are more likely to have worked in low status jobs characterized by sporadic work patterns and low earnings (Abbott, 1980; Anderson & Cottingham, 1981; Cain, 1976; Corcoran & Duncan, 1978; Gordon, Hamilton & Tipps, 1982; U.S. Bureau of the Census, 1980a; Hill, 1981; Montagna, 1978; Munnell, 1978). These handicapping work patterns over a lifetime have had negative effects on the economic well-being of Blacks as they reach old age (Abbott, 1980). Work in old age, in the same low-status jobs, becomes a necessity for many (Abbott, 1977). There is therefore a continuity of disadvantaged work patterns from their youth through their old age. It is this similarity of sporadic work patterns over the life course that may create for older Blacks a certain ambiguity of work and retirement. The ambiguity may in turn affect the very ways in which Blacks define retirement for themselves.

The level and source of income for Blacks in old age have also been affected by their lifetime work experiences (Abbott, 1980; Leon, 1986). Restriction to jobs characterized by instability, low earnings, and few benefits is directly related to low levels of retirement pension and Social Security benefits. Thus, the income packages of older Blacks compared to other groups contain a greater proportion of money from their own work and nonretirement sources (Abbott, 1977; Jackson & Gibson, 1985; Parnes & Nestel, 1981). Receiving income from one's work rather than the traditional retirement sources could also create a kind of uncertainty as to whether one is working or retired. This may complicate Blacks' adoption of the retirement role.

Retirement Versus Disability Role

The attractiveness, availability, and appropriateness of roles alternate to retirement may also interfere with Blacks' adoption of the retirement role. The role-theory literature lends some additional insights into reasons Blacks might actually prefer the disability to the retirement role (see Biddle & Thomas, 1966, and Sarbin & Allen, 1968, for thorough analyses of role theory). Role theory suggests, in general, that individuals select new roles either when forced out of an old role or when the new role is different or offers greater benefits than the old role. The inclination of Blacks to take on the retirement role might be interpreted within this general framework.

The identity theory of William James (1950) provides a point at which to begin. He posits that individuals change their self-identities when changes in the opportunities or demands of current social situations occur. They formulate different sets of expectations regarding appropriate or desirable self-meanings. Translated into terms of work and retirement, this means that changes in either demands or opportunities in the work sphere, or both, could encourage a search for more appropriate self-meanings such as the retiree role. Blacks experiencing few changes in their work spheres in old age, as pointed out earlier, would be less likely to search for or take on a new retiree identity.

Stryker (1968), expanding the identity theory of James, offers another framework in which to interpret Blacks' reluctance to adopt the retirement role. He suggests that individuals have a hierarchy of available roles, with the most salient in priority positions. Individuals change identities by selecting roles from this hierarchy that have the highest probabilities of (a) being invoked across situations and (b) congruence between the expectations of the individual and the expectations of society in regard to the appropriate behaviors of individuals within the role. Extrapolated to work and retirement roles, this might mean that when the work role is no longer available individuals choose the retirement role (a) if it is the most salient in their hierarchy of roles, (b) if it is applicable across a variety of life situations, and (c) if the individual and others agree on the behaviors of the retiree role. For older Blacks whose work is still contributing to their income and for whom the line between work and retirement is unclear, the retiree role would not have widespread applicability across life circumstances, nor would individual and societal expectations of retirement behavior coincide.

The theory that individuals give up and take on new roles according to the margin of benefits over costs that they perceive between the two roles offers yet another framework in which to examine the adoption of the retirement role by Blacks. This means that Blacks would adopt the retirement role if they perceive its benefits as outweighing the benefits of other available roles. The disability role compared to the retirement role may may have larger payoffs for older Blacks, as we shall see.

The special payoffs of the disability role for Blacks might be explained by modified versions of sick-role theory. One aspect of sick-role theory that is relevant to our purposes is that intolerable social and psychological conditions in individuals' lives encourage adoption of the sick role as an escape from a less desirable current role (Phillips, 1965; Thurlow, 1971). Even more relevant to the lives of older Blacks are recent interpretations of sick-role theory suggesting that the secondary *economic* gains of illness encourage adoption and maintenance of sick-role behavior (Lamb & Rogawski, 1978; Ludwig, 1981; Prince, 1978). Chirikos and Nestel (1983), in fact, show that reports of disability are related to economic need. Individuals with lower *expected* future wage rates are more likely than others to say they are work-disabled, and the influence of expected income on self-reported disability is greater for Blacks than for Whites.

Ellison (1968) extends the argument further and suggests that the sick role is an actual *substitution* for the retirement role, especially among blue-collar workers. Intolerable social and psychological experiences create for this group a "lack of fit" in the retirement role. The Chirikos and Nestel (1983) and Ellison studies taken together suggest that for disadvantaged workers the sick role has a better fit and greater economic benefits than the retirement role. The model seems particularly appropriate for older Blacks whose low levels of retirement benefits might make disability pay greater than retirement pay. The availability of disability pay might indeed be an important factor in Blacks' adopting the disability instead of the retirement role.

This review of the literature suggests that the self-defined retirement of Blacks may be a function not only of lifetime and current labor force experiences and source of income but also of the availability, attractiveness, and appropriateness of the disability role. In addition, assuming the disabled-worker role may have greater social, psychological, and economic payoffs than assuming the retirement role. Let us move now to see ways in which some characteristics of the Black elderly and their failure to call themselves retired might by definition screen them out of the major retirement research today.

Current Procedural Definitions of Retirement

Retirement definitions in current studies range from a simple dichotomy (retired/not retired) to a more complex definition that measures retirement in a number of objective and subjective ways. The simpler the definition, the greater the possibility of excluding the group of unretired-retired Black elderly. This does not mean, however, that complex definitions assure this group's inclusion, as we shall see.

Subjective retirement (calling oneself retired) is one of the newer constructs in retirement research and also the most complex because it involves choices on the part of the individual, which in turn require cognitive-motivational processes. Individuals generally call themselves retired if they experience noticeable decreases in time spent in work, income mainly from retirement sources, and greater rewards of the retirement than competing roles. Definitions of this genre would screen out that group of Black retired who do not view themselves as retired.

Parnes and Nestel (1981), analyzing the retirement process among Black and White men from the National Longitudinal Surveys of Labor Market Experience, used a quasi-objective definition of retirement that excluded two groups: those who did not report having stopped work at a regular job and those who leave one employer at a pensionable age and begin another job without reporting themselves retired. Blacks could be excluded disproportionately because they are more likely never to have had a regular job or to have left one job and begun another without reporting themselves as retired. Implicit if not explicit in the Parnes and Nestel findings is that the unretired-retired definition may be more prevalent among Black than White men due to a less distinct line between work and retirement for the Black men and their greater tendency to perceive themselves as disabled. Fully two-thirds of the Black

men 55 years old and over, in contrast to only half of the White men
that age, fail to say they are retired when asked reasons why they
are not working. The Black men are also more likely than the White
men to identify disability as the reason they are not working (three-
fifths of the Black men versus two-fifths of the White men). Kingson's (1982a) analysis of the Parnes data reveals much the same—a
larger proportion of Black than White men left work early for
health-related reasons. A careful examination of some of the tables
in the Parnes–Nestel study shows that part-time work patterns,
more characteristic of Blacks than Whites preretirement, are also
more likely to remain part-time among Blacks than Whites
postretirement. This means the Black men are more likely to show a
constancy of part-time work patterns and less likely than the White
men to show decreases in time spent in work. This could mean less
of a distinction between lifetime and old-age work patterns for the
Black men.

Palmore, George, and Fillenbaum (1984) used both subjective and
objective measures of retirement in analyzing data from seven longitudinal retirement studies: The Retirement History Survey, the
National Longitudinal Surveys, The Panel Study of Income Dynamics, The Duke Work and Retirement Study, The Duke Second Longitudinal Study, the Ohio Longitudinal Study, and the Michigan
Study of Auto Workers. Retirement was operationalized in four
ways. In the first measure, individuals employed fewer than 35
hours per week *and* receiving a retirement pension are considered
objectively retired. This definition would exclude two groups of
Black elderly: those receiving inadequate retirement benefits and
therefore working full-time and those who are working part-time
and not receiving any retirement benefits. The second definition,
age at retirement, measures whether the individual retired early,
on time, or late, with age 65 as the benchmark. The third measure is
based on a subjective report of retirement that could have excluded
retired Blacks who do not view themselves as retired. The final
measure is the total number of hours worked in the past year; the
more one works, the less one is considered retired. Blacks would be
excluded disproportionately because they are more likely than
Whites to be working and to be working greater numbers of hours
in old age. The range of definitions provided by Palmore et al.,
representing one of the most sophisticated approaches to retirement
research to date, may still have lost proportionately more retired
Blacks than Whites in their samples. A major contribution of this
study is that it demonstrates ways in which changing retirement
definitions change the factors that predict retirement.

Morgan (1980), examining actual and prospective retirement among individuals ages 45 and over from the Panel Study of Income Dynamics data, excluded several groups: those who did not report themselves retired, those ages 65 and over who were still working, those who were unemployed, and those who called themselves disabled rather than retired (the retired and disabled categories were mutually exclusive). A greater proportion of Blacks than Whites were undoubtedly in all of these excluded groups. Morgan's failure to find race differences in retirement experiences might be due to a loss of the disadvantaged unretired-retired Black elderly. His comparison groups might actually be Whites and better-off Blacks (groups that would have similar retirement experiences).

Atchley's (1980) procedural definition of retirement is objective and considers individuals retired if they are employed at a paying job less than full-time year-round *and* if income is at least in part from a retirement pension earned through prior years of employment. The definition would exclude those Blacks with no pension income.

Investigating the dynamics of retirement in the Cornell Study of Occupational Retirement, Streib and Schneider (1971) restricted their sample to those who retired from regular full-time jobs. Blacks, overrepresented among those who never had regular permanent jobs, would be disproportionately barred from the study.

Fillenbaum, George, and Palmore (1985), investigating race differences in the determinants and consequences of retirement, used three measures of retirement: self-reported retirement, the current amount of work combined with the receipt of pension income, and the total number of hours worked in the past year. There would be a race disparity in proportions screened out because Blacks are less likely to call themselves retired, more likely to be working greater numbers of hours, and less likely to be receiving pension income.

Two studies have focused exclusively on subjective retirement using predominantly white samples (Irelan & Bell, 1972; Murray, 1979). Murray, analyzing the Retirement History Survey data (RHS), examines the extent to which subjective assessments of retirement match objective measures and finds that the best predictors of subjective "complete" retirement (respondents feel they are completely rather than partially or unretired) are zero work hours and the receipt of a pension. Conversely, full-time work and no pension income predict "not retired at all." The in-between category, "partially retired," is least well predicted. This suggests that the less clear-cut the objective measures, the more difficult the subjective appraisal of retirement. Age is an important predictor only among those who are not working and not receiving pensions. Age might be used in self-defined retirement when other retirement criteria are in conflict. Race, demographic, and attitudinal factors have no bearing on self-defined retirement. Because separate regressions were not run by race, it is not known if the predictors of subjective retirement—current work hours, pension receipt, age, demographics, gender, and attitudinal factors—have the same relative and collective effects on the subjective retirement of Blacks and Whites.

The second study of subjective retirement (Irelan & Bell, 1972) represents the first attempt to understand ways in which retirement has different meanings for different people. Irelan and Bell find the best predictors of subjective retirement are being in the labor force, receiving Social Security (including disability and widow's benefits), and having health problems that limited work. Both Irelan and Bell and Murray (1979) find women and men different on certain factors that determine self-definitions of retirement. Although men and women are similar regarding the meaning of "not retired" (being in the labor force determines this meaning); they differ on "partial" and "complete" retirement. If a *man* is out of the labor force, regardless of the receipt of Social Security, he calls himself completely retired. But a *woman* out of the labor force had to also be receiving Social Security to identify herself as completely retired. In other words, women out of the labor force and receiving no Social Security do not think of themselves as retired.

This may be related to the fact that a number of these older women in the RHS sample, although not currently living with spouses, might have been lifetime housewives instead of workers. This gender difference may not exist to the same extent among Blacks because Black women have always been workers. Irelan and Bell also did not separate the races for analysis to determine whether labor force participation, Social Security payments, and work disability are of equal importance in determining the self-defined retirement of Blacks and Whites. Thus, Irelan and Bell's finding that race is not related to self-defined retirement may cover important paradoxes and countervailing trends in the Black and White data.

This review of the retirement research suggests that current operational definitions of retirement may allow needy groups of the Black elderly to drop through the cracks in the major retirement research today—individuals who have never had a regular job in life, those without pension benefits, those for whom there is no clear cessation of work, and those who do not choose to call themselves

retired. Moreover, studies of subjective retirement have inadequately examined the subjective retirement of Blacks. These studies
have not considered the ambiguity of work and retirement
when there has been a continuity of disadvantaged work patterns
over the lifetime, nor the special attractiveness of the disability role
for Blacks compared with the retirement role. Furthermore, the
subjective retirement studies using race simply as a predictor variable in the regression analyses may have covered important race
differences when measuring the relative influence of factors on
subjective retirement.

The Subjective Retirement of Black Americans

This brings us to a discussion of the present author's research,
which focused exclusively on the subjective retirement of Blacks
while taking into full account the uniqueness of their lifetime work
and retirement experiences (Gibson, 1986d). A description of the
NSBA sample utilized in this study follows.

The National Survey of Black Americans

The NSBA sample is a multistage probability sample of the Black
population consisting of 2,107 respondents. The sampling design
was based on the 1970 census, and each Black American residing in
an individual household within the continental United States had
an equal chance of being selected. The sample design is similar to
that of most national surveys but has unique features of primary
area selection and stratification to make it responsive to the distribution of the Black population. Eligibility for selection into this
household sample was based on citizenship and noninstitutionalized
living quarters within the continental United States. Reflecting the
nature of the distribution of the Black population, more than half
(44) of the 76 primary areas used for final selection of households
were located in the southern United States. Two methods of screen-
ing were developed to guarantee inclusion of Blacks (meeting selection criteria) in both high- and low-density areas (Jackson & Hatchett, 1985). The sample had a 69% response rate and all face-to-face
interviewing was conducted in 1979 and 1980 by Black interviewers
trained through the Survey Research Center of the University of
Michigan's Institute for Social Research.

The NSBA questionnaire was developed especially for use in the
Black population. Two years of pretesting and refinement preceded

actual use in the field. The instrument contains both open- and closed-ended items and takes approximately 2 hr 20 min to administer. Although the studies reported here are restricted to the retirement, work, and demographic sections, the questionnaire also includes the broad areas of neighborhood life, health, mental health, family, social support, racial and self-identity, religious experiences, and political participation. Thus, the data used in this study represent a rich, culturally relevant, and carefully collected source of information on the work and retirement experiences of the Black elderly.

The study explores the complexity of self-defined retirement for Black Americans by examining the influence of (a) an indistinct line between lifetime and current work patterns, (b) a large part of one's income stemming from one's own work, and (c) the availability of the disability role on calling oneself retired after accounting for gender and class. Nearly 40% of nonworking Blacks aged 55 and over did not view themselves as retired and constituted the very needy unretired-retired group of Black elderly. The unretired-retired compared to the retired (those who called themselves retired) were a more disadvantaged group economically and socially. They were more likely to be poor, poorly educated, and lifetime laborers or low-level service workers.

Not surprisingly, having worked discontinuous types of patterns over the lifetime, viewing oneself as disabled, and receiving income from one's own work and sources other than retirement pensions, annuities, or assets decreased the odds of calling oneself retired. A logit regression procedure was employed to predict this decision to call oneself retired (Hanushek & Jackson, 1977). Gender, urban residence, and social class (measured by income and education) were not important. Occupation is not a valid social class indicator for the present generation of older Black Americans because racial discrimination placed a ceiling on their occupational achievements. In a sense, the increasing validity of occupational status as a measure of social class among Blacks would be a good barometer of widening occupational opportunities for them. Self-defined retirement among Blacks appears to be more a matter of patterns of lifetime work experiences, source of current income, and choice of the disability role than one of gender or class.

Age was the most important predictor of subjective retirement, which is not surprising in and of itself. What seems to be the case, however, is that those not characterized by the more traditional markers of retirement, such as clearly defined work cessation or income from retirement pensions, are using chronological age as the single marker. As previously mentioned, Murray (1979) also found her respondents used age in defining retirement when other retirement criteria were less clear-cut.

Taking on a *disabled identity* was the second most important predictor. Those viewing themselves as disabled are not likely to also view themselves as retired, although they had the opportunity to do so. Let us focus specifically on those who identify themselves as disabled. Distinctions between two subgroups of the disabled fit rather nicely into sick-role theory—the disability role seems to fill more of the psychological and economic needs of the disabled unretired (those who called themselves disabled but not retired) than the disabled retired (those who called themselves *both* disabled and retired). The disabled unretired are more likely to feel powerless over their own fate, to feel less of a sense of life accomplishment, and to be less satisfied with life and less happy. Following sick-role theory, these individuals may be adopting the disability role to meet some special psychological needs. This role may serve to relieve them of responsibilities for themselves and to provide an excuse for perceived life failures. The disability role also seems to have larger financial payoffs for the disabled unretired because they are more likely to have disability pay as a *single* source of income. They are more dependent on disability pay. Thus, the disability role seems more appropriate and has larger economic *and* psychological payoffs for the disabled unretired than for the disabled retired.

Work history was the third most important predictor of subjective retirement. Quite expectedly, those who did not work all years full-time are less likely than others to call themselves retired. The unretired are more likely than the retired to have worked sporadically over the lifetime and also to be currently working between 11 and 19 hr per week. This special group of unretired disabled with a constancy of sporadic work from youth well into old age may in fact be the group to which Jackson (1980) referred when she stated that "Black Americans die from rather than retire from the work force." The retired, in contrast, are more likely to have worked continuously over the lifetime and not to be currently working at all or to be working very little (between 1 and 10 hr per week). Thus, there is a certain *sameness* of part-time work along the life course for the unretireds and more of a *decrease* in the amount of time spent in work among those who call themselves retired, suggesting that the unretired may not see as clearly the line between work and nonwork. The work history findings are curious because the oldest age cohort of elderly (65 and over) and the poorly educated are *more* likely than the youngest elderly cohort (55–64) and those with more education to have worked full-time all years.

Source of income was important. Not surprisingly, those receiving retirement pay, private pensions, or annuities are more inclined than those relying on their own work, Supplemental Security Income, Social Security, or other governmental sources to call themselves retired. The three governmental sources of income categories, in fact, have a common underlying factor, that is, *feeling* the necessity to work in order to supplement inadequate incomes. Individuals supported mainly or in part by the work of self, family, or friends; by Social Security, Supplemental Security Income, or welfare income feel similarly compelled to work intermittently. Those receiving private retirement pensions, investments, or annuities (better off financially) feel less of a compulsion to work. The Harris study (1979) also found those receiving pension benefits less likely than those not receiving benefits to say they wished to work (40% vs. 52%). Since Whites predominate in the Harris sample, this might be a class rather than a race phenomenon. A related finding was that of Jackson and Gibson (1985) who found lower morale among Black elderly who were *in* the labor force than among those who were *out* and receiving retirement pensions. The lower morale of the workers suggests that work was not by choice. The main point here is that not only is the *source* of income at issue with respect to calling oneself retired but the *feeling* of being compelled to work as well. Interpreted within our theoretical framework, work in old age among Black Americans without retirement pensions is more of an economic necessity than choice. Those Black elderly who feel the compulsion to work see less clearly the line between work and nonwork and therefore tend less to define themselves as retired.

Gender was not related significantly to subjective retirement. The lack of importance of gender in subjective retirement is contrary to the findings of Murray (1979) and Irelan and Bell (1972), both of whom found significant gender differences in the predictors of subjective retirement. These contrasting findings suggest a race difference in the effects of gender on self-defined retirement. Extensive gender analyses were conducted and are reported elsewhere (Gibson, 1986d). Some of the highlights of the gender findings are that (a) the failure to call oneself retired in this predominantly female group of nonworking Black elderly is not a matter of "traditional" sex differences in work histories, source of income in old age, and disability reporting; (b) whereas women are slightly less likely to have had full-time jobs, among those who have full-time jobs, the men are as likely as the women to have worked sporadically; and

(c) older Black men and women are not only similar in work and retirement but in other social and psychological characteristics as well and in this way may differ from their White counterparts, among whom gender is more of a discriminating factor.

Discussion

The research reviewed in this chapter suggests that the unretired-retired status among Black Americans is brought about by a combination of (a) an indistinct line between work in youth and work in old age, (b) the receipt of one's income from other than retirement pension sources, (c) a realization that one must work from time to time well into old age, and (d) the greater benefits of the disability over the retirement role. These findings have salience not only for the inappropriateness of the prevailing procedural definitions of retirement for a large segment of older Blacks, but also for the penalizing and damaging aspects of these definitions as well. They allow needy groups of the Black elderly to drop through the cracks in the major retirement research today. These are individuals who have some or all of the following characteristics: they never had a regular job in life, are without pension benefits, have not had a clear cessation of work, and do not choose to call themselves retired. Indeed, the very definitions of retirement need rethinking if this most disadvantaged group of the Black elderly is to be included in future retirement research, planning, and policy. Palmore et al. (1984) do, in fact, demonstrate that alternate definitions of retirement change the findings of retirement research. Expanding current definitions of retirement to include the unretired-retired Black elderly could change some of the past major findings of research, which found Blacks and Whites similar in retirement experiences. This calls into question some of the guiding paradigms of retirement research.

Particularly disturbing findings from the present author's study are that older cohorts, in spite of being more poorly educated, are better off than younger cohorts of Black elderly in regard to continuous types of lifetime work patterns. These findings suggest that education did not substantially improve employment patterns among these older Black Americans. Gordon et al. (1982), Jones (1973), and Gibson (1982), in fact, show that educational levels of attainment operate in negative ways on the continuity of employment for Blacks. These findings taken together might also mean that successive cohorts of older Blacks, even though better educated, will be less and less likely to have worked full-time over the life course. Coupling this set of findings with the high unemployment rates of Black teenagers (nearly 70% in some areas) causes great concern (Gibson, 1986a, 1986b, 1986c). If nothing is done to ameliorate the situation, millions of young Blacks will be even more disadvantaged when they reach old age than the present cohort of older Blacks in regard to continuous labor force participation. The group of unretired-retired Black elderly could increase substantially in the future.

It is also possible that this phenomenon of an increasing group of subjectively unretired Blacks is an omen for other groups of older Americans. Historically, negative social phenomena have occurred first in the Black community and then have moved on to become manifest in White America. Two good examples are drug abuse and the high incidence of out-of-wedlock births. If we take these as precedent, then we might even speculate that the changes in work and retirement patterns observed among Blacks are a kind of forewarning of the society at large. As work decreases for all Americans (as it is surely doing), the confusion over retirement status will increase, and retirement will eventually need redefinition not only for Blacks but for other groups as well. The ambiguity of work and retirement will not be exclusively a Black problem.

It is unsettling to realize that when the proposed age-of-eligibility changes take place under Social Security, for the unretired retired there will be an even longer wait than already exists between the end of work lives and the beginning of benefits. Raising the ages of eligibility also means that increasing numbers of Black males simply will not live long enough to collect their Social Security benefits. In view of the extreme economic need of the unretired retired, the question becomes whether they should be identified as retired, even though they do not meet the traditional criteria, in order to receive some type of retirement benefits. This becomes doubly important when we realize that this special group of Black elderly may never work again in any systematic or beneficial manner. Kingson (1982a, 1982b) offers some creative new solutions to this dilemma of very early retirement.

Gender is not an important factor in the subjective retirement of Black Americans. This is contrary to much of the retirement research on the majority population, in which there tend to be clear effects of gender. The striking ideas here are that Black men and women in the present elderly cohort, unlike their White counterparts, are remarkably alike in critical aspects of work. Both Black men and women are lifetime workers with discontinuous work pat-

terns, thus making gender less important in the retirement definitions of Blacks than of Whites. Extrapolating White gender
differences in retirement experiences to Blacks may hide important
similarities of the retirement experiences of Black men and women,
thus obscuring some important countervailing trends in Black retirement data.

These findings on the retirement of Black Americans can be
placed in the larger context of critical life events that occur earlier
for Blacks (e.g., the birth of first child, the onset of disability, the
loss of a spouse, and death) suggesting an earlier social aging of
Blacks. Retirement should perhaps now be added to the list of life
events that occur earlier for Blacks. Placing these findings within
that larger framework also raises a fundamental issue. Since Black
and other minority-group Americans age earlier socially than the
general population, age-based policies gauged to the life course
and life experiences of the majority population are generally inappropriate for them. Benefits are thus provided too late in life
spans that are truncated by high death rates at midlife or too late in
work lives that are shortened by disability and early labor force
withdrawal. The Advisory Council on Social Security (1979) offers
alternate interpretations of the issue. The Council concludes that
the evidence does not support the idea that minorities fare better
or worse than non-minorities in regard to Social Security benefits.
The reasons are that minorities are more likely to benefit from
(a) the adequacy tilt in the Social Security benefit formula and
(b) disability and survivor's protection. The fact remains, however,
that minority workers are less likely to reach early and normal
retirement ages and are therefore less likely to receive retirement benefits.

What these findings suggest is a model of the factors that contribute most significantly to the formation of the new type of Black
retiree, the unretired retired. This model should be tested across
national samples to see if Blacks, other minorities, and Whites
differ in the factors that influence perceptions of retirement. The
model should also be tested in longitudinal data to determine the
special effects of social change and civil rights legislation on these
meanings of retirement for minority groups. The relationships
among source of income, perceptions of disability, work history, and
subjective retirement undoubtedly form a more complex sociopsychological model than has been presented in this chapter. Therefore,
new research should expand the models to incorporate relevant
cognitive-motivational factors. In this way retirement research and
the policy stemming from that research will be more effective in
benefiting *all* elderly in our society.

17

Aging in an Ethnic Society: Policy Issues for Aging Among Minority Groups

Fernando Torres-Gil

The aging of the society and the attention given to the fast-growing elderly population in the United States has led to discussions, debates, and concerns about the impact of aging on domestic policy and the appropriate role of the public and private sectors. The cost of programs for older persons, the large federal deficit, and the shift of leadership from the federal level to the state level and private sector have created fiscal pressures and generational controversies that in turn are causing a fundamental reassessment of current aging policies. That reassessment, however, has not taken into account the unique circumstances of ethnic and minority elderly or the differential impact public policy actions and decisions might have on those groups.

The political and policy decisions made in the 1980s vis-a-vis older persons will affect the system of services and benefits not only to older persons in general, but to older members of ethnic and minority groups in particular. In some cases, those decisions may have a greater impact on older minorities. Just as important, those decisions and actions will have a major effect on younger members of ethnic and minority groups who can expect to live longer and become a large proportion of the elderly population after the year 2000. Yet no attention or examination has been given to the public policy issues affecting future generations of elderly ethnic and minority persons.

This chapter examines current policy actions, assesses the potential impact for the aging of minority groups, and suggests strategies for incorporating ethnicity and minority issues in analyzing the aging of American society. The chapter focuses on the four major national minority groups: Blacks, Hispanics, Asians and Pacific Islanders, and Native Americans. Collectively, they represent a large portion of American society and in some regions will become a majority of the population.

Research on Minority Elderly

Research on minority elderly issues has concentrated on the uniqueness of today's cohorts of older minority persons: those persons in their sixties, seventies, and eighties who are members of pre–World War II generations. The available information on that cohort shows that as a group they have low educational levels, lower life expectancy rates than Whites (with significant exceptions such as the Japanese), relatively high morbidity rates, and low-income levels (Jackson, 1980; Manuel, 1982; McNeely & Colen, 1983). They have low rates of pension coverage other than Social Security, they underutilize public services and benefits, and they are more likely to live in neighborhoods with serious crime and transportation problems (Cuellar & Weeks, 1980; Guttmann, 1980). In general, older minorities are at-risk populations who have higher poverty rates than White elderly.

What is unique about today's cohorts of older minorities is that, by and large, they retain the features of their early socialization: the language, culture, traditions, and rural life-styles prevalent at the turn of the century. They are generally part of large or extended families; they are more likely to receive support from family members compared with White elderly; they retain the cultural strengths of their ethnic group values, norms, and attitudes; and they live in stable communities (Cuellar et al., 1982; Gelfand, 1982; Langston, 1978). They are, in a sense, the survivors of their generation, having faced the effects of immigration to this country, with its relocation and disruption; they have endured and survived discrimination and racism and experienced the Depression of the 1930s.

A growing amount of information exists about the social, economic, and cultural status of today's minority elderly. However, there are significant gaps in the knowledge essential to understanding the factors affecting future cohorts of minority elderly. Several areas deserve mention: the politics of aging, public policy, and the aging of younger cohorts. In the first area, the politics of aging, much is known about the political behavior and political participation of older persons in general. With some exceptions, data about political participation and political behavior among older Blacks, Hispanics, Asians, and Native Americans are not available (Torres-Gil, 1983). In the second area, public policy, there remains inadequate information. Substantial literature exists describing the development of public policies for older persons, the creation of categorical programs, and the development of local and state programs for the elderly. Little attention has been given to the involvement of minority elderly and their advocates in the conceptualization, design, and implementation of those systems, or the effect the current system of public benefits and programs has on the unique culture and traditions of the minority elderly.

The third area is a reflection of the first two gaps in the literature. Because we know little about the political involvement of older minority persons and the effects of public policies on those groups, it is difficult to determine to what extent the situation of younger minorities should be taken into account as we plan for the aging of the baby boom generation and future cohorts of older persons. For example, will today's younger minority groups be a politically active minority elder movement? Will decisions made today to reduce educational and training programs for younger groups have a deleterious effect on their retirement security? Are decisions being made by the Congress and the executive branch, as well as state governments, that either enhance or work against the interests of younger minority groups as they age?

Changes and Trends

Those questions will become important and will require answers in the decades to come. Five important changes will occur in the composition of those four minority groups, changes that may lead to a different type of ethnic and minority elderly profile:

1. *Minority groups will grow dramatically in size, and in some parts of the country they will be the majority population.* In 1984, 91% of the 65-and-over population were White, and 9% were non-White, whereas in the total population, 85% were White and 15% were non-White (U.S. Senate, 1986). The elderly portion of each minority group over 65 included 7.9% for Blacks, 6% for Asians, and

4.9% for persons of Spanish origin (U.S. Bureau of the Census, 1980). Although minority elderly make up a relatively small proportion of their ethnic groups and a small percentage of the overall elderly populations, their numbers will increase in the next several decades. By 2025, 15% of the elderly population are projected to be non-White, and by 2050, 20% are likely to be non-White (AARP, 1986). Hispanic elderly, in particular, are aging at a faster rate than Whites; a greater percentage becomes 60 years old every year than in the White population (DHHS, 1981). In addition, the minority populations in general are increasing at faster rates than the White population. In some locations (e.g., California, Hawaii, Florida) minorities are expected to become a majority.

2. *Added to the high growth rates of minority groups and minority elderly is the continuing influx of immigrants and refugees arriving in this country.* The annual number of legal immigrants to the United States in 1984 was approximately 550,000, with 11.3% from Latin America and 47.1% from Asia (U.S. Bureau of the Census, 1985). The number of illegal immigrants is difficult to ascertain, but a recent study estimated about 2 million illegal immigrants, with about 1.1 million from Mexico (Warren & Passel, 1983). In 1984, 70,600 refugees arrived in the United States (U.S. Bureau of the Census, 1985). Much of the net increase of the U.S. population can now be attributed to immigration and fertility among minority groups.

3. *Assimilation of minorities will add to the heterogeneity of those groups.* Debate persists about the extent of assimilation among Hispanics and Asians, two of the largest ethnic groups, and the extent to which they retain their language, ethnic heritage, and attachment to the mother country. Although the rate of assimilation is uncertain, it appears to be occurring more slowly than the rate for earlier immigrant groups (Sowell, 1981). Most commentators would agree that Hispanics in particular have maintained a substantial ethnic cohesiveness over several generations. With the continuing influx of immigrants and refugees and the close proximity of their countries of origin, it will take longer for some of these groups to assimilate into American mainstream society. And as these groups assimilate into the population and are replenished by new immigrants, they will become more socially and culturally heterogeneous.

4. *A recognition of age as a social and political issue will develop among minorities.* What is unclear is the extent to which age consciousness will permeate and influence ethnic groups who previously have not had social and cultural mores based on age seg-

regation. Senior citizen centers and clubs are popular with Asian, Black, Hispanic, and Native American elderly, although their use may not be as high as for White elderly (U.S. Commission on Civil Rights, 1982). It can be expected that today's younger minorities, as they assimilate, will have greater age consciousness as they grow older.

5. *A politics of aging will develop among older minorities.* Assimilation and age consciousness will lead to increased political identity as members of elderly cohorts and perhaps as members of ethnic elderly cohorts. A "politics of minority aging" may develop among today's minority baby boomers who have a history of activism and have higher levels of education. If that happens, established aging organizations will need to integrate ethnic and minority concerns into their political agenda or face competing political priorities among minority elderly and White elderly groups.

Those five trends illustrate substantial changes that may create a distinctively different population of older persons after the year 2000. If that is the case, what does it portend for future cohorts of older persons? What are the issues, concerns, and tensions that may develop? What opportunities lie ahead to merge the common interests between ethnic and minority elderly and the larger aging population?

Aging Policies and Minority Groups

To understand the political and policy issues that may arise as minority populations age, it is useful to examine the background of current aging policy. The development of policies for older persons initially evolved without incorporation of race, ethnicity, or gender distinctions. This was to be expected because the first efforts to respond to the serious problems affecting older persons required a universal set of programs that met the income and health needs of all older persons. Social Security in 1935 and Medicare in 1965 provided important benefits to all older persons. The introduction of means-tested programs such as Medicaid and Supplemental Security Income, although not directed at racial and ethnic groups, especially assisted minorities and women, who were more likely to have low incomes.

There were other reasons why the unique circumstances of minorities were not a major factor in developing policies from the 1930s through the early 1970s. First, the numbers of older minorities were few. Second, with little age consciousness in those communities, it was not likely that spokespersons for minority communities would single out programs for older persons as a priority issue. Third, the effects of discrimination and segregation hindered the ability of minority advocates to influence the policymaking process.

By the early 1970s this began to change. The 1971 White House Conference on Aging brought together minority advocates who successfully lobbied to have their interests represented at that conference. Subsequently, each of the four major minority groups developed national organizations to represent their issues (Torres-Gil, 1982a). The Administration on Aging incorporated "set asides" for research and demonstration programs targeted at those populations. The Older Americans Act included preferences to those with "the greatest economic and social needs" that in turn helped to leverage resources for minority elderly. In addition, the expansion of benefits in Social Security, food stamps, Supplemental Security Income, Title XX Block Grants, and the increases in cost of living adjustments (COLAs) during the 1970s had a direct benefit for low-income elderly (Torres-Gil & Negm, 1980).

These policy responses relied on what was known about current cohorts of older minorities. To account for the unique characteristics of those groups, they relied on research studies that portrayed older minorities as groups either rural in background or reflecting the culture and language of their countries of origin. Thus, during the 1970s, bilingual and bicultural features were evident in many of the public benefits and services provided to minority populations. Social Security district offices hired bilingual staff people and developed informational material in Spanish. Advocacy groups pressured state and local governments to develop separate senior centers for Chinese, Japanese, Puerto Rican, and other ethnic groups. State and local Area Agencies on Aging required that ethnic meals be served in sites with large concentrations of ethnic elderly. There were even efforts to lower eligibility ages for certain minority groups (e.g., Blacks) with lower life expectancy rates on the supposition that they had been denied benefits because they did not live long enough to collect them.

Changing Directions in Aging Policies

The trend toward incorporating gender, race, language, and culture was abruptly derailed by the redirection of aging policies in the 1980s. The election of a national administration committed to reducing the role of the federal government had profound impact on the directions taken in the 1970s. The federal government moved away from enforcing the Voting Rights Act of 1965 and the Civil Rights Act of 1964 and reduced the effectiveness of the Equal Employment Opportunity Commission, and the U.S. Civil Rights Commission (Schroyer-Portillo, 1984).

Those efforts undercut the rationale and foundation for "set asides," targeting, and preferential treatment for ethnic and minority groups, as well as for women. In addition, and perhaps more important, a massive federal deficit, reductions in funding for federal programs, a consolidation of categorical programs through block grants, and retrenchment in the collection of data and statistics all served to weaken the federal government's ability to focus on subgroups of the elderly population. In turn, state governments were forced to choose between across-the-board cuts and selective targeting between groups most in need. Families, voluntary groups, corporations, and individuals were expected to take the lead in caring for older persons. The expansion of federal benefits and programs came to an abrupt halt, and Congress became less willing to pressure the executive branch to use race, gender, and ethnicity in determining where and how services would be placed.

This political and fiscal redirection is ongoing and has yet to sort itself out. The current approach to fiscal retrenchment, privatization, and reduced government may be a passing trend, or it may be around for the remainder of the century. However it develops during the 1980s, programs for older persons will be severely affected by this reassessment. For example, under the Gramm-Rudman-Hollings Amendment of 1986, COLAs for military and civil service retirement systems were scaled back. Social Security benefits are now taxed, and the Social Security retirement age will be raised. Medicare and Medicaid benefits and coverage have been reduced, and a larger portion of the programs' costs are placed on beneficiaries. Perhaps more important, the creation of policies and programs to meet the needs of a vastly expanding elderly population is not occurring. For example, long-term-care services are widely recognized as an absolute necessity for an increasing frail-elderly population; yet with the exception of a few demonstration projects and scattered state efforts, little is being done now to prepare for the long-term-care needs of elderly baby boomers after the year 2000.

Organizations representing older persons have been resisting the trends to reduce services and funding. In most cases, they have been unsuccessful, but at least they have held the line in critical areas. Under the Gramm-Rudman-Hollings Amendment, for example, they succeeded in exempting Social Security. They have forced Congress to maintain the basic structure of Medicare and Medicaid, and they have preserved the Older Americans Act as a categorical program. Whether they can continue to hold the line remains uncertain. But the political influence of the elderly may preserve those programs until a national administration is elected that is more favorable to their issues.

Throughout this political drama, little has been heard about the situation of ethnic and minority elderly vis-a-vis this redirection of policies. How are Black, Hispanic, and Asian elderly faring during this struggle? Are their representatives and advocates playing a major role as the Congress and executive branch debate the terms of aging and social policy? Unfortunately, these and other questions are not being asked or addressed in national policymaking. For example, during the 1983 reforms of Social Security no attention was paid to the impact of these policy changes on ethnic and racial groups. That appears to be the case as other policies and programs are scrutinized.

The remainder of this chapter points out some of those policy changes, assesses the potential impact for the aging of minority groups, and suggests areas for policy analysis and strategies for incorporating ethnicity and minority status in responding to the aging of the society. It looks at two key areas—political power and competition, and resource allocation and financial security—and draws out the issues and themes that provide clues about the future status of ethnic and minority aging and the conflicts, tensions, and opportunities that may occur as the reassessment of the 1980s plays itself out.

Political Power and Competition

Much has been written about the political influence of older persons. The "politics of aging" refers to the power and effectiveness of older persons as a constituency and age-based organizations as advocates and lobbyists. Although there is disagreement about the collective impact older persons have in the development of social policies for the aged, there is little disagreement that for elected officials, older persons are an extraordinarily important force. As a group they have high registration and voting rates and are more apt to write their elected officials and participate in political activities. For example, in 1982, 65% of persons 55 to 64 years old voted, compared with 60% of persons aged 45 to 54 and 52% of persons aged 35 to 44

(U.S. Congress, 1984). Some analysts argue that the elderly are not a voting bloc and that any claims to the effect that they wield inordinate power solely because of their collective numbers is a political bluff (Binstock, 1972). In part, this is accurate. Older persons are a diverse group whose members differ by gender, income, race, background, and class. They do not always have common concerns. However, on selective issues such as Social Security and Medicare, where they are directly affected as older persons, the elderly do tend to vote as a bloc and are an important political force (Pierce & Choharis, 1984). As organized interest groups, they are probably second only to the National Rifle Association in perceived and actual clout on Capitol Hill. They do not always have their way on matters of legislation and policies (funding for many elderly programs have been reduced), but at least they have managed to make it politically painful for the executive and legislative branches to reduce or eliminate public benefits and services.

The politics of aging among minority elderly is another matter. As a group, non-White elderly make up only 9% of the total elderly population in the United States. Registration and voting rates for minority elderly are low relative to the general elderly population. For example, in the 1982 election, for those between 65 and 74 years of age, 66.2% of Whites voted compared to 54.4% of Blacks and 29.3% of those of Spanish origin (U.S. Bureau of the Census, 1983b).

In addition, ethnic and minority elderly are further hindered by linguistic and citizenship barriers. Many Hispanic and Asian older persons are not citizens, do not speak English, or are illiterate in their native language (which mitigates the usefulness of ballots and election materials in their language). Some come from countries where there is no history of active civic participation, and others fear deportations or the repressive measures they knew in their countries (e.g., Central America, Vietnam) (Torres-Gil, 1982b). Still others, particularly Black elderly, retain memories of racism, which reduces their inclination to be active participants. Even if registration and voting rates equal to that of White elderly existed, their fewer numbers and tremendous diversity would limit their overall political impact. However, there do exist national organizations that represent those groups—e.g., National Caucus on Black Aged, National Hispanic Council on Aging—although they tend to be professional and academic in orientation. They do advocate for minority aged, but compared with the influence of larger organizations such as the American Association for Retired Persons, their impact is small.

On the other hand, minority elderly are members of populations with political influence. Blacks and Hispanics in particular are becoming important political forces in American Society. Their political organizations—The Urban League, Rainbow Coalition, LULAC, MALDEF, National Council of La Raza, NAACP—are recognized as effective political forces. The combined political power of the minority electorate in this country is increasing, as shown by the number of Black, Hispanic, and Asian elected officials at all levels of government. However, a major gap is that none of the organizations listed above have aging and senior citizen issues as key priorities. Aging policy is not a predominant issue for minority elected officials. In short, the elderly segment of the minority populations is not represented by its political leaders. There are some reasons for this. In the last 30 years, Blacks, Hispanics, Native Americans, and Asians have had to deal with pressing and immediate issues of jobs, education, and discrimination—issues that did not afford them the luxury of pursuing foreign affairs, environmental concerns, or demographic changes. In addition, they have traditionally been young populations with cultures that provided a measure of security and resources for their elders. Thus, the problems and needs of their elderly were not a highly visible concern. In addition, mainstream organizations such as the Gray Panthers, National Council on the Aging, and AARP did not actively promote membership among minority elderly. Thus, it is no surprise that although the elderly in general have substantial political influence, minority elderly in the 1980s do not have as much power. Will this be the case for future cohorts of elderly minorities?

There is evidence to suggest that today's minority baby boomers will have significantly greater levels of political involvement as they grow older. Although registration levels in the 1982 elections were 35% for Hispanics, 59% for Blacks, and 64% for Whites (U.S. Bureau of the Census, 1983a), those rates are increasing (Kirschten, 1983; Reid, 1982). The educational level of minorities, a key prerequisite to political interest and involvement, has increased, albeit still significantly lower than that of Whites (Boren, 1983; U.S. Department of Education, 1980).

The minority baby boom group, which will become the minority elderly after the year 2000, is also more assimilated than their parents and grandparents and already has a history of political involvement. They were the young student activists of the civil rights era in the 1950s, 1960s, and 1970s. They may also be the senior citizen activists at the turn of the century. Therefore, there is a real likelihood that, as the number of minorities who are elderly increases, their political activism and political influence will increase as well. What might be their political objectives and priorities?

In time, aging issues will almost certainly become a domestic policy concern for minority groups and minority political leaders. Just as older members of the general population have the highest voting rates, so it is with minority populations (U.S. Bureau of the Census, 1983b). Minority politicians eventually will recognize and seize on that statistical fact. Already we find that in local, state, and national elections, minority politicians make it a point to visit minority senior citizen centers to court their votes. As their size, educational levels, and assimilation rates increase, minority elderly will become a more sought-after group. Where they are predominant in numbers, they will be important political forces. In places like San Antonio, Detroit, Los Angeles, and San Francisco, the number of senior citizen clubs abound. We can expect them to have many of the same concerns that face all elderly. Adequate retirement income, fear of crime, the high cost of housing, adequate transportation, and health care coverage will be important issues for minority elderly. However, the future minority elderly may have issues that are distinct from that of older persons in general. Multilingualism and multiculturalism, maintaining their culture and language and involvement in the politics of their mother countries, will set their issues apart from nonminority elderly. Where discrimination and racism continue to segregate and polarize minority and nonminority populations, the elderly of both communities may also be segregated or polarized from each other. Thus, what faces the future politics of aging is that the current political profile of the elderly will change dramatically, becoming more heterogeneous along ethnic and linguistic lines. The general elderly population will no longer have the luxury to ignore or remain indifferent to the concerns of the ethnic and minority elders, whose numbers will ensure that they have a role to play in the politics of the aging. Whether that role is competitive, coalitional, integrative, or polarized remains to be seen.

There is another side to this equation. Although the percentage of elderly among minority groups will increase, the minority groups themselves will continue to remain younger than the general population, at least for the next several decades. The White population in the United States is close to zero population growth. Most of the net population gain is occurring because of immigration and high fertility rates of minority groups. Thus, minority populations will become a substantial part of the general population, creating the potential for tension. The elderly population will have age-related issues as their main concern—educating and training for later-life careers, protection of pension and retirement programs, affordable and comprehensive health care—and the political muscle to obtain what it wants. Minority populations, on the other hand, will continue to be plagued by high unemployment, poor educational attainment, deteriorating neighborhoods, and a growing underclass of alienated young people. Minority politicians will be forced to confront those needs, particularly in urban areas and states where minorities are in the majority. Will the elderly vote down public school bond measures that benefit young populations, particularly minorities? Will ethnic politicians vote to scale back municipal pension systems in order to pay for the urban infrastructures of cities that are essentially Third World? Will the labor force, increasingly dominated by minorities, be willing to tax itself to support age-related programs? These are sensitive and difficult questions that present various scenarios regarding what may occur.

The wild card in these scenarios is the direction in which the minority elderly of the future, a large and rapidly growing population after the year 2000, will lean. Will they support the priorities of their young ethnic populations, or will they attach priorities to senior citizens concerns? Will minority elderly develop coalitions with mainstream aging groups or with minority political organizations? These are intriguing and important questions that highlight the need to explore the situation of minority populations in an aging society. Unfortunately, the policy directions of the 1980s do not present an optimistic scenario.

Resource Allocation and Financial Security

In David Stockman's book *The Triumph of Politics* (Stockman, 1986), he argues that the Reagan revolution failed because the American people did not want to dismantle the "welfare state," with its entitlement programs and public subsidies. Whether or not he is correct in that analysis, it is true that during the 1980s those aging programs that were universal and were not means-tested carried popular support. Social Security, Medicare, and the Older Americans Act maintained their basic structure and benefits, although some of their benefits were scaled back and greater costs were placed on beneficiaries. On the other hand, programs that were means-tested and targeted toward low-income elderly took deeper cuts during this period. Food stamps, low-income energy subsidies, Section 202 and Section 8 housing supports were all drastically affected by cutbacks. Medicaid programs in many states were either frozen or reduced. Those programs that disproportionately aided low-income (and hence minority) elderly were scaled back at the very time when they were in great demand because of the increase of poverty among minority elderly. For example, among Black elderly, the poverty rate was triple (31.7%) and among Hispanic elderly was double (21.5%) that of White elderly (10.7%). Nearly half (45.6%) of all Black older persons had incomes below 125% of the poverty level (U.S. Senate, 1986). In addition, while the poor and minority elderly were feeling the brunt of reduction in vital social support programs, poverty among children was increasing at tremendous rates. By 1984, the poverty rate for the elderly had dropped to 12%, but for children it had grown to 21.3% (U.S. Bureau of the Census, 1984). This impoverishment was especially endemic among Black and Hispanic populations. The prevalence of young Black and Hispanic women as single heads of household had become a serious national problem; yet Aid for Families with Dependent Children (AFDC), day care, prenatal health care programs, and neighborhood health clinics were being reduced. Public education, the cornerstone of upward mobility, had become such a national disgrace that the president, the Department of Education, and many state governments were forced to concede that standards and resources required upgrading if the country was to avoid a decline in its educational standards. Still, there remained tremendous ambivalence among taxpayers about putting more revenues into inner-city public schools, which abetted the continuation of the erosion of educational supports for younger minority populations.

Those parallel trends—widespread support for entitlement programs to older persons, lesser support for low-income programs geared to poor elderly, and increased poverty among young minority populations—were creating some potentially divisive situations for America's aging society. Would the political power of the elderly continue to preserve and protect programs popular with the middle class (recognizing that they also provided critical support to minority and low-income elderly) while sacrificing the needs of the poor elderly? Would public support force choices between aging programs and youth-oriented services? It is uncertain whether young minority populations will lose out in the competition for scarce public dollars. But if they should, the future status of minority elderly may become more precarious. If young Blacks, Hispanics, Asians, and

Native Americans do not have the education, training, and employment opportunities to acquire jobs that provide pension and retirement coverage, then they will become more dependent on public welfare programs as they grow older. In their retirement years, they may face what their grandparents now face: dependence on Social Security and Supplemental Security Income for their retirement income and inadequate health care coverage because of reductions in Medicaid and Medicare benefits.

Again, a striking political feature stands out as these scenarios unfold: the political leadership of minority populations is not engaged in the critical public policy actions and decisions taking place in aging. No national group or organization purporting to represent minorities is playing a key role in the debates over Social Security, retirement and pension coverage, health care reform, or the development of long-term-care policies. To further complicate this equation, a new phenomenon has developed in the late 1980s: the notion that "generational conflict" exists between younger populations, particularly the baby boomers, and the elderly (Kingson, Hirschorn, & Harootyan, 1986; U.S. Congress, 1986). According to this notion, baby boomers fear that too large a proportion of the federal budget is going to older persons while they are being saddled with a large deficit and increased taxes to pay for entitlement programs. This view has major weaknesses, not the least of which is the fact that public opinion polls show strong support by young persons for aging programs. But here again, a consistent pattern exists whereby those individuals and their organizations, arguing for the rights of baby boomers, do not include the needs and concerns of young minority populations, nor do they distinguish between the needs and economic status of elderly in general and low-income and minority elderly in particular.

In an aging society, the continued existence of high rates of poverty among young and old minorities will raise serious issues about employment, labor-force participation, and education. But the more salient issue is the extent to which minority groups will be at greater risk when they age, given their present circumstances. How likely is it that, in an aging society, policy decisions are being made that affect the economic circumstances of future minority elderly? In 1983, for example, Congress instituted major structural changes to preserve the fiscal integrity of the Social Security system. It avoided benefit reductions for current recipients. But for future beneficiaries it raised the eligibility age for receipt of full benefits to age 67 for those individuals who will reach age 62 after the year 2022. This type of public policy action raises the prospect that future generations of older minorities may not have access to benefits now enjoyed by the elderly, particularly those groups with lower life expectancies.

Health policy is another area of concern. Health care delivery is developing into a two-tier system: one level for those with private health insurance, Medicare, or the means to pay for expensive medical treatment, and another for those forced to rely on Medicaid or public charity or do without health care altogether. The services provided at the second level are fewer and of lower quality. This situation is exacerbated by cutbacks in Medicaid, by the expansion of a for-profit medical-industrial system that caters to middle- and upper-income consumers, and by state and local government unwillingness or inability to provide health care to the poor.

Examination of pension coverage provides additional clues about the disparity in financial security for the aging of minority populations. In 1980, Hispanic civilian workers had the lowest rates of pension plan coverage (35%), followed by Blacks (40.9%) and Whites (45.5%) (Romero, 1984). Among workers participating in private pension plans, Hispanic and Black workers are less likely to have vested rights benefits than their White counterparts. The difference is particularly large among older participants, those getting ready to retire. Among all ages, 35% of Hispanics were vested and 41% of Blacks were vested, compared with 49% of Whites. In the 45-and-older range, 44% of Hispanics and 58% of Blacks were vested, compared with 66% of Whites (Rogers, 1982).

Issues

The issues of political power and competition, and resource allocation and financial security, point out the tensions, challenges, and opportunities for minority populations in an aging society. In particular, these issues suggest that several trends must be understood in comprehending the impact that current and future policy and political effects may have on the minority elderly of today and tomorrow: the situation of today's older minorities and the impact of current policy actions; the fundamental reassessment occurring today vis-a-vis public policies and benefits to older persons; the aging of young minority populations and the policy actions that hinder of help in their aging process; and the development of a more ethnically and racially diverse politics of aging after the year 2000.

Various scenarios may unfold depending on how each trend develops. For example, we know that today's older minorities face multiple jeopardies and that current policy actions are exacerbating their economic and social circumstances. We can surmise that the redirection of aging programs occurring in the 1980s does not bode well for today's elderly, both minority and nonminority; and if it continues into the 1990s, it does not bode well for future cohorts of minority elderly. What is uncertain is the extent to which there will be public and private sector investment in the economic, educational, and social needs of younger minority groups. To what extent will we invest in public education, job training programs, and health care services to children and families? Will discrimination, nativism, and racism continue to polarize and divide ethnic and racial groups? The answers to these and other questions will say much about how young minority populations age in this society. Therefore, the last issue, the future politics of aging, will be affected directly by the experiences encountered by the aging of young minority populations, groups that will become a large proportion of the elderly population after the year 2000 and who will be better educated, more assimilated, and hence more politically involved. Will that future elderly population find itself fragmented and divided along racial and ethnic lines? Will the minority elders of the next century ally themselves with the much larger ethnic populations, or will they see aging issues as their first priority? This last issue is subject to speculation and can only be guessed at. But it serves to emphasize that what occurs in the 1980s and 1990s regarding policy and politics will say much about the types of tensions, challenges, and opportunities that may unfold when the United States finds itself with an ethnically diverse elderly cohort comprising around 25% of its population.

There are various factors and variables that can complicate and alter these types of scenarios. The minority populations in the United States are extraordinarily diverse. Although Blacks and Hispanics comprise the two largest groups, they have major differences among themselves. For example, Hispanics include Cubans, Mexican Americans, Puerto Ricans, and Central Americans. Cubans tend to have the highest median ages and relatively high income and educational levels; Puerto Ricans and Central Americans have the lowest socioeconomic status. On cultural matters, they share some common goals, such as preservation of language, religion, and culture; but they differ on political issues. Cubans tend to be conservative, and Puerto Ricans tend to be liberal. Even Blacks differ greatly along urban/rural lines and increasingly are divided into Blacks from Africa and Blacks from the Carribean.

The other major minority groups are even more diverse. Asians and Pacific Islanders are the nation's fastest-growing groups but include subgroups as diverse as Japanese, Chinese, Vietnamese, Laotians, and Guamanians. The Japanese have a strong assimilationist ethos and the highest life expectancy rates, whereas Southeast Asians are very recent refugee groups who are only beginning to adjust in the United States. Native Americans comprise many different tribes and dialects and have a unique relationship with the federal government, having a more independent status vis-a-vis public services and benefits.

In addition to those differences, a growing division along gender and class lines exists. Women in those groups, as in the general population, live longer than men; and as their populations age, they will be a much larger portion of their populations. Although many of these groups retain traditional male/female patterns whereby men are the dominant force in their communities, women can be expected to benefit from advances in women's rights and to be increasingly outspoken. Class distinctions are becoming more pronounced among some of these groups, especially among Blacks and Hispanics. The civil rights and educational advancements of the last several decades have created a larger middle class, which has resulted in increasing numbers of well-educated and successful professionals in those populations. Yet a Black and Hispanic underclass continues to grow, and there is evidence that alienation and tensions are developing between the more successful elements of those populations and those who continue to be alienated and poor.

Conclusion

The effects of assimilation, ethnic diversity, and gender and class distinctions on the future aging of minority groups is difficult to assess. It does emphasize the need to examine closely a multitude of areas in order to better understand how to respond in a compassionate and productive manner to a growing minority elderly population. Yet research is practically nonexistent in those areas. Much of the research touching on those areas is either focused on today's minority elderly profiles or on the minority population as groups that will remain young and traditional. Unfortunately, a dichotomy among researchers interested in ethnic and racial issues has developed that begins and ends around age 60, whereby most look at minority issues as if aging is not an important continuum of the life cycle or examine aging issues as if minority elderly do not have a past. Neither approach examines the vital importance of longitudinal studies and trend analyses.

The issues raised in this chapter are so data-dependent that the type of data used and the collection of information becomes crucial to sound public policy. In the past, much of the data used to measure the economic status of different age groups and populations was cross-sectional. Comparison of successive cross-sections of a particular age group gives us a crude measure of their economic status. However, such static measures tell us little about the upward or downward mobility of individuals as they grow older. (For example, they don't always tell us how an aged person can be impoverished by long-term illness or the death of a spouse.) With respect to the aged in particular, it is essential that we examine longitudinal data in addition to the traditional static measure of well-being (like median income or an aggregate poverty rate) because the conclusions we come to can be very different. The availability of information becomes important in making policy decisions and determining resource allocations; however, the 1980s witnessed a disturbing trend. During that time, the federal government and many state governments reduced the requirements for collecting data and statistics, ostensibly to reduce paperwork requirements. But in fact, there was evidence that these actions were taken to make it more difficult for advocates to argue their cases for special preferences. If true, this adversely affects the ability to analyze and understand, and therefore respond to, the demographic trends and the manner in which the public sector responds.

How we define ethnicity will take on added meaning in investigating these profound social and demographic changes. The history of immigration to this country and the growth of minority populations will create new dimensions precisely because minorities are aging in a society that has yet to come to terms with its increasing cultural pluralism. In addition, the growing disparities between the poor and the affluent, the increasing tensions between ethnic and racial groups, and the emphasis during the 1980s on scaling back the public sector's responsibility for providing leadership on domestic matters, does not auger well for planning ahead. Nonetheless, scholars, policy analysts, and professionals involved in aging have an important role to play during this period by examining these trends and changes, defining the policy issues that must be addressed, and proposing solutions and recommendations. In time, minorities in general and minority elderly in particular will have political influence, and it is hoped that the nation will respond in compassionate and progressive ways, as it did during the depression of the 1930s and the civil rights struggles of the 1960s and the 1970s.

This chapter has pointed out the critical impact of policy and politics on public services to minority elderly and to the future aging of younger minority groups. Yet too few gerontologists, particularly researchers interested in ethnic and minority aging, are involved with policy analysis and applied policy research. Another area not normally investigated is that of the geopolitical circumstances affecting this nation and its diverse groups. Immigration, particularly the dramatic increase of Hispanics, Asians, and Pacific Islanders, will have major, albeit unpredictable, effects on the lives of minority groups in this country and on the attitudes of the general population toward ethnic diversity. The passage of a major immigration reform bill in 1986 will have major repercussions on illegal immigration and on the delivery of services to ethnic and minority elderly. The Pacific Basin and Latin America are also witnessing growing life expectancies and a growing aged population. What can the United States, with its growing numbers of older minorities, teach those countries about responding to aging in an increasingly industrialized, technological world?

In developing a better understanding of the aging of minority groups, several areas for research are important. Political behavior and participation will be a significant area for investigation, including the micro-subsystems and macro-issues that involve the interaction of political behavior, interest group politics, and public policy. Accounting for the effects of acculturation and assimilation will help us assess the effects of linguistic, cultural, and social changes among the myriad ethnic and racial groups, creating more accurate profiles of subgroup differences among and within ethnic and racial groups.

In conclusion, the future of the nation will be affected by two important trends: the aging of the society and the growing multiculturalism of its population. How we respond to both will say much about ethnicity and aging in this country.

Conclusion: Looking Back and Looking Ahead

Charles M. Barresi and Donald E. Gelfand

Looking Back

As we come to the end of this endeavor, it is time to take stock of where we have been and where we are going. A number of important themes are evident throughout the book. First is the emphasis on the uniqueness of cultural systems of meaning and the way in which these systems structure the aging experience for the individual. Understanding the realities of everyday aging from the point of view of the person reveals aspects that structural and sociopsychological approaches fail to consider. An important aspect of this approach, mentioned by several authors, is the salience of language in the creation of this everyday reality. Ethnic elderly not only use different words to describe their world and their needs in it, the words have a unique meaning that is not easily translatable into other languages. These ideas have implications that are also mentioned by other authors in regard to research and to practice and policy issues as well.

Second, the theory section provides a valuable contribution with its emphasis on the dynamics of ethnic identity as an adaptive technique in coping with the life-change events that accompany aging. In this sense, ethnicity is seen as not just a demographic variable that describes one's country of origin, race, or other cultural characteristics. Rather, it is considered as an integral part of the personality and a means of coping with a changing and sometimes hostile environment. Seen in this way, ethnicity becomes a dynamic mechanism that provides both continuity and the ability to adapt, as well as the means to the creation of a stable, ordered world. If this conception of ethnicity were to be integrated into the general theoretical framework used by many gerontologists, the knowledge base in ethnicity and aging would be greatly enhanced.

Third, the emphasis on ethnicity in the development of the life course should also be considered as one of the contributions of this book. Too often ethnicity is merely mentioned as an important variable in explaining the aging process without going into enough detail to provide a working knowledge. Several authors have demonstrated the utility of the life-course perspective in understanding ethnic aging. In the future, readers should not only be cognizant of the importance of this perspective but also be able to utilize these ideas and modify them to their own areas of interest in ethnicity and aging.

Many of the theoretical concerns raised in Part I are illustrated by the research chapters in Part II. The variety of topics treated in the latter section gives testimony to the range of research problems that encompass ethnic aging. In addition, by utilizing a number of methodological techniques, readers are provided with insights for future research.

The study of the Hmong portrays one of the newer ethnic groups in the United States and lends insight into the continuing salience of the ethnic issue in gerontology. The Hmong, like other newly immigrated groups from Asian and Latin American countries, show us how ethnicity continues to be problematic for several generations simultaneously. Each generation, whether young or old, is presented with dilemmas resulting from their being transplanted from one cultural setting to another. The contrast between these new groups and those that have been in the society for a longer time facilitates understanding of the dynamics of both. This understanding is abetted by the chapter on seldom studied groups such as the Greeks and the Amish.

The inclusion of chapters from Canadian gerontologists, illustrating the cross-national nature of the issues being investigated, is a unique contribution of this collection. Canada presents a rich setting for ethnic studies, and its population is now reaching a point where concern for the issues surrounding the aging of its ethnic populace are being translated into a wealth of information. Comparisons between the older ethnic population of the United States and the somewhat younger ethnic population of Canada will produce rich insights as scholars from the two North American countries continue to exchange ideas in the future.

The ultimate goal of any research-oriented discipline is to have its knowledge base become the foundation for understanding and implementing change in the subject matter with which it deals. Of course, it is assumed that the changes will be ones that ameliorate problems and contribute to clarification of issues and the means to deal with them. This is not to say that all science is, or must be, oriented toward practical ends. However, those who are involved with practice or legislative activities look to researchers for answers to assist them in their endeavors.

A problem that service providers often face with service delivery to ethnic elderly is the lack of literacy in the target population. The concept of bifunctionalism introduced in Part III suggests that before effective service delivery can occur, basic socialization in language and societal skills must take place. In this way the ethnic elderly persons who are being reached will not be culturally isolated and will instead be receptive and able to utilize the assistance they are given. This novel idea is fraught with problems, both practical and moral, but it is an attempt to innovate in the area of social work practice with ethnic elderly. Whether or not one agrees with this proposal, it does represent an attempt at providing a solution to the vexing problem of bringing services to elderly who are not literate and who are essentially hidden from the dominant culture.

The introduction of the concept of "socially constructed hardships" lends new directions for understanding the nature and scope of the problems involved in providing for the needs of the ethnic elderly. Identifying the social nature of social problems calls for solutions that address the problematic aspects of the community or group, not of the individual. This approach requires new strategies and policies, and in this way makes a positive contribution to problem solving.

Looking Ahead

There are a number of topics in ethnicity and aging that need further exploration. The first area of concern is continued theoretical development. That there is no adequate theory regarding ethnic aging is consistent with the general state of theory in gerontology. This collection takes up the important and necessary task of addressing this deficiency with an eye toward stimulating further attention and thought to remedy this situation.

Socioeconomic status and health account for a major part of the variation in behavior among the elderly. It is essential that gerontologists who study ethnic elderly concentrate more of their efforts in examining the effects of these two variables on aging. Many researchers who readily acknowledge the heterogeneity of the elderly in general ignore the fact that within any given ethnic group a wide range of socioeconomic status often exists.

Does ethnicity become less important as socioeconomic status increases? This question, when asked in relationship to aging, cannot yet be answered. It is often asserted that if the socioeconomic status of a middle-age cohort is higher than that of their parents, the ethnic culture may be altered and become more of a memory than an important factor in everyday life. At this point, however, that assertion cannot be fully proved nor dismissed.

In some cases it may not be the alterations in ethnic culture that we are witnessing but the fact that the ethnic culture fits very well into the majority culture and its demands on the individual intent on acculturation. Only a clear understanding of the traditional ethnic culture and how it has changed under immigration can provide us with the detail necessary to deal with this issue. We stress the change in the culture here because one of the major themes running through this volume is both the stability and change that occurs in ethnic culture.

The ethnic culture brought to a new country by immigrants may be the "traditional" culture, but it is not necessarily the same culture that binds Mexican Americans whose families have lived in the United States for five or six generations. On the other hand, a group such as Puerto Ricans may alter their cultural patterns even earlier because of the island's unique relationship to the U.S. mainland. Significant numbers of Puerto Ricans spend part of each year in both Puerto Rico and the mainland United States. This partial tenure in two distinct communities may affect the future configuration of this ethnic culture.

The important issues are not only the changes that differentiate present-day ethnic cultures from the traditional or "immigrant" culture but the values that form the core of the present ethnic culture. These values may produce less divergence between the ethnic culture and the majority culture. It is hoped that future research will explain the extent to which these changes are related to factors such as intergenerational succession and intermarriage, as well as explaining the consistency of these changes among all socioeconomic groups within the ethnic culture. With this knowledge in hand we can more accurately gauge the continuing or changing impact of ethnicity on aging.

The health issue also includes those aspects of groups that are seldom dealt with in the literature in gerontology: the frail, the physically handicapped, and the mentally retarded elderly. Investigation into these special groups of elderly can reveal insights that will advance our knowledge considerably. It is also imperative that we learn how various ethnic groups in our society respond to these problems as manifested by their elders. A related issue is the response of physicians, nurses, nursing home administrators, and other health-related personnel to the special needs and situations presented in the health and long-term-care needs of the ethnic elderly. In addition, knowledge regarding the attitudes and responses of family caregivers in ethnic communities is sorely needed.

The need for more information also extends to the services and policies of agencies serving ethnic elderly. These same concerns need to be addressed by decision makers regarding legislation that concerns ethnic elderly. Future research should focus on the present techniques of social service workers and the basic philosophies under which they operate. Given the uniqueness of ethnic groups, there is need to establish strategies of service delivery that take into consideration the respective differences among groups regarding intergenerational relations, status of elderly, gender differences, and other important characteristics. The openness of ethnic groups to assistance from social agencies also needs continued investigation. All of these issues should be addressed with the heterogeneity issue in mind so that differences within as well as among groups are not ignored.

Conclusion

This book was undertaken because of the need to update and accumulate the growing knowledge base in ethnicity and aging. Collections such as these are an important means of bringing together a variety of current issues that focus on a single theme. They not only provide an inventory of ideas and current thinking, they also create a stimulation to new directions in the field.

In order to accomplish these goals, our initial charge to the contributors to this book was to address not only the concerns of the particular ethnic group that they investigated but to broaden the application of their generalizations so they could be applied to other ethnic groups. In addition, all authors were encouraged to integrate their findings with existing theories so as to enlarge and extend their results beyond the present group or setting and to make their findings more useful for readers. We believe the result is a positive indication of the progress that has been made in the area of ethnicity and aging.

This progress can be accelerated if gerontologists who specialize in ethnicity come together to explore the theory accomplishments and deficits in their area of interest. Such concentrated attention would begin to highlight promising new directions of explanation and provide scrutiny of the relevance of present theoretical approaches to ethnicity.

An equal amount of attention should be centered on the research methods in ethnicity and aging. This includes issues relating to sampling techniques, data collection, and analysis. Some of the chapters in this book make contributions in this direction. Researchers in this area must understand how the unique characteristics of the ethnic group under investigation affect the research process. For example, knowledge of unique forms of relationship, address, and communication used in an ethnic group is crucial if researchers are to obtain results that are valid and meaningful. Although information on the language and culture of the study group is vital, knowing what data to collect and making sense of it afterward is equally important and is dependent on a thorough knowledge of gerontology as it relates to ethnicity.

The continued and growing interest in ethnicity in gerontology is a reflection of the significance of ethnicity in the general society. In the last decade policies have been predicated more on the decline of ethnicity than on its reemergence as a salient factor in defining significant social groups.

It was assumed by some that ethnicity was a disappearing and unimportant phenomenon because of the major decline in immigration from European countries. The aging and death of the last cohorts of individuals who entered the United States at Ellis Island was seen to signal the end of ethnicity as a phenomenon affecting behavior and values of older individuals. White ethnic groups had supposedly been totally assimilated into the American "melting pot." These White ethnic groups were also assumed to be doing so well economically that they did not need any formal assistance.

This could not be further from the truth. Not only do those groups that have been in this country for many years continue to require services but new groups from Southeast Asia and Latin America are steadily growing both in size and in demand for much needed help.

It is our hope that the interest in ethnicity that has been shown in gerontology will carry over into concerns by legislators and other decision makers for providing programs to assist the many persons needing assistance. It is imperative that gerontologists not only document the scope and direction of required programs but that they also evaluate the effectiveness of these programs once they are in place.

The addition of ethnicity as a variable in the field of aging can only mean further complexity and analytic problems in a field that is already long on problems and short on solutions. However, the return is worth the investment of time and effort. The resulting description will be a more accurate portrayal of the dynamic, pluralistic reality in which North Americans live, rather than the static, homogeneous society depicted as real by many writers. We can only hope that this book will contribute toward those ends through an increased awareness and knowledge of the ethnic dimensions of aging.

References

Aaltio, T. (1969). A survey of emigration to the United States and Canada. In R. Jalkanen (Ed.), *The Finns of North America, A social symposium.* Lansing, MI: Michigan State University Press.

Abbott, J. (1977). Socioeconomic characteristics of the elderly: Some Black/White differences. *Social Security Bulletin, 40,* 16–42.

Abbott, J. (1980). Work experience and earnings of middle-aged Black and White men, 1965–1971. *Social Security Bulletin, 43, 12,* 16–34.

Advisory Council on Social Security. (1979). *Social security financing and benefits—reports of the 1979 Advisory Council on Social Security.* Washington, DC: U.S. Government Printing Office.

Altergott, K. (1985). Marriage, gender, and social relations in late life. In W. A. Peterson & J. Quadagno (Eds.), *Social bonds in later life* (pp. 51–70). Beverly Hills, CA: Sage.

American Association of Retired Persons. (1986). A portrait of older minorities. *Minority Affairs Initiative.* Washington, DC: Author.

Andersen, R., Kravits, J., & Anderson, O. (1975). *Equity in health services: Empirical analysis in social policy.* Cambridge, MA: Ballinger.

Anderson, A., & Frideres, J. S. (1981). *Ethnicity in Canada.* Toronto: Butterworth.

Anderson, B. E., & Cottingham, D. H. (1981). The elusive quest for economic equality. *Daedalus, 110, 2,* 257–274.

Anderson, N., Patten, S., & Greenburg, J. (1980). *A comparison of home care and nursing home care for older persons in Minnesota* (Vol. 3). Minneapolis: University of Minnesota, Hubert H. Humphrey Institute of Public Affairs and Center for Health Services Research.

Anspoch, D. F. (1976). Kinship and divorce. *Journal of Marriage and the Family, 38,* 323–330.

Antonucci, T. C., & Depner, C. E. (1981). Social support and informal helping relationships. In T. A. Willis (Ed.), *Basic processes in helping relationships.* New York: Academic Press.

Areba, et al. (1972). International research and education in social gerontology—goals and strategies. *The Gerontologist, 12,* 49–83.

Atchley, R. C. (1971). Retirement and leisure participation: Continuity or crisis? *The Gerontologist, 11,* 13–17.

Atchley, R. C. (1980). *The social forces in later life: An introduction to social gerontology* (3rd ed.). Belmont, CA: Wadsworth.

Atchley, R. C. (1983). *Aging, continuity and change.* Belmont, CA: Wadsworth.

Atchley, R. C. (1985). *The social forces in later life* (4th ed.). Belmont, CA: Wadworth.

Attneave, C. (1982). American Indians and Alaska native families: Emigrants in their own homeland. In M. McGoldrick, J. K. Pearce, & J. Giordano (Eds.), *Ethnicity and family therapy* (pp. 55–83). New York: Guilford Press.

Back, K., & Bourque L. B. (1970). Life graphs: Aging and cohort effects. *Journal of Gerontology, 25,* 249–255.

Bahr, H. (1970). Aging and religious disaffiliation. *Social Forces, 49,* 59–71.

Baldwin, C. (1982). *Capturing the change.* Santa Anna, CA: Immigrant and Refugee Planning Center.

Barney, L. (1967). The Hmong of northern Laos. In *Indochinese refugee education guides.* Washington, DC: Center for Applied Linguistics.

Barresi, C. M. (1986). Ethnic elderly: Homogeneity or Pluralism? Presented at the Tenth Annual Professional and Scientific Conference on Aging, April, 4. Columbus OH.

Barresi, C. M. (1974). The meaning of work: A case study of elderly poor. *Industrial Gerontology, 1(N.S.),* 24–34.

Barresi, C. M., Ferraro, K. F., & Hobey, L. L. (1984). Environmental satisfaction, sociability, and well-being among urban elderly. *International Journal of Aging and Human Development, 18*(4), 277–293.

Barth, F. (1969). *Ethnic groups and boundaries: The social organization of cultural differences.* Boston: Little, Brown.

Bastida, E. (1983). Minority decision-making, accessibility and resource utilization in the provision of services: Urban-rural differences. In R. McNeely & J. Colen (Eds.), *Aging in minority groups.* Beverly Hills, CA: Sage.

Bastida, E. (1984). Reconstructing the social world at 60: Older Cubans in the United States. *The Gerontologist, 24,* 465–470.

Bastida, E. (1987). Sex-typed age norms among older Hispanics. *The Gerontologist, 27,* 59–65.

Becerra, R. (1983). The Mexican-American: Aging in a changing culture. In R. McNeely & J. Colen (Eds.), *Aging in minority groups.* Beverly Hills, CA: Sage.

Bengtson, V. (1979). Ethnicity and aging: Problems and issues in current social science inquiry. In D. Gelfand & A. Kutzik (Eds.), *Ethnicity and aging: Theory, research and policy.* New York: Springer Publishing Co.

Bengtson, V., Cuellar, J., & Ragan, P. (1977). Stratum contrasts and similarities in attitudes toward death. *Journal of Gerontology, 32,* 76–88.

Berger, P. E., & Luckman, T. (1966). *The construction of reality: A treatise in the sociology of knowledge.* Garden City, NY: Doubleday.

Berger, P., & Luckman, T. (1967). *The social construction of reality.* New York: Anchor Books.

Biddle, B., & Thomas, E. (Eds.). (1966). *Role theory: Concepts and research.* New York: John Wiley.

Biegel, D. E., & Sherman, W. R. (1979). Neighborhood capacity building and the ethnic aged. In D. Gelfand & A. Kutzik (Eds.), *Ethnicity and aging: Theory, research and policy.* New York: Springer Publishing Co.

Biggar, J., Longino, C., & Flynn, C. (1980). Interstate elderly migration: Impact on sending and receiving states, 1960–1965. *Research on Aging, 2,* 217–232.

Binstock, R. (1972). Interest group liberalism and the politics of aging. *The Gerontologist, 12*(Autumn), 256–280.

Blakemore, K. (1985). The state, the voluntary sector and new developments in provision for the old of minority racial groups. *Ageing and Society, 5*(2), 175–190.

Blenkner, M. (1965). Social work and family relationships in later life with some thoughts in filial maturity. In E. Shanas & G. G. Strieb (Eds.), *Social structure and the family.* Englewood Cliffs, NJ: Prentice Hall.

Bliatout, B. (1979). *Problems of acculturation of the Hmong in Hawaii.* Honolulu: Institute of Behavioral Sciences.

Boren, S. (1983). Education of Hispanics: Access and achievement. In *The Hispanic population of the United States: An overview.* (U.S. House of Representatives). Washington, DC: U.S. Government Printing Office.

Bornat, J., Phillipson, C., & Ward, S. (1985). *A manifesto for old age.* London: Pluto Press.

Bosse, R., & Ekerdt. (1981). Change in self-perception of leisure activities with retirement. *The Gerontologist, 21,* 650–654.

Branch, L. G. (1978). *Boston elders.* Program Report. Boston: University of Massachusetts Center for Survey Research.

Braun, P., & Sweet, R. (1984). Passages: Fact or fiction? *International Journal of Aging and Human Development, 18*(3), 161–176.

Brody, E. (1981). Women in the middle and family help to older people. *The Gerontologist, 21,* 472–480.

Brody, E. M. (1985). Parent care as a normative family stress. *The Gerontologist, 25,* 19–29.

Brody, E., Johnson, P., & Fulcomer, M. (1984). What should children do for elderly parents? Opinions and preferences of three generations of women. *Journal of Gerontology, 39,* 736–746.

Brody, E., Johnson, P., Fulcomer, M., & Lang, A. (1983). Women's changing roles and help to elderly parents: Attitudes of three generations of women. *Journal of Gerontology, 38,* 597–607.

Brotman, H. B. (1977). Population projections: Part 1. Tomorrow's older population (to 2000). *The Gerontologist, 17,* 203–209.

Bryant, E., & El-Attar, M. (1984). Migration and redistribution of the elderly: A challenge to community services. *The Gerontologist, 24,* 634–640.

Bryer, K. B. (1979). Amish way of death: Study of family support systems. *American Psychologist, 34,* 255–261.

Buhler, C., & Massarik, F. (Eds.). (1968). *The course of human life*. New York: Springer Publishing Co.

Butler, R. (1963). The life review: An interpretation of reminiscence in the aged. *Psychiatry, 26,* 65–76.

Butler, R. N. (1975). *Why survive? Being old in America*. New York: Harper and Row.

Cain, G. G. (1976). The challenge of segmented labor market theories to orthodox theory: A survey. *Journal of Economic Literature, 14,* 1215–1257.

Cantor, M. H. (1976). Effect of ethnicity on life styles of the inner-city elderly. In A. Monk (Ed.), *The age of aging: A reader in social gerontology*. Buffalo, NY: Prometheus Books.

Cantor, M. H. (1979). The informal support system of New York's inner city elderly: Is ethnicity a factor? In D. E. Gelfand & A. Kutzik (Eds.), *Ethnicity and aging: Theory, research and policy*. New York: Springer Publishing Co.

Cantor, M. H. (1983). Strain among caregivers: A study of experience in the U.S. *The Gerontologist, 23*(6), 597–604.

Carp, F. M., & Kataoka, E. (1976). Health care problems of the elderly of San Francisco's Chinatown. *The Gerontologist, 16,* 10–38.

Chen, P. N. (1979). A study of Chinese-American elderly residing in hotel rooms. *Social Casework, 60,* 89–95.

Chirikos, T., & Nestel, G. (1983). *Economic aspects of self-reported work disability*. Columbus, OH: Ohio State University, Center for Human Resource Research.

Chrisman, N. (1981). Ethnic persistence in an urban setting. *Ethnicity, 8,* 256–292.

Christensen, C. P. (1984). Social work and multiculturalism: An unmet challenge. *La formation en travail social au Quebec: D'une ecole a l'autre*. Montreal: Le regroupement des unites de formation universitaire en travail social du Quebec.

Cicirelli, V. (1981). *Helping elderly parents: The role of adult children*. Boston: Auburn House.

Clark, M. (1972). Cultural values and dependency in later life. In D. Cowgill & L. Holmes (Eds.), *Aging and modernization*. New York: Appleton-Century-Crofts.

Clark, M., & Anderson, B. (1967). *Culture and aging: An anthropological study of older Americans*. Springfield, IL: Charles C. Thomas.

Clark, M., & Mendelson, M. (1969). The Mexican-American aged in San Francisco: A case description. *The Gerontologist, 9,* 90–95.

Clausen, J. (1972). The life course of individuals. In M. Riley, M. Johnson, & A. Foner (Eds.), *Aging and society: A sociology of age stratification* (Vol. 3, pp. 475–514). New York: Russell Sage Foundation.

Cohen, A. (1981). Variables in ethnicity. In C. F. Keyes (Ed.), *Ethnic change* (pp. 307–331). Seattle: University of Washington Press.

Cohen, D. (1984). *The next Canadian economy*. Montreal: Eden Press.

Cohen, L. (1984). *Small expectations: Society's betrayal of older women*. Toronto: McClelland and Stewart.

Cohen, S. (1983). *American modernity and Jewish identity.* New York: Tavistock.

Cohler, B. J., & Grunebaum, H. U. (1981). *Mothers, grandmothers, and daughters: Personality and childcare in three-generation families.* New York: Wiley.

Cohler, B., & Lieberman, M. (1980). Social relations and mental health among middle-aged and older men and women from three European ethnic groups. *Research on Aging, 2*(4), 445–469.

Comptroller General of the United States. (1977). *The well-being of older people in Cleveland, Ohio.* Washington, DC: U.S. General Accounting Office.

Cool, L. (1980). Ethnicity and aging: Continuity through change for elderly Corsicans. In C. Fry (Ed.), *Aging in culture and society* (pp. 149–169). New York: Praeger.

Cool, L., & McCabe, J. (1983). The "scheming hag" and the "dear old thing": The anthropology of aging women. In J. Sokolovsky (Ed.), *Growing old in different societies: Cross-cultural perspectives* (pp. 56–68). Belmont, CA: Wadsworth.

Copeland, W. (1981). Early Finnish-American settlements in Florida. In M. Karni (Ed.), *Finnish diaspora II: United States.* Toronto: Multicultural Historical Society of Ontario.

Corcoran, M., & Duncan, G. J. (1978). A summary of part 1 findings. In G. J. Duncan & J. N. Morgan (Eds.), *Five thousand American families* (Vol. 6, pp. 3–46). Ann Arbor, MI: The University of Michigan.

Cowgill, D. (1985). *Aging around the world.* Belmont, CA: Wadsworth.

Cox, C. (1986, August). Physician utilization by three groups of ethnic elderly. *Medical Care, 24*(8), 667–676.

Cox, C., & Gelfand, D. (1987). Familial assistance, exchange and satisfaction among the ethnic elderly. *Journal of Cross-Cultural Gerontology, 2,* 241–256.

Crandall, R. C. (1980). *Gerontology: A behavioral science approach.* Reading, MA: Addison-Wesley.

Crawford, L. (1980). Aging, ethnicity and congregate shelter in Ontario. *Multiculturalism, 4,* 13–15.

Crouch, B. (1972). Age and institutional support: Perceptions of older Mexican Americans. *Journal of Gerontology, 27,* 524–529.

Crystal, S. (1982). *America's old age crisis.* New York: Basic Books.

Cueller, I., Harris, L., & Jasso, R. (1980). An acculturation scale for Mexican-American normal and clinical populations. *Hispanic Journal of Behavioral Science, 2,* 199–217.

Cueller, J., Stanford, E. P., & Miller-Soule, D. I. (Eds.). 1982. *Understanding minority aging: Perspectives and sources.* San Diego, CA: San Diego State University.

Cueller, J. B., & Weeks, J. (1980). *Minority elderly Americans: The assessment of needs and equitable receipt of public benefits as a prototype for area agencies on aging final report.* San Diego, CA: Allied Home Health Association.

Cullen, I., & Phelps, E. (1978). Patterns of behavior and responses to the urban environment. In W. Michelson (Ed.), *Public policy in temporal perspectives* (pp. 165–181). The Hague: Mouton.

Cumming, E., & Henry, W. (1961). *Growing old: The process of disengagement.* New York: Basic Books.

Daniels, D. (1977). Colonial Jewry: Religion, domestic and social relations. *American Jewish Historical Quarterly, 66,* 375–400.

Daniels, R. (1977). The Japanese experience in North America: An essay in comparative racism. *Canadian Ethnic Studies, 9,* 91–104.

Davis, D. L. (1976). Growing old black. In R. Atchley & M. Seltzer (Eds.), *The Sociology of aging: Selected readings* (pp. 263–276). Belmont, CA: Wadsworth.

Dimont, M. L. (1978). *The Jews in America.* New York: Touchstone Books, Simon and Schuster.

Dono, J., Falbe, C., Kail, B., Litwak, E., Sherman, R., & Siegel, D. (1979). Primary groups in old age: Structure and function. *Research on Aging, 1,* 403–433.

Dowd, J. (1981). Industrialization and the decline of the aged. *Sociological Focus, 14,* 255–269.

Dowd, J., & Bengtson, V. (1978). Aging in minority populations: An examination of the double jeopardy hypothesis. *Journal of Gerontology, 33,* 427–436.

Dohrenwend, B., & Dohrenwend, B. (1969). *Social status and psychological disorder.* New York: John Wiley and Sons.

Driedger, L. (1978). Introduction: Ethnic identity in the Canadian mosaic. In L. Driedger (Ed.), *The Canadian ethnic mosaic* (pp. 9–22). Toronto: McClelland & Stewart.

Dunlop, B. D. (1980). Expanded home-based care for the impaired elderly: Solution or pipe dream? *American Journal of Public Health, 70,* 514–519.

Eisenstadt, S. (1954). *The absorption of immigrants.* London: W. & J. Mackay.

Ell, K. (1984). Social networks, social support, and health status: A review. *Social Service Review, 58,* 133–149.

Ellison, D. L. (1968). Work, retirement and the sick role. *The Gerontologist, 8,* 189–192.

Eribes, A., & Bradley-Rawls, M. (1978). The underutilization of nursing home facilities by Mexican-American elderly in the Southwest. *The Gerontologist, 18,* 363–371.

Ericksen, E. P., Ericksen, J. A., & Hostetler, J. A. (1980). The cultivation of the soil as a moral directive: Population growth, family ties, and the maintenance of community among the old order Amish. *Rural Sociology, 45,* 49–68.

Ericksen, J. A., & Leon, G. H. (1978). *The fertility of the Old Order Amish.* Paper presented at the annual meeting of the American Sociological Association, San Francisco, Sept, 4–8.

Erickson, E. H. (1950). *Childhood and society.* New York: Norton.

Erickson, E. (1968). *Identity, youth and crisis.* New York: Norton.

Fandetti, D., & Gelfand, D. (1976). Care of the aged: Attitudes of white ethnic families. *The Gerontologist, 16,* 544–549.

Ferraro, K. (1981). Relocation designs and outcome among the elderly. *Research on Aging, 3*(2), 166–181.

Fillenbaum, G., George, L., & Palmore, E. (1985). Determinants and consequences of retirement among men of different races and economic levels. *Journal of Gerontology, 40*(1), 85–94.

Finney, J. M., & Lee, G. R. (1976). Age differences on five dimensions of religious involvement. *Review of Religious Research, 18*(2), 173–179.

Foster, T. W. (1981). Amish society. *The Futurist, 15,* 33–40.

Francis, D. (1981). Adaptive strategies of the elderly in England and Ohio. In C. Fry (Ed.), *Dimensions: Aging, culture, and health.* New York: Praeger.

Frank, G. (1984). Life history model of adaptation to disability: The case of a "congenital amputee." *Social Science Medicine, 19,* 639–645.

Freud, S. (1963). *An outline of psychoanalysis.* J. Strachey (Trans.). New York: Norton.

Friedman, E. H. (1982). The myth of the Shiksa. In M. McGoldrick, J. K. Pearce, & J. Giordano (Eds.), *Ethnicity and family therapy.* New York: Guilford.

Fry, C. (1979). Structural conditions affecting community formation among the aged: Two examples from Arizona. *Anthropological Quarterly, 52*(1), 7–18.

Fry, C. (Ed.). (1980). *Aging in culture and society: Comparative viewpoints and strategies.* New York: Praeger.

Fry, C. (1981). *Dimensions: Aging, culture, and health.* New York: Praeger.

Fry, C. L. (1984). *Aging in culture and society: Comparative viewpoints and strategies.* New York: Bergin.

Fujii, S. M. (1980). Minority group elderly: Demographic characteristics and implications for public policy. In C. Eisdorfer (Ed.), *Annual review of gerontology and geriatrics* (Vol. 12, pp. 261–284). New York: Springer Publishing Co.

Gambino, R. (1974). *Blood of my blood: The dilemma of the Italian-Americans.* New York: Doubleday.

Gans, H. (1962). *The urban villagers.* Glencoe, IL: The Free Press.

Gans, H. (1979). Symbolic ethnicity: The future of ethnic groups and cultures in America. *Ethnic and Racial Studies, 2,* 1–20.

Garcia, A. (1979). Factors affecting the economic status of elderly Chicanos. *Journal of Sociology and Social Welfare, 8,* 529–537.

Gardner, R., Robey, B., & Smith, P. (1985). Asian Americans: Growth, change and diversity. *Population Bulletin, 40*(4) (October).

Geddes, W. (1976). *Migrants of the mountains.* Oxford: Clarendon Press.

Gefro, M. (1980–1981). Three ways of reminiscence in theory and practice. *Journal of Aging and Human Development, 12,* 39–48.

Gelfand, D. (1981). The ethnic aged and social policy: A critical analysis. In C. Eisdorfer (Ed.), *Annual Review of Gerontology and Geriatrics* (Vol. 2, pp. 91–117). New York: Springer Publishing Co.

Gelfand, D. (1982). *Aging: The ethnic factor*. Boston: Little, Brown.

Gelfand, D. (1986). Assistance to the new Russian elderly. *The Gerontologist, 26,* 444–448.

Gelfand, D., & Fandetti, D. (1980). Suburban and urban white ethnics: Attitudes toward care of the aged. *The Gerontologist, 20,* 588–594.

Gelfand, D., & Fandetti, D. (1986). The emergent nature of ethnicity: Dilemmas in assessment. *Social Casework. 67,* 542–550.

Gelfand, D., & Kutzik, A. (1979). *Ethnicity and aging: Theory, research and policy*. New York: Springer Publishing Co.

Gelfand, D., & Olsen, J. (1979). Aging in the Jewish and Mormon family. In D. Gelfand & A. Kutzik (Eds.), *Ethnicity and aging: Theory, research and policy*. New York: Springer Publishing Co.

Gelfand, D., & Tow, M. (1978). Theoretical and applied inputs in mental health center research. *American Journal of Community Psychology, 6,* 81–89.

Gerber, L. M. (1983). Ethnicity still matters: Sociodemographic profiles of the ethnic elderly in Ontario. *Canadian Ethnic Studies 15,* 60–80.

Gibson, R. C. (1982). Race and sex differnces in the work and retirement patterns of older heads of household. *Scripps Foundation Minority Research Conference Monograph* (pp. 138–184).

Gibson, R. C. (1986a). Blacks in an aging society. *Daedalus, 115*(1), 349–371.

Gibson, R. C. (1986b). *Blacks in an aging society*. New York: The Carnegie Corp.

Gibson, R. C. (1986c). Perspectives on the Black family. In A. Pifer & L. Bronte (Eds.), *Our aging society: Paradox and promise*. New York: W. W. Norton.

Gibson, R. C. (1986d). The work, retirement and disability of older Black Americans. In J. S. Jackson (Ed.). *Research on aging Black populations*. New York: Springer Publishing Co.

Glaser, B. (1978). *Theoretical sensitivity: Advances in the methodology of grounded theory*. Mill Valley, CA: The Sociology Press.

Glaser, B., & Strauss, A. (1967). *The discovery of grounded theory: Strategies for qualitative research*. Chicago: Aldine.

Glazer, N. (1980). Toward a sociology of small ethnic groups. *Canadian Ethnic Studies, 12,* 1–16.

Glock, C. Y. (1962, July–August). On the study of religious commitment: Review of recent research bearing on religion and character education. *Religious Education,* pp. 98–110.

Glock, C. Y., & Stark, R. (1965). *Religion and society in tension*. Chicago: Rand McNally.

Golant, S. M. (1984). Factors influencing the nighttime activity of old persons in their community. *Journal of Gerontology, 39,* 935–941.

Goldscheider, C. (1982). The demography of Jewish Americans: Research findings, issues, and challenges. In M. Sklare (Ed.), *Understanding American Jewry*. New Brunswick, NJ: Transaction Books.

Goldscheider, C. (1986). *Jewish continuity and change*. Bloomington, IN: Indiana University Press.

Goldstein, S. (1981). The Jews in the United States: Perspectives from demography. *American Jewish Yearbook*, 3–59.

Gordon, H. A., Hamilton, C. A., & Tipps, H. C. (1982). Unemployment and underemployment among Blacks, Hispanics, and women. (Clearinghouse Publication No. 74). Washington, DC.

Gordon, M. M. (1964). *Assimilation in American life*. New York: Oxford University Press.

Gould, R. L. (1978). *Transformations: Growth and change in adult life*. New York: Simon & Schuster.

Greeley, A. M. (1972). *That most distressful nation*. Chicago: Quadrangle.

Greeley, A., & McCready, W. (1974). *Ethnicity in the United States: A preliminary reconnaissance*. New York: John Wiley and Sons.

Greeley, H. (1976). Why can't they be more like us? In R. Krieks (Ed.), *Nursing the American dream: White ethnics and the new populism* (pp. 262–272). Bloomington, IN: Indiana University Press.

Gubrium, J. (1975). *Living and dying at Murray Manor*. New York: St. Martin's Press.

Guemple, L. (1980). Growing old in Inuit society. In V. Marshall (Ed.), *Aging in Canada: Social perspectives*. Toronto: Fitzhenry and Whiteside.

Guillemard, A. M. (1982). Old age, retirement, and the social class structure: Toward an analysis of the structural dynamics of the latter stage of life. In T. K. Hareven & K. J. Adams (Eds.), *Aging and life course transitions: An interdisciplinary perspective* (pp. 221–243). New York: Guilford Press.

Guttmann, D. (1976). The cross-cultural perspective: Notes toward a comparative psychology of aging. In J. E. Birren & K. W. Schaie (Eds.), *Handbook of the psychology of aging* (pp. 302–326). New York: Van Nostrand Reinhold.

Guttmann, D. (1979). Use of informal and formal supports by the ethnic aged. In D. Gelfand & A. Kutzik (Eds.), *Ethnicity and aging: Theory, research and policy*. New York: Springer Publishing Co.

Guttmann, D. (1980). *Perspective on equitable share in public benefits by minority elderly: Executive summary*. (Administration on Aging Grant No. 90-A1671). Washington, DC: The Catholic University of America.

Hagestad, G., & Neugarten B. (1985). Aging and the life course. In R. Binstock & E. Shanas (Eds.), *Handbook of aging and the social sciences* (pp. 35–55). New York: Van Nostrand Reinhold.

Haines, D., Rutherford, D., & Thomas, P. (1981). Family and community among Vietnamese refugees. *International Migration Review, 15*, 312–321.

Handlin, O. (1973). *The uprooted*. Boston: Little, Brown.

Hanushek, E., & Jackson, J. (1977). *Statistical methods for social scientists*. New York: Academic Press.

Harbert, A., & Ginsberg, L. (1979). *Human services for older adults*. Belmont, CA: Wadsworth.

Harel, Z., (1985). Nutrition site service users: Does racial background make a difference. *The Gerontologist, 25*, 286–291.

Harel, Z. (1986). Ethnicity and aging: Implications for service organizations. In C. Hays, R. Kalish, & D. Guttmann (Eds.), *European-American elderly: A guide to practice*. New York: Springer Publishing Co.

Harel, Z., Jackson, M., Deimling, G., & Noelker, L. (1983). Racial differences on well-being among aged and disabled public housing residents. *Journal of Housing for the Elderly, 1*, 45–62.

Harel, Z., Noelker, L., & Blake, B. (1985). Planning services for the aged: Theoretical and empirical perspectives. *The Gerontologist, 25*, 644–649.

Harel, Z., Wyatt, J., & Luick, M. (1984). Older Americans Act service consumers: A contrast between the homebound and users of nutrition programs. *Journal of Gerontological Social Work, 6*, 19–34.

Hareven, T. (1978). *Transitions: The family and the life course in historical perspective*. New York: Academic Press.

Harris, L. H., & Associates. (1979). *The myth and reality of aging in America*. Washington, DC: National Council on the Aging.

Hays, C., Kalish, R., & Guttmann, D. (1986). *European-American elderly: A guide to practice*. New York: Springer Publishing Co.

Heenan, E. F. (1972). Sociology of religion and aged. *Journal of Scientific Study of Religion, 11*, 171–176.

Heinbach, E. (1983). Interview with author.

Hempel, C. (1952). *Fundamentals of concept formation in empirical science*. Chicago: University of Chicago Press.

Hendricks, J., & Hendricks, C. D. (1979). Theories of social gerontology. In J. Hendricks & C. D. Hendricks (Eds.), *Dimensions of aging* (pp. 191–208). Cambridge, MA: Winthrop.

Hepworth, P. (1985). *Reappraising priorities for aging in Canada: A personal view*. Paper presented at the International Congress of Gerontology, New York, July 12–14.

Hershkowitz, L. (1976). Some aspects of the New York Jewish merchant community, 1654–1820. *American Jewish Historical Quarterly, 66*, 10–34.

Hertzberg, A. (1979). *Being Jewish in America*. New York: Schocken.

Hess, B., & Markson, E. (1980). *Aging and old age*. New York: Macmillan.

Hill, M. S. (1981, January). *Trends in the economic situation of U.S. families and children: 1970–1980*. Paper presented at the Conference of Families and the Economy, Washington, DC.

Hochschild, A. (1973). *The unexpected community*. Englewood Cliffs, NJ: Prentice-Hall.

Hoglund, W. (1960). *Finnish immigrants in America, 1880–1920*. Madison, WI: University of Wisconsin Press.

Holmes, T., & Rahe, R. (1967). The social readjustment rating scale. *Journal of Psychosomatic Research, 11*, 213–218.

Holzberg, C. S. (1982). Ethnicity and aging: Anthropological perspectives on more than just the minority elderly. *The Gerontologist, 22,* 249–257.

Hooker, K., & Ventis, D. G. (1984). Work ethic, daily activities, and retirement satisfaction. *Journal of Gerontology, 39,* 478–484.

Hooyman, N., Gonyea, J., & Montgomery, R. (1985). The impact of in-home services termination on family caregivers. *The Gerontologist, 25,* 141–145.

Hostetler, J. A. (1980). *Amish society* (3rd ed.). Baltimore: The Johns Hopkins University Press.

Hoyt, D., & Babchuck, N. (1981). Ethnicity and the voluntary association of the aged. *Ethnicity, 8,* 67–81.

Hsieh, T., Shybut, J., & Lotsof, E. (1969). Internal versus external control and ethnic group membership. *Journal of Consulting and Clinical Psychology, 33,* 122–124.

Huntington, G. E. (1981). The Amish family. In C. H. Mindel & R. W. Habenstein (Eds.), *Ethnic families in America* (2nd ed.) (pp. 295–325). New York: Elsevier.

Irelan, L. M., & Bell, D. B. (1972). Understanding subjectively defined retirement: A pilot analysis. *The Gerontologist, 12,* 354–356.

Isajiw, W. (1981). *Ethnic identity retention.* (Research Paper No. 125). Toronto: University of Toronto Centre for Urban and Community Studies.

Jackson, J. (1971). Sex and social class variations in Black aged parent-adult child relationships. *Aging and Human Development, 2,* 96–107.

Jackson, J. J. (1980). *Minorities and aging.* Belmont, CA: Wadsworth.

Jackson, J. J. (1985). Race, national origin, ethnicity and aging. In R. Binstock & E. Shanas (Eds.), *Handbook of aging and the social sciences* (2nd ed.) (pp. 269–303). New York: Van Nostrand Reinhold.

Jackson, J. S. (1979). The national survey of Black Americans. Institute for Social Research, The University of Michigan, Ann Arbor, MI.

Jackson, J. S., & Gibson, R. C. (1985). Work and retirement among the Black elderly. In Z. Blau (Ed.), *Current perspectives on aging and the life cycle, Vol. 1* (pp. 193–222). JAI Press.

Jackson, J. S., & Hatchett, S. J. (1985). Intergenerational research; Methodological considerations. In N. Datan, A. L. Green, & H. W. Reese (Eds.), *Intergenerational networks; Families in context.* Hillsdale, NJ: Erlbaum Associates.

Jackson, M., & Harel, Z. (1983). Ethnic differences in social support networks. *Urban Health, 9,* 35–38.

Jacobs, J. (1974). *Fun city: An ethnographic study of a retirement community.* New York: Holt, Rinehart and Winston.

Jalali, B. (1982). Iranian families. In M. McGoldrick, J. K. Pearce, & J. Giordano (Eds.), *Ethnicity and family therapy* (pp. 289–309). New York: Guilford Press.

Jalkanen, R. (Ed.). (1969). *The Finns of North America: A social symposium.* Lansing, MI: Michigan State University Press.

James, W. (1950). *The principles of psychology.* New York: Dover. Original work published 1910.

Joe, V. (1971). Review of the internal-external construct as a personality variable. *Psychological Reports, 28,* 619–640.

Johnson, C. L. (1983). Dyadic family relations and social support. *The Gerontologist, 23,* 377–383.

Johnson, C. L., & Catalano, D. (1983). A longitudinal study of family supports to impaired elderly. *The Gerontologist, 23,* 6'1–6'8.

Jones, B. A. (1973). *The contribution of Black women to the incomes of Black families: An analysis of the labor force.* Unpublished doctoral dissertation, The University of Michigan, Ann Arbor, MI.

Juster, F. T., Courant, P., Duncan, G. J., Robinson, J. P., & Stafford, F. P. (1977). *Time use in economic and social accounts.* Ann Arbor, MI: University of Michigan, Survey Research Center.

Juster, F. T., & Stafford, F. P. (1985). *Time, goods, and well-being.* Ann Arbor, MI: University of Michigan.

Justin, M. (1970). Culture, conflict and Mexican-American achievement. *School and Society, 98,* 27–28.

Kadushin, A. (1972, May). The racial factor in the interview. *Social Work,* pp. 88–98.

Kahana, E. (1975). A congruence model of person-environment interaction. In T. O. Byerts, M. P. Lawton, & J. Newcomer, (Eds.), *Theory development in environments and aging.* Washington, DC: Gerontological Society.

Kahana, E. (1974). Matching environments to needs of the aged: A conceptual scheme. In J. Gubrium, (Ed.), *Late life: Recent developments in the sociology of aging.* Springfield, IL: Thomas.

Kahana, E., & Kahana, B. (1971). Theoretical and research perspectives on grandparenthood. *Aging and Human Development, 2,* 261–268.

Kahana, E., & Kahana, B. (1984). Jews. In E. Palmore (Ed.), *Handbook on the aged in the United States.* Westport, CT: Greenwood Press.

Kalish, R. A., & Moriwaki, S. (1973). The world of the elderly Asian American. In J. Hendricks & C. D. Hendricks (Eds.). Dimensions of aging (pp. 264–277). Cambridge, MA: Winthrop Publishers.

Kamikawa, L. (1982, Spring). Expanding perceptions of aging. *Generations,* pp. 26–27.

Kaminsky, M. (1978). Diagnostic implications of reminiscence theory. *Journal of Gerontological Social Work, 1,* 19–32.

Kart, C. S., & Beckham, B. L. (1976). Black-White differentials in the institutionalization of the elderly: A temporal analysis. *Social Forces, 54,* 901–910.

Kart, C., & Engler, C. (1985). Family relations of aged colonial Jews: A testamentary analysis. *Ageing and Society, 5,* 289–304.

Kart, C., Palmer, N., & Flaschner, A. (1986). *Aging and religious commitment in a midwestern Jewish community.* Paper presented at annual meeting of the North Central Sociological Association, April 17–19, Toldeo, OH.

Kastenbaum, R. (1971). The missing footnote. *Aging and Human Development, 2,* 155.

Kastenbaum, R. (1979). Reflections on old age, ethnicity, and death. In D. E. Gelfand & A. J. Kutzik (Eds.), *Ethnicity and aging: Theory, research, and policy*. New York: Springer Publishing Co.

Kaufman, S. (1981). Cultural components of identity in old age: A case study. *Ethos, 9,* 51–87.

Keith, J. (1980). Old age and community creation. In C. Fry (Eds.), *Aging in culture and society*. New York: Praeger.

Kephart, W. M. (1981). *The family, society, and the individual* (5th ed.). Boston: Houghton Mifflin.

Kephart, W. M. (1982). *Extraordinary people* (2nd ed.). New York: St. Martin's Press.

Kerkhoff, A. (1966). Family patterns and morale in retirement. In I. Simpson & J. McKinney (Eds.), *Social aspects of aging* (pp. 173–192). Durham, NC: Duke University Press.

Kikumura, A., & Kitano, H. H. L. (1981). The Japanese American family. In C. H. Mindel & R. W. Habenstein (Eds.), *Ethnic families in America* (2nd ed.) (pp. 43–60). New York: Elsevier.

Kingson, E. R. (1981). Disadvantaged very early labor force withdrawal. *Policy issues for the elderly poor*. Washington, DC: Office of Policy Planning and Evaluation, Community Services Administration. (CSA Pamphlet 6172–8) pp. 23–30.

Kingson, E. R. (1982). The health of very early retirees. *Social Security Bulletin, 45*(9), 3–9.

Kingson, E., Hirschorn, E. B., & Harootyan, L. (1986). *The common stake: The interdependence of generations*. Washington, DC: Gerontological Society of America.

Kirschten, D. (1983). The Hispanic vote: Parties can't gamble that the sleeping giant won't awaken. *The National Journal, 11,* 2410–2416.

Kitano, H. H. L. (1969). *Japanese Americans: The evolution of a subculture*. Prentice Hall: Englewood Cliffs, NJ.

Koivukangas, O. (1986). Finnish emigration to the USA: An introduction. In S. Sinkkonen & A. Milen (Eds.), *Towards equality: Proceedings of the American Finnish Workshop on Minna Kanth*. Kuopio, Finland: University of Kuopio.

Kopan, A. T. (1981). Greek survival in Chicago: The role of ethnic education, 1890–1980. In P. d'A. Jones & M. G. Holli (Eds.), *Ethnic Chicago*. Grand Rapids, MI: W. B. Eerdmans Publishing Co.

Kopan, A. T. (1982). The way it was. In S. Diacov (Eds.), *Hellenism in Chicago* (pp. 89–91). Chicago: The United Hellenic American Congress.

Krout, J. A. (1983). Correlates of service utilization among the rural elderly. *The Gerontologist, 23,* 500–504.

Kuhn, M. (1980). Foreword. In J. Levin & W. C. Levin, *Ageism: Prejudice and discrimination against the elderly*. Belmont, CA: Wadsworth.

Kutza, E. A. (1986). A policy analyist's response. *The Gerontologist, 26*(2), 147–149.

Lamb, H. R., & Rogawski, A. S. (1978). Supplemental security income and the sick role. *American Journal of Psychiatry, 135,* 1221–1224.

Langston, E. (1978). The role and value of natural support systems in retirement. In E. P. Stanford (Ed.). *Retirement: Concepts and realities of ethnic minority elders*. San Diego: The Campanile Press.

Larson, R. (1978). Thirty years of research on subjective well-being of older Americans. *Journal of Gerontology, 33,* 109–125.

Lawton, M. P. (1976). The impact of the environment on aging and behavior. In J. E. Birren & K. W. Schaie, (Eds.), *Handbook of the psychology of aging*. New York: Van Nostrand Reinhold.

Lazerwitz, B. (1962). Membership in voluntary associations and frequency of church attendance. *Journal of Scientific Study of Religion, 2,* 74–84.

Lazerwitz, B., & Harrison, M. (1979). American Jewish denominations: A social and religious profile. *American Sociological Review, 44*(4), 656–666.

Leake, C. D. (1962). Social status and aging. *Geriatrics, 17,* 785.

Lebowitz, B. (1973). *Age and religiosity in an urban ethnic community*. Paper presented at the annual meeting of the Gerontological Society, Miami Beach, FL.

Lee, C. F. (1985, May). *A current demographic profile of the Euro-American elderly*. Paper presented at the National Conference on Euro-American Elderly, Washington, DC.

Lee, G. R. (1979). Children and the elderly: Interaction and morale. *Research on Aging, 1,* 335–360.

Lefcourt, H. (1966). Internal-external control of reinforcement: A review. *Psychological Bulletin, 68,* 152–157.

Lefcourt, H. (1976). *Locus of control: Current trends in theory and research*. New York: Wiley.

Lefcourt, H., & Ladwig, G. (1966). Alienation in Negro and white reformatory inmates. *Journal of Social Psychology, 68,* 152–157.

Lenzer, A. (1961). Sociocultural influences on adjustment to aging. *Geriatrics, 16,* 631–640.

Leon, J. (1986). A recursive model of economic well-being. *Journal of Gerontology, 40,* 494–505.

Leroy, X., & Deliege, D. (1982). Time-budget of the Belgian physician nowadays and in the future. In Z. Staikov (Ed.), *It's about time*. Sofia: Bulgarian Academy of Sciences.

Lessing, E. (1969). Racial differences in indices of ego functioning relevant to academic achievement. *Journal of Genetic Psychology, 115,* 153–167.

Levin, J., & Levin, W. C. (1980). *Ageism: Prejudice and discrimination against the elderly*. Belmont, CA: Wadsworth.

Levinson, D. (1978). *The seasons of a man's life*. New York: Alfred Knopf.

Lewis, M., & Butler, R. (1972). Why is women's lib ignoring old women? *Aging and Human Development, 3,* 223–231.

Lieberman, M., & Tobin, S. (1983). *The experience of old age*. New York: Basic Books.

Liton, J., & Olstein, S. (1969). Therapeutic aspects of reminiscence. *Social Casework, 50,* 263–268.

Little, V. C. (1984). An overview of research using the time-budget methodology to study age-related behavior. *Aging & Society, 4,* 3–20.

Litwak, E. (1985). *Helping the elderly: The complementary roles of informal networks and formal systems.* New York: Guilford Press.

Longino, C. (1979). Going home: Aged return migration in the United States, 1965–1970. *Journal of Gerontology, 3,* 736–745.

Longino, C., & Biggar, C. (1981). The impact of retirement migration on the south. *The Gerontologist, 21,* 283–290.

Lopata, H. (1973). *Widowhood in American society.* Cambridge, MA: Schenkman.

Lopata, H. (1976). *Polish-Americans.* Englewood Cliffs, NJ: McGraw-Hill.

Lopata, H. Z. (1981). Polish American families. In C. H. Mindel & R. W. Habenstein (Eds.), *Ethnic families in America* (2nd ed.) (pp. 17–42). New York: Elsevier.

Lowenthal, M., & Robinson, B. (1976). Social networks and Isolation. In R. Binstock & E. Shanas, (Eds.), *Handbook of Aging and the Social Sciences.* New York: Van Nostrand Reinhold.

Lowenthal, M. F., Thurner, M., & Chiriboga, D. (1975). *Four stages of life.* San Francisco: Jossey Bass.

Ludwig, A. (1981). The disabled society? *American Journal of Psychotherapy, 35*(1), 5–15.

Lukas, J. A. (1985). *Common ground.* New York: Alfred Knopf.

Lum, D., et al. (1980). The psychosocial needs of the Chinese elderly. *Social Casework, 61,* 100–106.

MacLean, M. J. (1987). Ageism in the United Kingdom and Canada. *Critical Social Policy, 18,* 52–57.

MacLean, M. J., & Bonar, R. (1986). Ethnic elderly people in long-term care facilities for the dominant culture: Implications for social work practice and education. *International Social Work, 29*(3), 227–236.

Maddox, G. (1979). Sociology of later life. *Annual Review of Sociology, 5,* 113–135.

Madsen, W. (1964). *Mexican-Americans of South Texas.* New York: Holt, Rinehart & Winston.

Mann, A. (1979). *The one and the many: Reflections on the American identity.* Chicago: University of Chicago Press.

Mannheim, K. (1936). *Ideology and utopia.* New York: Harcourt.

Manson, S., & Callaway, D. (1985). *Health and aging among American Indians: Issues and change for the biobehavioral sciences.* Unpublished monograph.

Manton, K. G., & Stallard, E. (1984). *Recent trends in mortality analysis.* New York: Academic Press.

Manuel, R. (Ed.). (1982). *Minority aging: Sociological and social psychological issues.* Westport, CT: Greenwood Press.

Markides, K. S. (1982). Ethnicity and aging: A comment. *The Gerontologist, 22,* 467–470.

Markides, K., & Vernon, S. (1984). Aging sex role orientation and adjustment: A third generation study of Mexican-Americans. *Journal of Gerontology, 39,* 586–591.

Markle, G. E., & Pasco, S. (1977). Family limitation among the old order Amish. *Population Studies, 31,* 267–280.

Markson, E. (1979). Ethnicity as a factor in the institutionalization of the ethnic elderly. In D. Gelfand & A. Kutzik (Eds.), *Ethnicity and aging: Theory, research and policy.* New York: Springer Publishing Co.

Marshall, V. W. (1978–1979). No exit: A symbolic interactionist perspective on aging. *International Journal of Aging and Human Development, 9,* 345–357.

Marshall, V. W. (1980). *Reflections on the Canadian research scene.* Paper presented at the Conference on Research in Gerontology, Winnipeg, Canada.

Matthews, S. H. (1979). *The social world of old women.* Beverly Hills, CA, and London: Sage Publications.

McGill, D., & Pearce, J. K. (1982). British families. In M. McGoldrick, J. K. Pearce, & J. Giordano (Eds.), *Ethnicity and family therapy* (pp. 457–479). New York: Guilford Press.

McGoldrick, M. (1982). Ethnicity and family therapy: An overview. In M. McGoldrick, J. K. Pearce, & J. Giordano (Eds.), *Ethnicity and family therapy* (pp. 3–30). New York: Guilford Press.

McGoldrick, D., Pearce, P., & Giordano, J. (Eds.). (1982). *Ethnicity and family therapy.* New York: Guilford Press.

McNeely, R., & Colen, J. (1983). *Aging in minority groups.* Beverly Hills, CA: Sage Publications.

Meyer, J., & Speare, A. (1985). Distinctive elderly mobility: Types and determinants. *Economic Geography, 61,* 79–88.

Michelson, W. (1984). *The empirical merger of objective and subjective aspects of daily life.* Paper presented at the International Conference on Studies of Time Use, August, 8–10, Helsinki, Finland.

Mindel, C. H., & Habenstein, R. W. (1981). Family lifestyles of America's ethnic minorities: An introduction. In C. H. Mindel & R. W. Habenstein (Eds.), *Ethnic families in America: Patterns and variations* (2nd ed.) New York: Elsevier.

Mindel, C. H., & Vaughn, C. E. (1978). A multidimensional approach to religiosity and disengagement. *Journal of Gerontology, 33,* 103–108.

Mindel, C. H., & Wright, R. (1982). The use of social services by Black and White elderly: The role of social support systems. *Journal of Gerontological Social Work, 4,* 107–125.

Mirowsky, J., & Ross, C. (1983). Paranoia and the structure of powerlessness. *American Sociological Review, 48,* 228–239.

Moberg, D. O. (1972, January). Religion and the aging family. *The Family Coordinator,* pp. 47–60.

Moitoza, E. (1982). Portuguese families. In M. McGoldrick, J. Pearce, & J. Giordano (Eds.), *Ethnicity and family therapy* (pp. 412–437). New York: Guilford Press.

Montagna, P. D. (1978). *Occupations and society: Toward a sociology of the labor market.* New York: Wiley and Sons.

Moore, J. (1971). Situational factors affecting minority aged. *The Gerontologist, 11,* 88–93.

Morgan, J. N. (1980). Retirement in prospect and retrospect. In G. Duncan & J. Morgan (Eds.), *Five thousand American families—patterns of economic progress* (Vol. 8) (pp. 73–107). Ann Arbor, MI: University of Michigan, Institute for Social Research.

Morgan, L. (1976). A re-examination of widowhood and morale. *Journal of Gerontology, 31,* 687–695.

Moriwaki, S. Y., & Kobata, F. S. (1983). Ethnic minority aging. In D. S. Woodruff & J. E. Birren (Eds.). *Aging: Scientific perspectives and social issues* (2nd ed.). Monterey, CA: Brooks/Cole.

Moskos, C. C., Jr. (1980). *Greek Americans: Struggle and success.* Englewood Cliffs, NJ: Prentice-Hall.

Moss, M., & Lawton, M. (1982). Time budgets of older people: A window on four lifestyles. *Journal of Gerontology, 37,* 115–123.

Munnell, A. H. (1978, January/February). The economic experience of Blacks: 1964–1974. *New England Economic Review,* pp. 5–18.

Murase, K. (1982). *Help seeking behavior and attitudes of Southeast Asian refugees.* San Francisco: San Francisco State University, Pacific-Asian Mental Health Research Project.

Murray, J. (1979). Subjective retirement. *Social Security Bulletin, 42*(11), 20–25, 43.

Mutran, E. (1985). Intergenerational family support among Blacks and Whites: Response to culture or to socioeconomic differences. *Journal of Gerontology, 40,* 382–389.

Myerhoff, B. (1978). *Number our days.* New York: Dutton.

Myerhoff, B., & Simic, A. (1978). *Life's career—aging: Cultural variations on growing old.* Beverly Hills, CA: Sage.

Neugarten, B., & Datan, N. (1973). Sociological perspectives on the life cycle. In P. Baltes, & K. Schaie (Eds.), *Life span developmental psychology: Personality and socialization.* New York: Academic Press.

Neugarten, B., & Hagestad, G. (1976). Age and the life course. In R. Binstock, & E. Shanas (Eds.), *Handbook of aging and the social sciences.* New York: Van Nostrand Reinhold.

Neugarten, B., Moore, J., & Lowe, J. (1965). Age norms, age constraints, and adult socialization. *American Journal of Sociology, 70,* 710–717.

Neugarten, B., & Weinstein, K. (1964). The changing American grandparent. *Journal of Marriage and Family, 26,* 199–204.

Noelker, L., & Poulshock, W. (1982). *The effects on families of caring for impaired elderly in residence.* Cleveland, OH: The Benjamin Rose Institute.

Norman, A. (1985). *Triple jeopardy: Growing old in a second homeland.* London: Centre for Policy on Ageing.

Nydegger, C. N. (1983). Family ties of the aged in cross-cultural perspective. *The Gerontologist, 23,* 26–32.

Nye, F. (1979). Choice, exchange and the family. In W. Burr, R. Hill, F. Nye, & I. Reiss (Eds.), *Contemporary theories about the family, Vol. 2.* New York: Free Press.

Office of Refugee Resettlement (1981).

Olson, J. (1979). *The ethnic dimension in American history.* New York: St. Martin's Press.

Orbach, H. (1961). Aging and religion. *Geriatrics, 16,* 534–540.

Paden, J. (1967, November). *Situational ethnicity in urban Africa with special reference to the Hausa.* Paper presented at the African Studies Association meeting, New York.

Padgett, D. (1980). Symbolic ethnicity and patterns of ethnic identity assertion in American born Serbs. *Ethnic Groups, 3,* 55–77.

Padilla, A. M. (1980). *Acculturation: Theory, models, and some new findings.* Boulder, CO: Westview Press.

Padilla, A., Ruis, R., & Alvarez, R. (1975). Delivery of community mental health services to the Spanish speaking/surnamed population. *American Psychologist, 30,* 892–905.

Palmore, E. (1983). Cross cultural research: The state of the art. *Research in Aging, 5,* 45–57.

Palmore, E. B., George, L. K., & Fillenbaum, G. G. (1984). Consequences of retirement. *Journal of Gerontology, 39*(1), 109–116.

Pampel, F. I., Levin, J., Louviere, R., Meyer, R., & Rushton, G. (1984). Retirement migration decision-making: The integration of geographic, social and economic preferences. *Research on Aging, 6,* 139–162.

Parnes, H., & Nestel, G. (1981). The retirement experience. In H. Parnes (Ed.), *Work and retirement: A longitudinal study of men* (pp. 155–197). Cambridge, MA: MIT Press.

Patton, M. (1980). *Qualitative evaluation methods.* Beverly Hills, CA: Sage.

Pavalko, R. (1981). The spatial dimension of ethnicity. *Ethnic Groups, 3,* 111–125.

Payne, B. (1982). Religiosity. In D. J. Mangen & W. A. Peterson (Eds.), *Research instruments in social gerontology: Vol. 2. Social roles and social participation.* Minneapolis: University of Minnesota Press.

Peacock, J. (1968). *Rites of modernization: Symbolic and social aspects of Indonesian proletarian drama.* Chicago: University of Chicago.

Pelto, P., & Pelto, G. (1978). *Anthropological research: The structure of inquiry.* Cambridge: Cambridge University Press.

Penti, M. (1986). Piikajutut: Stories Finnish maids told. In C. Ross & K. Wargelin-Grow (Eds.), *Women who dared: The history of Finnish-American women.* St. Paul, MN: University of Minnesota, Immigration History Research Center.

Phillips, D. (1965). Self-reliance and the inclination to adopt the sick role. *Social Forces, 43,* 555–563.

Phillipson, C. (1982). *Capitalism and the construction of old age.* London: MacMillan Press.

Piaget, J. (1932). *The moral judgement of the child.* London: Kegan Paul.

Pierce, N., & Choharis, P. C. (1984). Gray power. *National Journal, 14*(37) 1559–1962.

Place, L. (1981). The ethnic factor. In F. Berghorn & D. Schager (Eds.), *The dynamics of aging: Original essays in the processes and experiences of growing old.* Boulder, CO: Westview Press.

Potter, G., & Whirin, A. (1982). Traditional Hmong birth customs. In B. T.

Downing & D. Olney (Eds.), *The Hmong in the West*. Minneapolis: University of Minnesota Press.

Prince, E. (1978). Welfare status, illness and subjective health definition. *American Journal of Public Health, 68,* 865–871.

Quadagno, J. S. (1981). The Italian American family. In C. H. Mindel & R. W. Habenstein (Eds.), *Ethnic families in America* (2nd ed.) (pp. 61–85). New York: Elsevier.

Ralston, P. A. (1984). Senior center utilization by Black elderly adults: Social, attitudinal, and knowledge correlates. *Journal of Gerontology, 39,* 224–229.

Reid, J. (1982). Black America in the 1980's. *Population Bulletin, 37*(4), 1–39.

Rein, M., & Morris, R. (1962). Goals, structure, and strategies for community change. *Social work practice*. New York: Columbia University Press.

Riley, M. W. (1987). On the significance of age in sociology. *American Sociological Review, 52,* 1–14.

Riley, M. W., Johnson, M. E., & Foner, A. (Eds.). (1972). *Aging and society: A sociology of age stratification* (Vol. 3). New York: Russell Sage Foundation.

Rives, N., & Serow, W. (1981). Interstate migration of the elderly. *Research on Aging, 3,* 259–278.

Robinson, J. P. (1977). *Changes in Americans' use of time: 1965–1975.* Cleveland, OH: Cleveland State University, Communication Research Center.

Rogers, G. (1982). *Private pension coverage and vesting by race and Hispanic descent, 1979*. Washington, DC: U.S. Department of Health and Human Services, Social Security Administration.

Romero, F. (1984). *The Hispanic population in the United States: Increasing numbers and increasing poverty*. Unpublished report.

Rosenberg, M. (1981). *Conceiving the self*. New York: Basic Books.

Rosenthal, C. J. (1986). Family supports in later life: Does ethnicity make a difference? *The Gerontologist, 26,* 19–24.

Rosow, I. (1974). *Socialization to old age*. Berkeley: University of California Press.

Ross, C. (1986). The feminist dilemma in the Finnish immigrant community and servant girls, community leaders. In C. Ross & K. Wargelin-Brown (Eds.), *Women who dared: The history of Finnish-American women*. St. Paul, MN: University of Minnesota, Immigration History Research Center.

Ross, J. (1977). *Old people, new lives*. Chicago: University of Chicago Press.

Rossi, P. (1969). Theory, research and practice in community organization. In R. Kramer & H. Specht (Eds.), *Readings in community organization practice* (pp. 49–61). Englewood Cliffs, NJ: Prentice-Hall.

Saloutos, T. (1980). Greeks. In S. Thernstrom (Ed.), *Harvard encyclopedia of American ethnic groups* (pp. 430–440). Cambridge, MA: Belknap Press.

Sapir, E. (1929). The status of linguistics as a science. *Language, 5,* 207–214.

Sarbin, T., & Allen, V. (1968). Role theory. In G. Lindzey & E. Aronson (Eds.), *Handbook of social psychology* (2nd ed.), (Vol. 1, pp. 488–567). Reading, MA: Addison-Wesley.

Saunders, L. (1954). *Cultural difference and medical care: The case of the Spanish-speaking people of the Southwest*. New York: Russel Sage Foundation.

Schooler, C. (1976). Serfdom's legacy: An ethnic continuum. *American Journal of Sociology, 81,* 1265–1285.

Schreiber, W. I. (1962). *Our Amish neighbors*. Chicago: University of Chicago Press.

Schroyer-Portillo, J. (1984). *Civil rights in crisis: The Reagan administration's reforms*. Washington, DC: National Council of La Raza.

Schutz, A. (1973). *Collected papers: I. The problem of social reality*. The Hague: Martinus Nijhoff.

Scott, G. (1982). Practical implications of the continuing ethnic solidarity. *American Anthropologist, 56.*

Scott, J., & Phelan, J. (1969). Expectacies of unemployed males regarding source of control of reinforcement. *Psychological Reports, 25,* 911–912.

Shanas, E. (1979a). The family as a support system in old age. *The Gerontologist, 19,* 169–174.

Shanas, E. (1979b). Social myth as hypothesis: The case of the family relations of old people. *The Gerontologist, 19,* 3–9.

Shragge, E., & MacLean, M. J. (1983). Canadian pension policy: A critical analysis. *Canadian Social Work Review, 1,* 77–92.

Silberman, C. (1985). *A certain people: American Jews and their lives today*. New York: Summit Books.

Silverstein, N. M. (1984). Informing the elderly about public services: The relationship between sources of knowledge and service utilization. *The Gerontologist, 24*(1), 37–40.

Simmons, L. W. (1945). *The role of the aged in primitive society*. New Haven, CT: Yale University Press.

Sinnott, J., Harris, C., Block, M., Collesano, S., & Jacobson, S. (1983). *Applied research in aging*. Boston: Little, Brown.

Sklare, M., & Greenblum, J. (1979). *Jewish identity on the suburban frontier* (2nd ed.). Chicago: University of Chicago Press.

Sontag, S. (1975). The double standard of aging. In *No longer young: The older woman in America*. Occasional Papers in Gerontology No. 11. Institute of Gerontology: The University of Michigan–Wayne State University.

Sowell, T. (1981). *Ethnic America*. New York: Basic Books.

Stark, R. (1968). Age and faith: A changing outlook as an old process. *Sociological Analysis, 29,* 1–10.

Stark, R., & Glock, C. Y. (1968). *American piety: The nation of religious commitment*. Berkeley, CA: University of California Press.

Stein, B. (1980, February 22). *The refugee experience: An overview of refugee research*. Paper presented at the Royal Anthropological Institute, London.

Steinberg, S. (1981). *The ethnic myth: Race, ethnicity and class in America.* New York: Atheneum.

Stockman, D. (1986). *The triumph of politics: How the Reagan revolution failed.* New York: Harper & Row.

Stoller, E. (1983). Parental caregiving by adult children. *Journal of Marriage and the Family, 45,* 851–858.

Strassburger, R. B., & Hinke, W. J. (1934). *Pennsylvania German pioneers.* Norristown, PA: Pennsylvania German Society.

Streib, G., & Schneider, G. (1971). *Retirement in American society.* Ithaca, NY: Cornell University Press.

Strickland, B. (1971). Delay of gratification as a function of race of the experimenter. *Journal of Personality and Social Psychology, 22,* 108–112.

Stryker, S. (1968). Identity salience and role performance: The relevance of symbolic interaction theory for family research. *Journal of Marriage and the Family, 30,* 558–562.

Sue, D., & Sue, S. (1972). Ethnic minorities: Resistance in being researched. *Professional Psychology, 3,* 11–17.

Sue, S., Ito, J., & Bradshaw, C. (1982). Ethnic minority research: Trends and directions. In E. Jones & S. Korchin (Eds.), *Minority mental health.* New York: Praeger.

Sue, S., & Morishima, J. (1982). *The mental health of Asian Americans.* San Francisco: Josey-Bass.

Szalai, A. (1972). *The use of time.* The Hague: Mouton.

Szalai, A. (1984). The concept of time budget research. In A. S. Harvey, A. Szalai, D. H. Elliott, P. J. Stone, & S. M. Clark (Eds.), *Time budget research, an ISSC workbook in comparative analysis* (pp. 17–35). Frankfurt: Campus Verlag.

Tate, N. (1983). The Black aging experience. In R. McNeely & J. Colen (Eds.), *Aging in minority groups.* Beverly Hills, CA: Sage.

Taylor, R. J. (1985). The extended family as a source of support to elderly blacks. *The Gerontologist, 25,* 488–495.

Teaff, J. F., Lawton, M. P., Nahemow, L., & Carlson, D. (1978). Impact of age integration on the well-being of elderly tenants in public housing. *Journal of Gerontology, 33,* 126–133.

Thao, C. (1982). Hmong migration and leadership in Laos and in the United States. In B. T. Downing & D. Olney (Eds.), *The Hmong in the West.* Minneapolis: University of Minnesota Press.

Thurlow, H. J. (1971). Illness in relation to life situation and sick role tendency. *Journal of Psychosomatic Research, 15,* 73–88.

Tornstam, L. (1982). Gerontology in a dynamic society. In T. K. Hareven & K. J. Adams (Eds.), *Aging and life course transitions: An interdisciplinary perspective.* New York: Guilford Press.

Torres-Gil, F. (1982a). *The politics of aging among elder Hispanics.* Washington, DC: University Press of America.

Torres-Gil, F. (1982b). The special interest concerns of the minority professional: An evolutionary process in affecting social policies for the minority aged. In Ron Manuel (Ed.), *Minority aging: Sociological and social psychological issues.* Westport, CT: Greenwood Press.

Torres-Gil, F. (1983). Political involvement among older members of national minority groups: Problems and prospects. In R. McNeely & J. Colen (Eds.), *Aging in minority groups* (pp. 226–236). Beverly Hills, CA: Sage.

Torres-Gil, F. (1986). An examination of factors affecting future cohorts of elderly Hispanics. *The Gerontologist, 26*(2), 140–146.

Torres-Gil, F., & Becerra, R. M. (1977). The political behavior of the Mexican-American elderly. *The Gerontologist, 17*(5), 392–399.

Torres-Gil, F., & Negm, M. (1980). Policy issues concerning the Hispanic elderly. *Aging,* Nos. 305–306, 2–5. Washington, DC: Office of Human Development Services.

Trela, J., & Sokolovsky, J. (1979). Culture, ethnicity, and policy for the aged. In D. Gelfand & A. Kutzik (Eds.), *Ethnicity and aging: Theory, research and policy* (pp. 117–136). New York: Springer Publishing Co.

Trevino, F. (1982). Vital and health statistics for the U.S. Hispanic population. *American Journal of Public Health, 72*(9), 979–981.

Turner, J. (1986). *The structure of sociological theory.* Chicago: The Dorsey Press.

Uhlenberg, P. R. (1974). Cohort variations in family life cycle experiences of United States females. *Journal of Marriage and Family, 36,* 284–292.

Ujimoto, K. V. (1985a). The allocation of time to social and leisure activities as social indicators for the integration of aged ethnic minorities. *Social Indicators Research, 16,* 253–266.

Ujimoto, K. V. (1985b). The allocation of time to social, organizational, and leisure activities by aged Asian Canadians. *Tsukuba Journal of Sociology, 9,* 56–68.

U.S. Bureau of the Census. (1980a). *The social and economic status of the Black population.* (Current Population Reports, Series P-23 No. 80). Washington, DC: U.S. Government Printing Office.

U.S. Bureau of the Census. (1980b). *General population characteristics: U.S. summary population survey, Persons by age, race, Spanish origin and sex.* (Census of Population, Table 43). Washington, DC: U.S. Government Printing Office.

U.S. Bureau of the Census. (1983a). *America in transition: An aging society.* (Current population reports, Series P-23, No. 128). Washington, DC: U.S. Government Printing Office.

U.S. Bureau of the Census. (1983b). *Voting and registration in the election of November, 1982.* (Population Characteristics, Series P-20). Washington, DC: U.S. Government Printing Office.

U.S. Bureau of the Census. (1984). *Demographic and socioeconomic aspects of aging in the United States.* (Current Population Reports, Series P-23, No. 138). Washington, DC: U.S. Government Printing Office.

U.S. Bureau of the Census. (1985). *Statistical abstract of the United States: 1986.* (106th ed.) Washington, DC: U.S. Government Printing Office.

U.S. Bureau of the Census. (1986). *Money, income and poverty status of families and persons in the U.S.* Washington, DC: U.S. Government Printing Office.

U.S. Commission on Civil Rights. (1982). *Minority elderly services: New programs, old problems.* Washington, DC: U.S. Government Printing Office.

U.S. Congress. House. Select Committee on Aging. (1986). *Investing in America's families: The common bond of generations.* Washington, DC: U.S. Government Printing Office.

U.S. Congress. Senate. Special Committee on Aging. (1984). *Aging America: Trends and projections.* Washington, DC: U.S. Government Printing Office.

U.S. Department of the Army. (1970). *Minority groups in Thailand.* (Pamphlet No. 550–107). Washington, DC: Author.

U.S. Department of Education, National Center for Educational Statistics. (1980). *Fall enrollment in higher education.* Washington, DC: U.S. Department of Education.

U.S. Department of Health and Human Services, Administration on Aging. (1981). Characteristics of the Hispanic elderly. *Statistical reports on older Americans.* Washington, DC: U.S. Government Printing Office.

U.S. Department of Health and Human Services, Social Security Administration. (1982). *Private pension coverage and vesting by race and Hispanic descent, 1979.* Prepared by Gayle Thompson Rogers. Washington, D.C.: U.S. Government Printing Office.

U.S. Senate Special Committee on Aging, American Association of Retired Persons, and Administration on Aging. (1986). *Aging America: Trends and projections.* Washington, DC: U.S. Government Printing Office.

Valle, R. (1983). The demography of Mexican-American aging. In R. McNeely & J. Colen (Eds.), *Aging in minority groups.* Beverly Hills, CA: Sage.

Valle, R., & Martinez, C. (1981). Natural networks of elderly Latinos of Mexican heritage: Implications for mental health. In M. Miranda & R. Ruiz (Eds.), *Chicano aging and mental health.* (Publication # (ADM) 81-952). Washington, DC: U.S. Department of Health and Human Services, National Institute of Mental Health.

Valle, R., & Mendoza, L. (1978). *The older Latino.* San Diego, CA: The Campanelle Press.

Vang, T. (1981). *The Hmong of Laos.* Hawthorne, CA: Cultural Friendship Center.

Varghese, R., & Medinger, F. (1979). Fatalism in response to stress among the minority aged. In D. Gelfand & A. Kutzik (Eds.), *Ethnicity and aging.* New York: Springer Publishing Co.

Walker, A. (1982). Dependency and old age. *Social Policy and Administration, 16*(2), 115–135.

Wan, T., & Arling, G. (1983). Differential use of health services among disabled elderly. *Research on Aging, 5,* 411–431.

Ward, R. (1984). *The aging experience* (2nd ed.). New York: Harper and Row.

Wargelin-Brown, K. (1986a). A closer look at Finnish-American women's issues. In C. Ross & K. Wargelin-Brown (Eds.), *Women who dared: The history of Finnish-American women*. St. Paul, MN: University of Minnesota, Immigration History Research Center.

Wargelin-Brown, K. (1986b). The legacy of Mummu's granddaughters: Finnish-American women's history. In S. Sinkkonen & A. Milen (Eds.), *Towards equality: Proceedings of the American-Finnish workshop on Minna Canth*. Kuopio, Finland: University of Kuopio.

Warren, R., & Passel, J. (1983). A count of the uncountable: Estimates of undocumented aliens counted in the 1980 U.S. Census. Unpublished paper.

Watanabe, C. (1973). Self expression and the Asian American experience. *Personnel and Guidance Journal, 51,* 390–396.

Welts, E. P. (1982). Greek families. In M. McGoldrick, J. Pearce, & J. Giordano (Eds.), *Ethnicity and family therapy* (pp. 269–288). New York: Guilford Press.

Westermeyer, J. (1985). Mental health of Southeast Asian refugees: Observations over two decades from Laos and the United States. In T. C. Owan (Ed.), *Southeast Asian mental health: Treatment, prevention, services, training, and research* (pp. 65–89). Rockville, MD: National Institute of Mental Health.

Whitmore, J. (1979). *An introduction to Indochinese history, culture, language and life*. Ann Arbor, MI: University of Michigan Press.

Whorf, B. L., (1956). *Language, thought, and reality*. Cambridge, MA: MIT Press.

Wictorowicz, B. (1980). Toronto's ethnic elderly: Their participation in voluntary associations. *Multiculturalism, 4,* 15–24.

Wiggins, G. (1986). *Targeting services for the minority elderly*. Washington, DC: National Association of Area Agencies on Aging.

Wilson, W. (1980). The declining significance of race. Chicago: University of Chicago Press.

Wingrove, C. R., & Alston, J. (1974). Age, aging and church attendance. *The Gerontologist, 11*(4), 356–358.

Wiseman, R. (1980). Why older people move: Theoretical issues. *Research on Aging, 2,* 141–154.

Wiseman, R., & Roseman, C. (1980). A typology of elderly migration based on the decision-making process. *Economic Geography, 55,* 324–337.

Woehrer, C. (1978). Cultural pluralism in American families: The influence of ethnicity on social aspects of aging. *The Family Coordinator, 27,* 329–339.

Woehrer, C. (1982). The influence of ethnic families on intergenerational relationships and later life transitions. *Annals of the American Academy of Political and Social Sciences, 464,* 65–78.

Wright, R., Saleebey, D., Watts, T., & Lecca, P. (1983). *Transcultural issues in the human services: Organizational issues and trends*. Springfield, IL: Charles C. Thomas.

Wu, F. (1975). Mandarin-speaking aged Chinese in the Los Angeles area. *The Gerontologist, 15,* 271–275.

Yancey, W., Ericksen, E., & Juliani, R. (1976). Ethnicity: A review and reformulation. *American Sociological Review, 41,* 391–403.

Yinger, J. M. (1985). Ethnicity. *Annual Review of Sociology, Vol. 11.*

Young, K. (1982). An agenda for Sir George: Local authorities and the promotion of racial equality. *Policy Studies, 3*(1), 54–69.

Zambrana, R. E., Merino, R., & Santana, S. (1979). Health services and the Puerto Rican elderly. In D. Gelfand & A. Kutzik (Eds.), *Ethnicity and aging: Theory, research and policy.* New York: Springer Publishing Co.

Zay, N. (1978). Old age and aging in Canada's ethic population. Paper prepared for the National Symposium on Aging. Ottawa, CA.

Zbrowski, M. (1952). Culture components in response to pain. *Journal of Social Issues, 8,* 16–23.

Zuniga-Martinez, M. (1983). Social treatment with the minority elderly. In R. McNeely & J. Colen (Eds.), *Aging in minority groups.* Beverly Hills, CA: Sage.

Index